COMING TO TERMS
WITH DEMOCRACY

COMING TO TERMS WITH DEMOCRACY

Federalist Intellectuals and the Shaping of an American Culture

➤➤ MARSHALL FOLETTA

University Press of Virginia
CHARLOTTESVILLE AND LONDON

THE UNIVERSITY PRESS OF VIRGINIA
© 2001 by the Rector and Visitors of the University of Virginia
Printed in the United States of America

First published 2001

∞ The paper used in this publication meets the minimum requirements of
the American National Standard for Information Sciences—Permanence of
Paper for Printed Library Materials, ANSI Z39.48-1984.

Library of Congress Cataloging-in-Publication Data
Foletta, Marshall, 1955–
    Coming to terms with democracy : Federalist intellectuals and the shap-
ing of an American culture / Marshall Foletta.
        p. cm.
    Includes bibliographical references and index.
    ISBN 0-8139-2059-0 (cloth : alk. paper)
    1. United States—Politics and government—1789–1815.   2. United
States—Politics and government—1815–1861.   3. United States—Intellectual life—19th century.   4. New England—Intellectual life—19th century.   5. Intellectuals—New England—Political activity—History—
19th century.   6. Federal Party (U.S.)—History.   7. Politics and literature—United States—History—19th century.   8. North American review—History.   9. Political culture—United States—History—19th century.   I. Title.
E338 .F65 2001
973.5—dc21   2001026067

111501-3960X6

For Khris

Contents

Illustrations

Acknowledgments

➤➤ Scholarship is usually a very private affair, requiring hours of solitary study and the acceptance of personal responsibility for whatever shortcomings exist in the end. This attempt is no different. But like most others it has also benefited from the contributions of others. At the University of California at Berkeley, where this book began as a doctoral dissertation, the contributions of my committee were invaluable. Richard Hutson encouraged me to believe, correctly I hope, that a certain naïveté regarding American literature might not prove too great a disadvantage. Robin Einhorn's energetic reading of early drafts helped me place my narrative within a far richer context. Most importantly, Jim Kettner allowed me the freedom to work through my own questions and supported me with the gentle encouragement that characterizes all fine teachers.

At various stages other individuals — most notably Henry May, Charles Royster, and Daniel Howe — read at least some portion of the manuscript and contributed more than they probably realized. At the University Press of Virginia, Richard Holway provided a reassuring appreciation for my questions and an unfailing sense of how to strengthen my answers.

My family, extended and immediate, assisted in more personal ways. Most rewarding was the support of my children, who were a part of this project from its inception. Lucas, a night owl since birth, provided late-night company as I began my research. John, who read the first chapter when he was twelve and the last just before heading off to college, reassured me that both my narrative and analysis were worth reading. Anna helped pack my bags when I took off on writing retreats and through frequent calls kept me in touch with the personal history that was always most important.

But above all others, I am indebted to my wife, Khris. As collaborator, editor, and critic, she left her mark on most every page. In more ways than she knows, but only she could begin to realize, this work is as much hers as it is mine. For this reason it is dedicated to her.

COMING TO TERMS
WITH DEMOCRACY

CHAPTER I

1815

➤➤ In January 1815 Harrison Gray Otis left Hartford, Connecticut, for Washington, D.C. Having spent several weeks in Hartford discussing with his Federalist colleagues their opposition to the present war with England, he now carried the convention report to President Madison. The president, and the nation, waited uneasily for this report. New Englanders had opposed the war at its inception in 1812, and their opposition had intensified as their trade was proscribed and their coastal towns came under attack. By 1815 public protest was vehement, and threats of secession were tossed about regularly. Within this atmosphere Otis traveled to the nation's capital. Surrounded by charges of treason and attacked as the symbol of New England's disloyalty, he arrived just in time to hear of Jackson's victory at New Orleans and the signing of a treaty at Ghent.

In March 1815 another prominent Bostonian, William Tudor, announced the publication of the first issue of the *North American Review*. Joined in this inaugural effort by Willard Phillips and Richard Henry Dana, Tudor would soon draw to the *Review* New England's most prominent young intellectuals. Declaring it their intention to review and discuss every work of significance published in America and abroad, the contributors somewhat more privately discussed their hope of freeing American letters from a slavish dependence on foreign opinion and a too ready subordination to partisan purposes. Applauding these ambitions, its readers welcomed the *Review* as a refreshing and portentous contribution to American letters.

On the surface, these events held little in common. Indeed, the closer one looks, the less these events seem to share. Otis's trip and the convention that preceded it appear now to be among the low points of New England history and the pivotal episode in the Federalist Party's doomed struggle for survival. The arrival of the convention's report in Washington alongside news of the Treaty of Ghent and Jackson's victory at New Orleans cast the Federalist delegates at Hartford in the role of jaded malcontents—poor judges of geopolitical affairs and hopelessly out of touch with the more optimistic and nationalistic popular mood. A generation of Federalist statesmen were forced into immediate retirement, and allusions to these events would continue to embarrass the region for years. The publication of the *North American Review,* on the other hand, marked the beginning of a literary journal that would enjoy recognition throughout the century as among the most distinguished in America. Its contributors would be recognized as the aristocracy of American letters, and their optimistic and ambitious agenda would inspire a generation of New England intellectuals.

With one event marking the end and the other a beginning, one reflecting political regionalism and partisan desperation, while the other voiced a more optimistic, national cultural agenda, the two events could be hardly more different. Perhaps even more striking is the contrasting ages of the participants. In 1815 Otis was forty-nine. With one exception, the delegates to the Hartford Convention were between forty-seven and sixty-three. Tudor, on the other hand, was thirty-six and among the oldest contributors to the *North American Review.* The group of intellectuals who wrote for this journal, as well as its next several editors, Jared Sparks, Edward Tyrrel Channing, and Edward Everett, were all in their twenties.

The differences between the two events and their principal players were indeed great. But if in many ways these events and the men behind them were distinguished by their differences, in one very significant way they were similar. Tudor, like Otis, identified himself as a Federalist. Although he only briefly held public office, he actively supported Federalist candidates and in the first editions of the *North American Review* voiced sympathy for Federalist concerns. Dana, Phillips, Sparks, Channing, and Everett all also identified themselves as Federalists. Although the temper and focus of their efforts suggest a far different outlook than that of Otis, they defined themselves politically in similar terms.

To a certain extent this is not surprising. In 1815 Federalism was still a powerful force in New England. To find that Boston's most prominent intellectuals, its best-educated and most widely respected cultural figures, identified with this political tradition is no great surprise. But the differing moods, efforts, and perspectives of the two groups, groups which are also defined generationally, present an interesting contrast and raise some questions regarding just what it meant to call oneself a Federalist and just what Federalism itself represented.

Federalism is a well-traveled subject. The Federalist Party and its somewhat brief but significant history have been explored in detail. The domestic and foreign policies that defined its agenda, the international crises that forged its organizational structure, its leading figures, areas of greatest strength, and ultimate decline, have all been explored. But a full understanding of Federalism rests in the recognition that Federalism was always far more than a political party, far more than just a set of political objectives and candidates. Underlying the Federalist Party was a distinct set of ideas, beliefs, and attitudes that defined the political agenda and united its members. Fully understanding Federalism rests in the recognition that more than just a political party, Federalism represented a distinct political culture—a distinctive philosophy of man and the communities in which he lived; a constellation of religious, moral, and economic principles more profound and culturally entrenched than any mere party agenda.[1]

This understanding of Federalism as culture as well as party is hardly new, and to argue its importance here is far from innovative. It is implicit in much of the existing literature surrounding the party. James Banner, for example, has argued that party politics "followed—they did not precede—the growth and definition of the political culture." The political agenda of the Federalist Party, moreover, was never a complete representation of the breadth of Federalism. Beyond its legislative vision Federalism represented a multidimensional critique of "the unrestrained liberal capitalism of the middle class," a critique, in effect, of the emerging American character. Moreover, historians of American political behavior have long noted the range of cultural factors—religious, ethnic, racial, and class—underlying and directing political participation. In examining a later political party with strong New England roots, Daniel Walker Howe argued that the American Whigs were best understood in these terms. Concluding that in many ways the political culture of Whiggery was more successful and powerful than the party it created, he defined culture as "an evolving system of beliefs, attitudes, and techniques for solving problems, transmitted from generation to generation and finding expression in the innumerable activities that people learn: religion, child-rearing customs, the arts and professions, religion, and, of course, politics."[2]

It is much the same argument that I would make for Federalism. Although most visibly represented in the Federalist Party, it is more usefully understood as a set of beliefs and attitudes—a set of ideas about the world and man's place within it, a set of ideas that was passed from generation to generation and expressed not only in politics but also in religion, work, and domestic life. And like Whiggery, the culture of Federalism was perhaps more powerful, and certainly more enduring, than the party. Although the political arm of the Federalist culture would fail in the early nineteenth century, the culture would persist as a vital force in American affairs. The political organization would collapse, but the ideology of Federalism would survive.

At the core of this Federalist culture lay an understanding of society as an organic web of reconcilable interests, tended and brought into harmony by the judicious leadership of the best educated and most virtuous. When translated into the political arena, this expressed itself in an advocacy of egalitarian self-government and aristocratic rule that modern sensibilities often find confusing. Federalists claimed to be democratic and supported a broad and liberal suffrage. A wide electoral base lent stability to society and swathed the government and its policies in the security of consensus. But at the same time Federalists believed that the offices of political leadership ought to be narrowly restricted. Public office was reserved for those they most commonly referred to as "the wise and the good," a designation that tended to identify not only the best educated but also the more affluent.

Connecting and reconciling these elements of democracy and elitism within the Federalist ideology were the twin notions of deference and virtue. Deference was the social quality that assured the social, cultural, and political elites their proper recognition. It ensured that business leaders were respected and that their behavior was emulated. Deference promised that members of the clergy were awarded the audience and respect they required. And deference guaranteed the elevation of the proper sorts to public office. It was the force of habit that induced a politically empowered public to accept aristocratic leadership. Virtue was the force that guided the general public in the exercise of its submissive duties. Virtue reconciled the masses to the limitations within their roles and the sacrifices required of good citizenship. It led them to a respect for authority and the law, even law generated by elites.

It was Federalists' emphasis on the importance of virtue and their support for popular participation in politics that allowed them to describe themselves without embarrassment as republicans. In these emphases members of the Federalist Party joined Republicans and actually questioned which party was more deserving of the mantle of "true republicanism." But beneath this semantic similarity there were significant differences. While Federalists depended on deference to guide the public's social and political behavior, most Republicans placed confidence in the public's "common sense." Drawn from the Scottish Enlightenment, the Republicans' "common sense" philosophy recognized in man a universal ability to make basic decisions about politics and morality. And whereas Federalists depended upon virtue to breed submission to law, Republicans saw virtue as the prerequisite to the public creation of law. Beneath these differences, moreover, lay a view of human nature more fundamental and profound. For the Federalist, deference was rooted in tradition. Like virtue it was the product of training and education. Without such formation the individual was a political and social liability. For the Republican, the common sense that guided political behavior and the virtue that informed social and moral judgment were inherent.

For Federalists the acquired nature of deference and virtue meant that the preservation of social order involved the efforts of more than just political leaders. The clergy, in particular, had an important part to play in forming the public's values and preserving the appropriate traditions. The New England clergy had inherited from their Puritan ancestors a compelling sense of political and social responsibility. This sense had been heightened and more sharply focused by the Revolutionary War. By the last quarter of the eighteenth century, a fully politicized Federalist clergy considered political commentary a central part of their ministerial role. Supplementing their efforts were those of a more broadly defined community of business persons and professionals — men of education, breeding, and status whose privilege and position incurred responsibilities to the cause of good order.

Working together, these interlocking groups were responsible in Federalist theory for the governance of the political and social order. More precisely, this meant they were entrusted to identify the general good and steer society toward its realization. Here again Federalism distinguished itself from its cultural and political rival. A politics of the general welfare, as opposed to one of self-interest, was one of the principal tenets of classical republicanism. But somewhat ironically, Democratic Republicanism, under the guidance of James Madison, defined government's role more modestly. Government, as outlined in *The Federalist Papers,* served to provide a forum in which various interests might contest for influence. Although Madison believed that America's size and diversity would prevent any of these specific interests from dominating the forum and thus directing public policy, his was nevertheless a more wary vision of government's purposes and one contrary to classical republican thought.[3]

Federalism, with its argument that the essence of leadership was not to moderate but rather to harmonize varying interests and extrapolate from them the general good, was truer to the tradition of classical republicanism. Not all Federalists maintained this theoretical purity. John Adams, the most notable innovator, distrusted the aristocracy's integrity in separating their personal interests and the general welfare.[4] And contemporary and modern skeptics have noted that for many Federalists, self-interest and the public welfare tended rather fortuitously to coincide. Nevertheless, on the level of theory if nothing else, this sense of government not only distinguished Federalism from emerging democratic philosophy but also solidified the party's sense of purpose.

The confidence underlying this sense of society and government was reenforced by the composition of New England society. Massachusetts in the late eighteenth century was marked by social and cultural homogeneity. Its population was almost universally white, of English extraction, and Protestant. Enhancing this social and cultural homogeneity was a sense of itself and its history which James Banner has labeled the "myth of New England exclusiveness." Massachusetts's Puritan origins, its central place in the Revolutionary conflict, and its continued prominence in government and learning led the state, and particularly Boston, to a sense of historical primacy and exceptionalism.[5]

In retrospect this sense of exceptionalism can seem little more than provincialism. Massachusetts was suspicious of most regions outside of New England, in particular the Quaker-founded and more cosmopolitan Philadelphia, the distant and "immoral" District of Columbia, and the "slavocratic" and rivaling state of Virginia. Yet whether exceptional or merely provincial, this sense of itself, shared at most levels of society, reenforced the ideological consensus that was Federalism. In society and politics this meant a persisting hierarchical order, held together by deference, nurtured by clerical and social elites, and governed by the wise and the good.

This broader definition of Federalism makes it perhaps more understandable that it could find expressions that were independent of, and even out of sync with, the political party. Given the fact that Federalism meant more than the Federalist Party, it is more understandable that Tudor and his colleagues at the *North American Review* could voice an ambitious and optimistic agenda amid the political despair and defeat of Otis and his colleagues. Even so, the question as to how these differences emerged remains. What was it that led to the formulation of such different agendas? What led to such different conceptions of purpose? How did this culture generate such contrasting conceptions of the social and political environment and the opportunities for Federalism within it?

What follows is an attempt to answer these questions—an explanation as to why 1815 saw the end of one Federalist tradition and the emergence of another; why one form of Federalist activity failed and another rose in its place; why, more precisely, the failure of one expression of the Federalist ideology made necessary the rethinking of that ideology and application of its principles in new ways. And as these differences corresponded to generational divisions, it is a description of how one generation of Federalism gave way to another; how, in fact, the failure of one generation produced new opportunities for, and perhaps even the success of, the next.

It is a story that is significant at several levels. For starters, it contributes to the much-needed clarification of Federalism's response to its political trials. The argument that Federalism completely collapsed during the Jeffersonian era has been challenged for some time. David Hackett Fischer first pointed out that although one generation of Federalist statesmen faded away despondent and inflexible, another generation of "young Federalists" adapted to the new political realities and persisted as a force in American politics. His argument makes an important correction, but even in his treatment the integrity of the Federalist political culture does not fare well. His young Federalists appear almost nonideological in their willingness to compromise traditional Federalist values. Their "only question," he suggested, "was whether the ideals of the old-school gentlemen should be abandoned in part or dropped altogether."[6] In their subsequent pursuit of issues through which electoral victories could be secured, they appear as shameless political opportunists grotesquely juxtaposed against the Federalist tradition.

Other historians of Federalism have added further to the revision, but they also have tended to link the political adaptations too unconditionally to ideological compromise or disintegration. James Banner disagreed somewhat with Fischer regarding the generational character of Federalism's political adaptation. Far more "old school" Federalists made the transition to party politics, Banner argued, than Fischer acknowledged. For every one that retreated or withdrew, another adapted and persisted. For every George Cabot and Fisher Ames, there was a Caleb Strong or John Brooks. But he agreed with Fischer that these adaptations unsettled the ideological consistency of Federalism and led to the destabilization of the broader Federalist society. Its cultural and literary arm, as represented by the Anthology Society, pulled back in disgust from political activism, while the Federalist clergy deplored the excessive materialism that seemed to accompany the growing commercialism promoted by Federalist economic policies. Meanwhile, Federalist politicians grew increasingly irritated with the impolitic rhetoric of the orthodox churches, especially in their attack on the Bavarian Illuminati. As a result, although the party may have survived, the ideological consensus that had earlier defined it was shattered. And as the culture that had previously given it strength and coherence unraveled, the party's significance, according to Banner, grew negligible.[7]

Linda Kerber went furthest in acknowledging the cultural basis of Federalism. Even Federalists themselves, she has argued, recognized that the two parties "were separated on practical issues because they were separated on intellectual ones." Their distrust of Jeffersonians, she added, was grounded "not only in political objection, but in disagreement that was ideological in the broadest possible sense." But Kerber, too, concluded that the political events of the early nineteenth century reduced the culture to reaction and despair. What distinguished Federalists from their Jeffersonian rivals, she argued, was their inability to redefine the "terms of the golden age" within the realities of the growing Republic. Clinging inflexibly to the literary and political prescriptions of a fading era, they grew bitter, "not merely because they had lost office, patronage, and power in the election of 1800, but because America appeared to be developing a civilization which they did not understand and of which they certainly did not approve."[8]

The conclusions of Fischer and Banner regarding the ideological confusion of the Federalist Party are convincing. But they overstate their case in suggesting that the ideological compromises of the party completely destroyed the culture of Federalism. Similarly Kerber's assessment is limited by the time frame in which she examined the culture of Federalism. Although an accurate portrayal of one generation of Federalists, it does not represent the spirit of the next. An examination of the young Federalists of the *North American Review* suggests that the political expressions of the Federalist culture are not the best place to look for its persistence in the first decades of the nineteenth century. Similarly, this examination demonstrates that any assessment of Federalist culture must draw a line between its literary voices of the eras before and after the War of 1812. Such an examination indicates that the more creative and principled adaptations took place outside the political arena—that Federalism found voices outside politics after 1815 truer to its traditions, voices that managed to adapt without compromising and that succeeded in applying the ideology of Federalism to the new social and political realities without sacrificing its integrity.

The creativity of this response should offer evidence to correct yet another of the long-standing misconceptions within the historiography of New England. For over a century New England's early national culture was stigmatized by Ralph Waldo Emerson's pronouncement that "from 1790 to 1820 there was not a book, a speech, a conversation, or a thought in the state."[9] Emerson credited the *Review*'s Edward Everett with contributing to the breaking up of this intellectual sterility. Everett's eloquence in the classroom bred an interest in oratory and lecturing that proved "of the first importance to the American mind." But even this praise was tempered by qualification. "It was not the intellectual or the moral principles . . . it was not thoughts" that Everett offered. "His power lay in the magic of form."[10] The *North American Review*, as the preeminent literary expression of this culture, received equally harsh criticism. Contemporary with Emerson's condemnation, the *Boston Chronotype* complained that "Europe is on fire, and questions of moment are welding hot in our own country, yet the *North American Review* is either admiring the tails of tenth-rate comets, or sprinkling a little Attic salt without any pepper on a dish of cucumbers."[11] Thoreau labeled the *Re-*

view a "venerable cobweb" which for too long had escaped the broom, while Edgar Allan Poe summarily condemned the critics and contributors of the *North American* to death by hanging.[12]

Just as damaging, generations of scholars including V. L. Parrington and Robert Spiller have echoed this assessment. "Except for Channing," Spiller argued, "this Boston group did little to break away from England or her literature and to discover the roots of American life."[13] Described as intellectually unambitious and literarily provincial, the thinkers and writers of this period have been reduced to cultural irrelevancies awaiting the renaissance of the 1840s. Nor has the criticism been directed only at the era's literary contributions. Peter Hall and other historians who have looked more broadly at cultural and institutional development during these years have similarly concluded that while other regions embraced messianic agendas of national reform, "Bostonians were, on the whole, concerned only with perpetuating their preeminent position in the affairs of Boston and its environs."[14]

In more recent years numerous scholars have challenged what Lewis Simpson first labeled the "myth of New England's intellectual lapse." Lawrence Buell, for example, has argued that American literary historians have failed to appreciate the contributions of this era to American culture because of a bias against its Federalist and neoclassical character. Benjamin Spencer has suggested that although powerful forces did serve to inhibit American letters during the first years of the nineteenth century—the absence of an international copyright agreement, the conservative cultural inheritance, and residual Puritan suspicions of literature and art—American culture was not as sterile as many have argued. In these years one can detect the beginnings of a national literature amid encouragement from literary critics anxious to break free of imported standards. Even the *North American Review* has been more favorably reassessed. Within its pages, Spencer argued, this nascent American literary criticism "found a stable though not wholly indigenous base." Daniel Howe made the argument even more fully in crediting the Unitarian intellectuals who hovered around Joseph Stevens Buckminster and eventually founded the *Review* with a "small-scale counter-reformation" that "laid the groundwork for New England's literary Renaissance."[15]

Yet among historians there has persisted the tendency to oversimplify the intellectual character of the region and the Federalist culture that continued to shape it—the tendency to write Federalism quickly out of the history of early America, or at best to reduce its voice to the bitter cant of a frustrated elite. Thus in Joyce Appleby's rich portrait of "the first generation of Americans," Federalists assume the most minor of roles—cautious and stodgy, all but irrelevant, and hopelessly out of step with the dynamic, expansive, and raucous rhythms of the new America. Unable to cope politically and "deeply offended by the crass self-assertion of the common folk," Appleby's Federalists embrace refinement "as an end in itself," all the while "strengthening their ties with the English world from whence they took their values." She acknowledged them as America's "first cultural critics" but characterized their efforts—"their laments"—as those "of a spurned elite dispossessed of its admiring following." Similarly Peter Field has recently revisited the *Monthly Anthology*—the parent journal of the *North American Review*—only to contrast the "haughty elitism" of Boston's Federalist Brahmin culture with the flexibility and creativity of Ralph Waldo Emerson's generation. Ignoring the *North American Review* completely, Field contrasted the "sour grapes" of young Federalists Joseph Buckminster, Edward Everett, and George Ticknor with the later generation that "sensed America's democratic promise." While Everett, Ticknor, and their circle took advantage of fortuitous marriages and the patronage of Boston's merchant elite to shape a "smug exile," it was left to the next generation—Emerson, Theodore Parker, and Elizabeth Peabody—"to forge new bonds between themselves and the nation."[16]

The attitude and contributions of the young Federalists of the *North American Review*, however, challenge these conclusions. Their efforts reflect a genuine and in many ways effective attempt to adapt to the emerging democratic society. Their work suggests not only that Emerson and company misjudged their contributions but that the "renaissance" of American letters so frequently posited in contrast was actually dependent on the efforts of these young Federalists. And further, a look at the sort of institutional reforms they advocated, the sorts of reforms they envisioned and outlined in the *North American Review* for American education and the law, as well as their efforts to strengthen American universities, professionalize the fields of medicine and law, establish graduate professional schools, and even reform the American legal system, reveals that their vision was far more national and progressive than historians like Hall have acknowledged.

The story of the young Federalists of the *North American Review* thus does a great deal to correct certain misunderstandings regarding the intellectual vitality of New England during the early nineteenth century. But the record of their attempts to preserve and apply the culture of Federalism despite its political failures is significant beyond the resurrection of the region's reputation. Their story contributes also to our understanding of the forces shaping American culture and society during that century.

In many ways Federalism did march wildly out of step with the expansive and egalitarian tendencies of nineteenth-century America. In an age when many of the forces within politics and culture were working to liberate the individual, Federalism stood for the subordination of the individual to the community and the surrender of self-interest to the public welfare. In an age marked by increasing pluralism and powerful centrifugal forces in religion, politics, and society, Federalism suggested that the centripetal forces necessary to reconcile and harmonize these disparate interests could be identified and nurtured. Finally, in an age that celebrated the common man, Federalism argued the importance and necessity of elite governance. Amid the calls for increased democratization, Federalists suggested that ultimate responsibility for the management of society rested with the wise and the good.

Although largely in disagreement with the main currents of the nineteenth century, these young Federalists were not simply unthinking reactionaries trying to preserve the outdated cultural prescriptions of the eighteenth century. They recognized the need to adapt to the changing forces that surrounded them. They understood that preserving a place in American affairs meant moving forward, not backward. In addition, neither the content of their thought nor the complexities of nineteenth-century ideology warrant so simple an assessment.

If the long and convoluted debate among historians regarding republicanism and liberalism has told us anything, it is that these two philosophical and ideological constructs cannot be overly simplified or placed in too rigid opposition. The argument that during the nineteenth century the communitarian philosophies of classical republicanism contested but gradually succumbed to the radically individualistic doctrines of liberalism has been demonstrated to be far too simple. It is now clearer that eighteenth- and nineteenth-century Americans did not think in so rigid or consistent terms. It is now clear that they drew upon both webs of thought simultaneously; that individuals on both ends of the ideological spectrum drew upon the values and principles at the other extreme, and that these philosophies were more malleable than rigid; that individuals appropriated from them selectively and shaped their premises to fit personal and historical conditions.[17]

With this understanding it becomes further clear that to equate the communitarian and elitist rhetoric of Federalism too exclusively with the eighteenth century is inaccurate, to characterize its emphases on virtue and self-sacrifice, communal responsibility and the common good, as the tired rhetoric of an earlier era is far from true. Instead we must look at these reformulations of Federalist ideology undertaken in the *North American Review* as elaborations of a living body of thought, as attempts to adapt this pliable set of beliefs to the realities of a more democratic America. The efforts of these young Federalists thus represent not simply an attempt to impose upon a changing America the prescriptions of an earlier era but a reformulated version of republicanism, an elaboration, a modernizing, of the ideology that continued to exercise an influence on American culture well beyond the eighteenth century. Although their version of republicanism may not have become the dominant voice in American culture, one can recognize vestiges of this culture as a powerful undercurrent in American life periodically surfacing in reform agendas and political visions, in movements as removed in time as Progressivism and the New Deal.

James MacGregor Burns, in writing Franklin Roosevelt's biography, was struck by the juxtaposition of a certain conservative temperament alongside a reformist disposition, an elitist approach to questions of governance paired with a progressive approach to matters of policy. In Roosevelt, Burns identified a form of conservatism which could not be reduced to a reactionary force or equated narrowly with the interests of big business, evangelical religion, or moral fundamentalism. It was a conservatism defined by ideology, an ideology which envisioned

> an organic view of society, compelling a national and social responsibility that overrides immediate class or group interest; a belief in the unity of the past, the present, and the future, and hence in the responsibility of one generation to another; a sense of the unknowable, involving a respect for the limits of man's knowledge and for traditional forms of religious worship; a recognition of the importance of personal property as forming a foundation for stable human relationships;

personal qualities of gentility, or gentlemanliness, that renounce vulgarity and conspicuous display and demands sensitivity to other persons' needs and expectations; and an understanding of the fact that while not all change is reform, stability is not immobility.[18]

Burns concluded that this particular form of conservatism was rooted in the British tradition. But an examination of these young Federalists of the *North American Review* suggests that Roosevelt's brand of conservatism could have been fed by native sources. We need not cross the Atlantic to find a persisting and viable conservative ideology after the eighteenth century; American culture generated one of its own. It was a conservatism that combined elitism and social responsibility, traditionalism and adaptation, a respect for the individual and the belief that the self is only fully realized within the context of community.

The origins and durability of a conservative tradition in America have been broadly debated in academic circles. But it is possible these questions are of more than academic interest, for if contemporary political philosophers like Michael Sandel are correct, certain principles within this conservative ideological construct are of continuing relevance. In their eyes it is the eclipse of these more communitarian forms of republicanism by the individual-serving philosophies of the "procedural republic" that has left many Americans feeling disempowered and ill at ease. It is the ascendance of a political philosophy that values the "right over the good," the substitution of a political structure that seeks to establish fair procedures rather than particular ends, that has contributed to the widespread sense that the moral character of our communities is deteriorating. It is the ignorance among statesmen of the "formative" responsibilities of politics, their failure to recognize that government has an obligation to help cultivate in citizens "the qualities of character self-government requires," that has bankrupted our political discourse. It is the modern belief that a government is measured by how successfully it enables individuals to pursue their private goals rather than by how effectively it enables citizens to deliberate collectively regarding the common good and to participate in its realization that has produced the prevailing sense that as the moral character of our communities deteriorates, we are powerless against the forces that surround us.[19]

Sandel's argument, in particular, suggests that these Federalist intellectuals offer a great deal to contemporary questions of citizenship and political philosophy, but to focus excessively on the political ramifications of their thought may skew their importance. Although clearly their views on the proper relation of individual to communal goals offer something to contemporary political discourse, the cultural vehicles through which these men sought to apply this Federalist ethic suggest that their story is less about politics than about the history—the troubled history—of the intellectual in America.

For the better part of two centuries, American intellectuals have wrestled with their place in American life. Unsettled by fears of marginalization, offended by a culture seemingly indifferent to their efforts, they have struggled to strengthen their voice and carve out roles within public affairs appropriate to their talents and achievements. Understandably, historians have been fascinated by the plight of these intellectuals. Generally sympathetically, perhaps even therapeutically, they have described the frustrations of these intellectuals and their oftentimes awkward attempts to gain greater public acceptance and participate more fully in public affairs.

The lamentations of Henry Adams, the alienation of Henry James, and Randolph Bourne's anomalous pursuit of experience have provided historians with the material for often pathetic narratives of marginalization and unappreciation. Compelling in themselves, these accounts have been rendered even more so by the suggestion that during earlier periods—in the seventeenth and eighteenth centuries, and even the early nineteenth century—intellectuals enjoyed a different position in American life. If over the last century writers, academics, scientists, and artists have felt themselves isolated, their frustration has been sharpened by their sense that in these earlier periods the highly educated clergymen enjoyed greater prestige and influence, the eloquence and erudition of the scholar could be a springboard to public office, and philosophers were elected president.

There is a romantic appeal to this portrait of the unappreciated intellectual. One can read in their displacement the reckless forces of democratization—America's most talented and best educated tragically caught in the wake of frontier revivals and log cabin campaigns. Or a bit less nostalgically, these intellectuals can be viewed as the unfortunate casualties of modernization, their rejection the lamentable but necessary cost of cultural and social progress, victims to the emergence of a more open society which deferred less to the talents and skills of a privileged elite.

Yet a closer look at American history reveals a more complex picture. To begin with, the intellectual's place in early American culture was far from unchallenged. There was more than a hint of anti-intellectualism in the Great Awakening of 1740, and for many, Thomas Jefferson's philosophical bent was more a political liability than an expression of presidential fitness. Nor has the intellectual's story in the twentieth century been an unbroken tale of disfranchisement. In 1912 a professor and college administrator was elected to the presidency, while in 1932 Franklin Roosevelt turned to the "brain trust" to guide the country back to prosperity. In the 1960s John Kennedy looked to "the best and the brightest" to revitalize American government, and even more recently a former history professor turned Speaker of the House rivaled the president in his power and visibility.

The picture is further clouded by the recognition that some of the most damaging attacks on intellectuals and intellectualism have come not from the agents of popular culture but from intellectuals themselves. Jefferson's philosophical temperament was questioned first not by frontier politicians but rather by New England Federalists. The suggestion that his scientific and philosophic disposition left him ill suited for the presidency emanated not from the backwoods of Tennessee but from the New England bastions of American high culture.

Nor was this self-feeding restricted to the early nineteenth century. Richard Hofstadter, in his provocative but at times overwrought study of anti-intellectualism in American life, argued that anti-intellectualism has historically depended on the efforts of intellectuals. There is considerable truth in this. But his reduction of these critics to "marginal intellectuals, would-be intellectuals, unfrocked or embittered intellectuals, the literate leaders of the semi-literate," misrepresents a more complex reality. One of the more powerful indictments of twentieth-century intellectuals and their misanthropic "detachment from life," their ironically fanatical attachment to intellectual freedom, which leaves them "blinded . . . to the social character of life," came not from a "would-be" intellectual but from Reinhold Niebuhr, perhaps the most important theologian of the century.[20]

Anti-intellectualism has, in fact, been a recurring subtext of American intellectual life. Thomas Jefferson, too philosophical for many, himself contributed to the arsenal of anti-intellectualism with his defense of common sense philosophy. Put a moral question to a professor and a plowman, he argued, and you will quite often get a more cogent response from the latter. Uncorrupted in his thinking by "artificial rules," the farmer's take on basic questions of morality and even politics was often more sound than the scholar's. Romanticism and transcendentalism contributed their own anti-intellectual premises in the first half of the nineteenth century, just as did realism and naturalism at the end of the century. Whether it was an emphasis on emotion over reason or intuition over intellect, whether the concern was overcivilization or cultural effeminacy, nineteenth-century intellectuals offered repeated challenges to intellectualism. When fin-de-siècle intellectuals embraced spontaneity and the martial spirit, when they scorned the contemplative and the analytical and lauded chivalric virtue and redemptive violence, they posed a greater challenge to nineteenth-century intellectualism than dime novels or itinerant fundamentalist preachers.[21] Oliver Wendell Holmes Jr., Boston Brahmin, Harvard educated, summed up most powerfully the self-deprecating tendencies of American intellectuals when he confessed in 1884: "I do not know what is true. I do not know the meaning of the universe. But in the midst of doubt, in the collapse of creeds, there is one thing I do not doubt, that no man who lives in the same world with most of us can doubt, and that is that the faith is true and adorable which leads a soldier to throw away his life in obedience to a blindly accepted duty, in a cause which he little understands, in a plan of campaign of which he has no notion, under tactics of which he does not see the use."[22]

Beyond this tendency among American intellectuals to contribute to their own disregard, their actual status has been clouded by the fact that it is intellectuals themselves who are most responsible for chronicling their story of displacement. One wonders whether their perception of their own status is altogether accurate. For example, the recent perception of the intellectual's status was shaped, to a large extent, in the decades following World War II. The rise of the university alongside the hysteria of McCarthyism, the sharp increase in those pursuing graduate degrees alongside the expansion of the corporate economy, the emergence of an artistic counterculture alongside a broader tendency toward cultural complacency and conformity, helped shape the modern sense of the intellectual's embattled place in American life.

This conflict was given a gladiatorial quality in the presidential contests of the 1950s. When the "egghead," Adlai Stevenson, challenged the "old general," Dwight Eisenhower, the competing strands in American cul-

ture seemed to find their champions. Both candidates made intellectualism something of an issue. Stevenson pointed to the transferal of political
power from one cultural elite to another when he lamented the transition
from the New Dealers to the car dealers. And Eisenhower tapped popular
cynicism when he defined an intellectual as "a person who takes more
words than necessary to say more than he knows." Consequently, Stevenson's defeat took on more than political significance for many intellectuals. In the ascendance of the inarticulate war hero, intellectuals saw
proof of their own displacement, further evidence of a dominant culture
hostile to their sensibilities and unappreciative of their contributions.

But here again the reality was far more complex. Seymour Lipset
noted, even at the time, that intellectuals' sense of their déclassé status
was out of step with popular perceptions. Surveys of popular attitudes
suggested instead that college professors, for example, ranked second
only to physicians in occupational status. Writers, artists, and musicians
ranked almost as high.[23] Furthermore, academia continued to represent
a prestigious career direction for children of professional and business backgrounds. Just as the manufacturing and mercantile barons of
nineteenth-century New England finalized their climb up the social ladder by ushering their children into academic and other intellectual careers, successful professionals and business persons of the 1950s steered
their children toward intellectual pursuits in disproportionate numbers.[24]

If intellectuals have not suffered a steady erosion of status and influence, if their own worst enemy is often themselves, if popular attitudes
do not seem to square with their own sense of reality, then the romantic
portrait of the unappreciated intellectual needs reconsideration. It need
not be rejected altogether, for clearly on some level the intellectual of the
1790s stood in different relation to American life than the intellectual of
today. It is a difference reflected perhaps most fundamentally in the very
term itself. In the 1790s the word *intellectual* did not designate a type or
class of individuals. Literary and intellectual pursuits did not identify
particular individuals or groups but rather complemented other contributions to public life made by clergymen, judges, physicians, merchants,
and statesmen.

But beyond this, it is difficult to speak without considerable qualification regarding the position or power of intellectuals in America. Some
would even go so far as to argue that the existence of anti-intellectualism
in America and the resulting sense of unappreciation among intellectuals

are more a reflection of intellectuals' continued status than any loss of public stature, that intellectuals' laments about declining influence are rooted in their continued access to public power and perhaps even their disproportionate influence.

There are plenty of examples to support this argument. The strident anti-intellectualism that accompanied fundamentalist attacks on modernism in the late nineteenth century was clearly an expression of fundamentalists' own sense of disfranchisement. It was the institutional entrenchment of the intellectual mainstream, their control over the academic and literary establishment, in effect, their positions of cultural influence and prestige, that incited this attack on intellectuals.

More recent concerns about the security of intellectualism in America seem similarly rooted. Fears of resurgent anti-intellectualism in the wake of attempts to restructure and even dismantle the National Endowment for the Humanities mask an important fact—no previous generation of intellectuals has enjoyed comparable access to funding and institutional support. The efforts of conservative politicians and citizen groups to impose limits on the sorts of projects funded may indeed be interpreted as a form of anti-intellectualism, but it is an attack on a fairly well entrenched position. Since the mid-1990s the NEH has distributed over $100 million annually in grants, and over $3.1 billion since the agency's inception in 1965. As many of these grant dollars required the acquisition of matching funds, the NEH further claims to have stimulated more than $1.5 billion in private support for intellectual and cultural efforts.[25] Despite the vitriolic attacks on the agency, moreover, a 1993 survey found 73 percent of those questioned agreeing with the statement that "in spite of economic hardship, public and private support of the arts and humanities should not be curtailed."[26] Federal support for the arts and humanities may be minuscule compared with that provided other government endeavors, it may even pale in comparison to the monies allocated the National Science Foundation; nevertheless, the NEH, coordinating the distribution of several billion dollars, self-administered by intellectuals, historically unfettered by political manipulation, speaks to the status of letters, academic research, and the arts in American society over the past quarter century.

So what has been the place of intellectuals in American life? Have they enjoyed access to public affairs, has the dominant culture respected their achievements and contributions? Or has anti-intellectualism crippled their efforts? Have the highest levels of public life been closed to their influence, has the dominant culture been indifferent or even hostile to their work and their values? Have intellectuals generally been relegated to the margins of American society, and if so, to what extent have they been responsible for their own marginalization?

It is toward answering these questions that the story of the young New England intellectuals who founded the *North American Review* has the most to offer. Clearly, so narrow a study cannot offer too definitive a set of answers to such sweeping questions, but there is much in the experience of these intellectuals that speaks to the experience of American intellectuals more broadly. To begin with, it seems that the questions regarding the place of intellectuals in American life hold a particular poignancy for this region and time. On the one hand, it was in colonial New England that ministers enjoyed their greatest prestige. It was colonial New Englanders who paid the most homage to intellectual pursuits— prided themselves on their commitment to education and founded the first colleges and libraries. And it was in New England that an aloof political theorist like John Adams could achieve political power, just as did his scholarly son. But it was also New England intellectuals who complained most loudly of their isolation and disfranchisement by the end of the nineteenth century. It was Boston's intellectual establishment that retreated most completely behind the fortress of "high culture." It was Boston's Henry James who suggested that the person of literary sensibilities had no place in the bustle of American society. And it was John and John Quincy Adams's heir Henry who wrote the intellectual's most elaborate monody of obsolescence and marginalization.

In between these two eras stood the young Federalist intellectuals of the *North American Review.* In between the integration of John Quincy Adams and the alienation of Henry Adams stood William Tudor and George Ticknor, Edward and Alexander Everett, Jared Sparks, William Hickling Prescott, and several other young Federalists anxious to preserve their Federalist heritage and stake out a place for the intellectual in American life.

The story of these young Federalists thus holds meaning at a variety of levels. For students of American politics, it offers something on the history of the first party system and the resilience of its political ideology. For the student of American culture, their views on literature and its importance for the new Republic form an important chapter in the history of American letters. For the student of American society, the institutional reforms they advocated hold significance for nineteenth-century social development. And for students of all sorts, their attempts to achieve through cultural vehicles the type of influence their fathers exercised through political channels—to carve out a meaningful public role for men of advanced education and literary sensibilities—hold a significance as much personal as historical.

Nor in exploring the social and political forces that framed their place and sense of place in America can the human dimensions of their story be ignored. For underneath it all, theirs was a story about meaning and purpose, about conscience and sense of self. It was a story, moreover, worked out within the context of conflicting generations—generations united by their beliefs about man and society and the responsibilities incurred by the "wise and the good" but separated by their willingness and ability to adapt to the changing character of American life. Just as poignantly, because it occurred within the complicated context of antebellum culture, where questions about self were often textured by questions about manhood, this pursuit of position and place took on even greater pathos. When this group of young intellectuals introduced their new journal in 1815, theirs was no uncomplicated task—they set out not only to establish a new voice for Federalism but also to secure a place for themselves as useful citizens, as their fathers' sons, and as men.

CHAPTER 2

FATHERS

➤ For the Federalists of Harrison Gray Otis's generation, the events surrounding 1815 were as unexpected as they were grim. The embarrassment of Hartford and the subsequent collapse of the party were not a part of the world they expected to inherit. They had come of age in a time when the principles and position of Federalism had been securely established. In the pulpit and the schools of late eighteenth-century New England, Federalist values were canonized and sustained. The New England clergy, although somewhat divided theologically, were still united in their commitment to Federalist principles of deference and authority. New England's schools—with Harvard the proud centerpiece—remained largely resistant to the pressures of curricular reform, and consequently their traditional classical course of studies reenforced the hierarchical standards of Federalism. Politically the principles of Federalism seemed on equally secure ground. The Federalist Party dominated the national government and enjoyed an almost unrivaled hegemony in most New England states. Its policies had been legislated into law, its economic principles had been firmly established through the efforts of Alexander Hamilton, and its long-term interests seemed secured by the strengthening of the judicial branch.

For Federalists like Otis, the future was promising. Later toasted as "the first scholar of the first class of a new nation," he graduated from Harvard in 1783, and his entry into adulthood was celebrated with a portentous mingling of personal and national destiny.[1] The record of his earliest forays into the public arena suggests this optimism was not misplaced. His regular participation at town meetings and the approving nods of elder Federalist statesmen reflect the confidence and even arrogance of a political culture secure in itself.

There were some troubling signs of insurrection during the last decade and a half of the eighteenth century. The Jeffersonian faction was gathering strength. The political and philosophical heresies emanating from France were increasingly visible. And the perhaps always present challenges to the social consensus surfaced violently in the rebellion of west Massachusetts farmers under Daniel Shays. But in the late 1790s a Federalist could still believe that the traditional Federalist culture would prevail. Shays' Rebellion of 1786 was summarily subdued. Otis and the Federalist volunteers of the Independent Light Infantry helped fend off this challenge to good order and subsequently were awarded the honor of escorting President Washington on his trip to Boston. By 1798 the worst of the French threat had passed, with even the ever-gloomy Fisher Ames agreeing that "folly has nearly burnt out its fuel." The forces of Jeffersonianism, albeit growing, still seemed manageable. Otis's attack on Albert Gallatin in 1795 won him party applause as proof of the security of Federalism. Dismissing this critic of the Jay Treaty as a "vagrant foreigner who . . . ten years ago came to this Country with a second shirt to his back," Otis "met Democracy in its citadel," crowed his biographer, and prevailed.[2]

But in 1800 the confidence of this culture and the party that represented it met a challenge less easily dismissed. In the election of Thomas Jefferson, the Federalists of Otis's generation faced a challenge that was both political and cultural. As a result, the confidence and arrogance that had characterized their earlier assumptions of hegemony were replaced with unequivocal alarm. Portraying him in Robespierrean terms, they attacked Jefferson as a demagogue and a tyrant, a man who held little respect for the Constitution or the people who had been duped into supporting his election. They ridiculed him as a radical and a dreamer, a hopeless visionary incapable of disciplined thought, much less effective leadership.[3]

A few Federalists managed to retain a certain smug confidence in the persisting influence of the party. Josiah Quincy, the Federalist congressman from Massachusetts, even managed to turn defeat into victory and find affirmation in Republican imitation. The Republicans, he charged, "have found nothing in the general organization of their system to alter, scarcely anything, which they have even pretended to improve." The revolutionary dangers Federalists had anticipated in their Republican opponents had proved a paper tiger. They were not the formidable agents of international revolution but rather the spineless reflections of the public's mood—"federalist, or democrat, or jacobin, or republican, according to the varying breath of popular humour."[4]

But by 1804 even this residual confidence had vanished. In that year Jefferson carried Massachusetts, and Republican candidates made significant gains in congressional and state legislative campaigns. Republicans took control of the state legislature in 1806 and captured the governorship in 1807. During these years the hegemony of Massachusetts's Federalist Party was shattered, and up to the outbreak of war in 1812, they essentially shared power with the Republicans, with no party polling more than 51 percent in any gubernatorial election.[5]

Amid these local defeats the Federalists were little able to appreciate the gestures of moderation that Jefferson offered from Washington. Many historians have argued that they were well placed in their skepticism. According to these scholars Jefferson acted forcefully to undo the Federalist legacy, aggressively removing Federalists from office in the process. Still others have argued that he was genuine in his pledge of moderation, changing the established processes of government little and exercising his patronage powers with restraint.[6] But all agree that Republicans at the state and local level, including Massachusetts, were more aggressive in exercising their patronage powers. As Federalists and Republicans swapped positions with every election and new hostile elements entered the political arena in the wake of each Republican victory—religious dissenters, institutional reformers, upstate squatters—the Federalist sense of social and political security faded quickly.[7]

It was within this context of increasing local insecurity that Republican national policies took on their heightened significance. The Louisiana Purchase in 1803, for example, portended nothing but trouble for Federalists. The prospect of several new states, agricultural and instinctively Republican, threatened to reduce the already waning Federalist influence. This fear was exacerbated by an old grievance, the three-fifths clause. This constitutional travesty, it was charged, had given the election to Jefferson in 1800 and tilted the national government toward the slave-invested South. Massachusetts attempted to eliminate this clause in 1805 but saw in the defeat of its efforts further proof of the political imbalance.[8] Against this background Jefferson's restrictive commercial policies introduced in 1806 represented only the latest in a series of hostile measures from the Republican administration.

These policies, designed in an attempt to avoid war by removing American shipping from the seas, were, in retrospect, perhaps ill conceived but hardly discriminatory in their intent or effects. Southern planters suffered equally in the restriction of their crops from European markets, and many New Englanders actually benefited from the increased opportunities the Embargo created in the coastal peddling trade. But these nuances were neither recognized nor appreciated by Federalist critics. Nor did the peddling trade prove sufficient to carry the entire New England economy.[9] By 1808, as exports backed up, unemployment rose, and the entire town of Boston wilted under the pressure of commercial stagnation, Federalist criticism grew united and vehement.[10]

The economic crisis induced by these measures should not be minimized. New England had legitimate grievances with Jefferson's, and later Madison's, policies. But it is also true that Federalist complaints during this period assumed a tone and breadth that were informed by more than just these current issues. The entire list of Federalist concerns, from the Louisiana Purchase to the three-fifths clause, from the refusal to renew the Jay Treaty to the rejection of the Monroe-Pinckney Treaty, from the submission to the Berlin Decree to the series of restrictive measures culminating in the Embargo of 1807, were all identified as part of a single program. Amid the increasing tension of local politics and the economic pressure of commercial restriction, Federalists perceived not just a series of policy disagreements but the irrefutable proofs of regional prejudice and Republican conspiracy.

John Lowell noted in 1810, just as Quincy had in 1805, the adoption of Federalist policies by Republican opponents. Hamiltonian finance, the National Bank, and naval construction were all offered as proof of Republican co-optation. For Lowell, however, this was no cause for complacency. The Republicans were far from harmless imitators but rather "violent theorists." Thomas Jefferson was nothing other than a "Frenchman in manners, sentiments and feelings," a participant in a conspiracy to destroy British commerce using American shipping as "the instrument of his warfare and intrigues." The *Chesapeake* affair and the diplomatic intrigue surrounding Francis Jackson, the British minister to the United States, were offered as further proof of Jefferson's conspiratorial intent.

Hardly cautious attempts to secure American interests, as Jefferson described them, they demonstrated the "undeviating pursuit of a system of measures hostile to commerce."[11]

Why Americans should demonstrate a recurring tendency to place political conflicts within conspiratory frameworks is a question with which historians have not fully come to terms. Bernard Bailyn and Alan Heimert both noted the recurring appeal and potency of conspiracy theories in the eighteenth century.[12] Whether this tendency should be traced to the popularity of radical Whig literature in the colonies, as Bailyn suggested, or the persistence of Calvin's cosmological dualism, as Heimert argued, Federalists of the early nineteenth century were as willing to employ these interpretive frameworks as their eighteenth-century compatriots. Just as American Revolutionaries had seen in efforts of the British ministry an insatiable grasping for power, Federalists saw in the Republican administration a lust for power which "lives by corruption . . . [and] hastens to glut its ravening appetite on our morals, that it may devour our liberties, at its leisure."[13] Just as American patriots had seen in the actions of Britain's Parliament a systematic attack on their liberty, Federalists saw in Republican commercial policies a conspiracy to "embarrass commerce and annihilate its influence . . . part of a system, which has for its objects, the present advancement of their personal views and the permanent elevation of the interests of the planting States over the commercial."[14]

This penchant for analysis via conspiracy may have been an American tradition, but it was wholly out of character for the Federalists. Prudent, cautious, and self-consciously sensible, Federalists loathed extremism and emotional hyperbole. As heirs of what Henry May has labeled the "Moderate Enlightenment," they sought balance and reason in all things. The tone and the content of their rhetoric during this crisis represented thus not just the revival of an American tradition but the expressions of a party and an ideology under stress.[15]

The mounting pressure upon Federalist ideology was reflected most strikingly in the increasingly apocalyptic view of democratic politics. The acceptance of popular participation had always been, for many Federalists, more an unpleasant concession to political realities than the result of ideological commitment. This concession had always depended upon a certain confidence in the persisting power of social deference. But as the political tension of the decade increased, this Federalist confidence weakened, and their latent fears of democratic politics rose to the surface.

Among the more eloquent early critics of democracy was Fisher Ames. Born in 1758, he cut his political teeth on Shays' Rebellion and consequently developed a distrust of the people that grew pathological over time. For Ames democracy was flawed on several counts. For starters it was inherently unstable. Resting as it did on the "approbation of the majority . . . the first murmurs of sedition excite doubts of that approbation."[16] Sound government, in Ames's thought, required a transcendent source of authority—some institution or historical assumption of authority that transcended particular peoples or periods. But among democrats, he lamented, "there is nothing so fixed that they may not change it; nothing so sacred that their voice, which is the voice of God, would not unsanctify and consign to destruction."[17] To an extent he seems to have believed this a particular failing of the American people. Noting the devotion of British and French citizens to their countries, he mourned the American lack of "national prejudice."[18] But he seems also to have believed faithlessness a problem inherent in the democratic mentality. Fickle and lacking both education and breeding, the people "can only destroy; they cannot rule." Indiscriminate in their political passions, they became, inevitably, "blind instruments in the hands of ambitious men."[19]

Despite these doubts Ames claimed that he and most other Federalists were "essentially democratic."[20] He did not share the usual Federalist confidence in deference but did hold hope that the failings of popular government might be offset by institutional restraints, such as an independent judiciary. But for the pessimistic Ames even these hopes were short-lived. The Constitution, he concluded in 1804, had only bred complacency. Federalists had unwisely concluded that its system of institutional restraints, "once fairly engrossed in parchment, was a bridge over chaos that could defy the discord of all its elements."[21]

The Constitution held little long-term promise for Ames. Nor did any of the other political theories "so dear to our vanity."[22] The progressive refinement of public tastes through the diffusion of knowledge also promised little. America's high level of literacy, in fact, bode more harm than good. Widespread literacy and a popular press that provided an "endless stimulus to their imagination and passions" left the public "susceptible of every transient enthusiasm, and of more than womanish fickleness of caprice." Nor could love of country be counted on to maintain public discipline. "We may as well talk," said Ames, "of loving geometry."[23]

Ames was influenced not only by a pessimistic view of human nature but also by a mechanistic sense of history. Such a view of history was common in the late eighteenth century at all points on the political spectrum from Ames to Jefferson.[24] "The political sphere," Ames argued, "like the globe we tread upon, never stands still, but with a silent swiftness accomplishes the revolutions which, we are too ready to believe, are effected by our wisdom, or might have been controlled by our efforts." But whereas Jefferson envisioned, at least for the proximate future, a course of progress, Ames saw the United States drawn within the "revolutionary suction of Niagara." While Jefferson waxed eloquent on the perfectibility of the human race, Ames's historical vision was filled with nothing but despair. "Our days are made heavy with the pressure of anxiety, and our nights restless with visions of horror. We listen to the clank of chains, and overhear the whispers of assassins. We mark the barbarous dissonance of mingled rage and triumph in the yell of an infatuated mob, we see the dismal glare of their burnings and scent the loathsome steam of human victims offered in sacrifice."[25]

Ames was revered throughout the New England states. His name was often mentioned in tones more usually reserved for George Washington and Alexander Hamilton. He was heralded as "the American Burke," and his death in 1808 was proclaimed a tragedy of national proportions.[26] But it seems that this reverence did not signify agreement with all points of his political vision. He himself lamented that so few Federalists recognized the dire situation confronting the American experiment.[27] Among a caste cautious and conservative by nature, his apocalyptic rhetoric no doubt proved excessive. But if perhaps more moody and melodramatic, he was far from unique. Benjamin Wells, in complaining of the town halls filled with "the breath of fat and greasy citizens," was able to match Ames's contempt and his rhetoric.[28] More importantly, the resolution of a Boston town meeting in 1812 suggests that as the political crisis grew, Ames's apocalyptic vision came to reflect more closely the general Federalist mood. Confronted by the specter of mob violence in the attack on a Federalist paper in Baltimore, the citizens of Boston saw "a prelude to the dissolution of all free government and the establishment of a reign of Terror. The mob erects its horrid crest over the ruins of liberty, of property, of the domestic relations of life and of civil institutions; untill satiated or fatigued with slaughter it resigns its bludgeons and its pikes at the feet of a dictator, and raises its bloody hands to worship some God of Idolatry."[29]

This was not the language of a self-confident elite. This was not the posture of a party secure in its position or its beliefs. Nor was this fear of democratic chaos the only evidence of ideological strain. It was further reflected in the adoption of decidedly non-Federalist positions. One such example was the increasing acceptance among Federalists of party politics. Traditional Federalist ethics condemned the formation of partisan factions—the curse of republican government—and held that politicking was beneath the dignity of the true statesman. But as David Hackett Fischer first pointed out, a number of "young Federalists" quickly adapted to the new political realities and imitated the tactics of their more successful Republican rivals.[30]

This foray into party organization and active political campaigning began cautiously. Ranking Federalists emphasized the ad hoc nature of their earliest caucuses and instructed local committees to pursue tactics commensurate with the party's dignity and reputation. But by 1810 the party machinery was firmly established, and party zealots were actively engaging in a far less restrained range of electioneering methods. Immigrants and minors were illegally registered, and workers were cajoled by their Federalist employers. Liquor was distributed freely on election day, loans were made readily available to individuals unable to satisfy the registration requirement, and sailors were taxied to the polls by their Federalist shipmasters. Viciously partisan newspapers were inaugurated, and even public rallies, the trademark of Jacobinism, were held to drum up support.[31]

These adaptations brought the Federalist Party some electoral success, but they were not without their ideological costs. Ames worried about the dangers of a runaway press; George Cabot feared more a runaway public.[32] Another old Federalist saw in these developments "the very thing we condemn," and Thomas Dwight refused to "resort to those contemptible measures which distinguish the exertions of its enemies." Some thus retired from public life rather than yield to the demands of modern politics, but others, perhaps most, responded like Cabot, who accepted the new political realities while lamenting the descent "into the vortex of politics, which I wish to shun."[33]

Further evidence of ideological strain, or rather reversal, was reflected in the increasing provincialism of the party. In response to Jefferson's election in 1801, Fisher Ames urged Federalists to "entrench themselves in the State governments, and endeavour to make State justice and State power a shelter of the wise, and good, and rich."[34] An element of provincialism had always existed within New England Federalism. But the party had formed itself around the principle of national strength and the necessity of a strong federal government. It had forged party unity around the nation-building economic policies of Alexander Hamilton, and it exploited regional disorder in the case of the Whiskey Rebellion as a means of increasing federal strength. Ames's advice, set against this tradition, amounted to a repudiation of past principles, a defederalization, in effect, of Federalism.

The confusion expressed ideologically was exacerbated by a series of internal conflicts. Federalism was distinctive in the late eighteenth century because of its surprising degree of unity. Social and political leaders, the clergy, and the commercial elite united, with considerable public support, behind a broad ideological consensus. But during the first decade of the nineteenth century, a series of intra-Federalist schisms undermined this unity and compounded the sense of disarray. One of these separated moderates from ultraists on the subject of Republican commercial policies and British duplicity. While extremists such as Timothy Pickering absolved the British of all responsibility, even in the wake of the *Chesapeake* affair, moderates like Otis were puzzled by the British Orders in Council and not uncritical of Britain's stubborn adherence to them.[35]

A second schism was drawn between traditionalists who criticized the increasing materialism of the age and a capitalist class taking full advantage of its opportunities. In between stood more clever politicians who traced even materialism to the policies of Jefferson. Speaking of the Louisiana Purchase, the Massachusetts House of Representatives observed, "This extension of territory has already excited a spirit of cupidity and speculation, which is among the causes of our present troubles."[36] But such explanations only veiled a growing tension between capitalists and traditionalists.

The pressure of Republican commercial policies created yet another division within the Federalist ranks. While the Embargo and Non-Intercourse Acts stifled transoceanic trade, frustrated capital developed new outlets in domestic manufacturing and a coastal, or "peddling,"

trade. The significance of this new trade became apparent when merchants of the latter sort broke ranks with the former and objected to a
too narrow and too belligerent approach to Republican measures. An intemperate response might antagonize southern merchants and jeopardize
these new commercial opportunities.[37]

Yet another schism, one ultimately of still greater importance, was
inspired by the emergence within New England Congregationalism of
Unitarianism. Liberals and orthodox Calvinists had clashed repeatedly
within the Congregationalist establishment since the founding of Massachusetts Bay, but the second half of the eighteenth century saw relatively little open conflict as conservatives and liberals united behind broad
doctrinal principles and compelling political concerns. In 1803, however,
the death of David Tappan, Harvard's orthodox professor of divinity, unsettled this rapprochement. The selection of the Unitarian Henry Ware
to replace Tappan, shortly followed by the election to the college presidency of Samuel Webber, another liberal, placed the college firmly in the
hands of the liberals and prompted two decades of institutional and cultural conflict. Complete schism would be postponed for several years. As
Daniel Howe has noted, "As long as deism and Jacobinism threatened,
the two wings of the established church made common cause in defense
of true religion and good order."[38] But the unity of the religious establishment was fractured nonetheless. The persisting polemics had the
additional effect of alienating members of the lay elite. Although the
Unitarians seemed on their part somewhat reluctant to enter into open
combat, the forces of orthodox Calvinism were not. But far from winning
supporters, their acrimonious attacks on Unitarians, coupled with their
crusade against the Bavarian Illuminati, only served to undermine their
credibility as moderate custodians of social order.[39]

Thus by 1812 Federalism was neither the united nor the ideologically
coherent force it had once been. Buffeted by Republican commercial
policies, concerned with the deterioration of their legislative strength,
unnerved by theories of social and political disintegration, and torn by internal division, Federalists looked out upon the political and social landscape with considerable anxiety. To an extent Federalists drew a blank
in explaining the confusion that surrounded them. What had brought
about this "strange condition . . . that the new states govern the old; the
unsettled the settled," asked Josiah Quincy. What could make a Christian
people elect to the presidency a "despiser of their holy religion," pondered

John Lowell. But more often they converted their own confusion to partisan purpose and traced it to Republican policies. Republican success and the excitement of the French Revolution had brought to the surface, argued Richard Henry Dana, "all those characters hanging loose on society." Jefferson's commercial policies, added Lowell, served to drive out of business the honorable merchant and leave in his place "needy and desperate adventurers." Right and wrong had been turned upside down by Republican rule, social distinctions had become blurred—Jefferson's policies "tended to confound moral distinctions, to lessen the respect that belongs to the wise and good," and generally brought about a "debasement of national character." "The whole is awfully confused," summed up William Sullivan more poetically; "effects without causes; ends without means; all is mystery, sophistry, delusion, madness!"[40]

It was thus a frightened and ideologically confused but rabidly partisan party that confronted Madison's declaration of war in 1812. Federalists cringed at Republicans' "hypocritical" defense of "free trade and sailors' rights" and ridiculed their sudden conversion to naval development. The willingness of Republicans to ignore French duplicity offered further proof of a biased and viciously partisan administration. Most importantly, Madison's willingness to pursue war and alienate New England's primary trade partner, even after Britain repealed its Orders in Council, reaffirmed suspicions of an anticommercial bias.[41]

Again, Federalists insisted that these current grievances were only part of a much greater problem. "The evils we suffer," stated a group of Federalists gathered at Northampton, "are not wholly of a temporary nature, springing from the war, but some of them are of a permanent character, resulting from a perverse construction of the Constitution of the United States."[42] The three-fifths clause, the Louisiana Purchase, and Jefferson's Embargo drew equal fire in their comprehensive critique of Madison's war. Thus synthesizing old fears with new grievances, Federalists launched their opposition.

This opposition took a variety of forms. New England towns sent off petitions of redress by the handful. Vermont attempted to recall its state militia from the service of the federal government. Massachusetts rallied to Vermont's defense and similarly refused to cooperate with federal troop requests. The culmination of this opposition came in 1814 when three states—Massachusetts, Connecticut, and Rhode Island—sent delegates to Hartford to consider a more effective course of action.

Harrison Gray Otis, by Gilbert Stuart, 1809. (Courtesy of the Society for the Preservation of New England Antiquities)

Their specific objectives in meeting were somewhat ambiguous. Hard-line Federalists like Timothy Pickering urged the delegates to explore secession. Moderates like Harrison Gray Otis hoped to avoid this extreme and to secure more limited goals—constitutional revisions and state control over their own militia and defense. Otis confided yet a third objective in a letter to a friend. This convention, he hoped, would provide an outlet for popular steam and give moderates time to win concessions from the administration.[43]

Regardless of these differences, to nonparticipants, Republicans in particular, the objectives and significance of this convention seemed clear. Massachusetts's Republican press labeled the convention delegates "mischievous men" and their activities treasonous. According to Boston's *Independent Chronicle,* this convention recklessly sabotaged the peace negotiations and strengthened the enemy by "holding out to that foe, the evidence of our being a divided people."[44] As much as Federalists tried to defend the convention as the judicious and moderate course of responsible leadership, the patently non-Federalist character of this renegade assembly left them ideologically compromised and politically vulnerable.

To a certain extent Republicans attacked the Federalist opposition in traditional ideological terms. The restricted participation and secret meetings were condemned, for example, as typical Federalist elitism. But just as often Republicans twisted the debate and used the Federalists' own principles to condemn their current actions. Federalists were criticized as animated by "the spirit of party" and guided by narrow parochial interests. Not among these, ironically, was a concern for the public debt. Republicans portrayed the party of Hamilton as insensitive to the questions of finance and credit raised by their convention. Federalist foreign affinities were also turned on their head as Hartford recalled for Republican critics the "groans of revolutionary France." In yet another ironic twist, Federalist machinations were linked to the turmoil of 1786, as Federalist conspirators, the *Chronicle* charged, summoned the public to "the standard of insurrection, bearing the devices which waved on the standard of Daniel Shays."[45]

This attack on the Federalists as sowers of discord and threats to the Constitution provided the Republicans with their most potent weapon. Although moderates like Otis denied such secessionist intentions, the threat of secession, which had lurked on the edges of Federalist rhetoric for years, was now far too prevalent to deny. John Lowell, who had called the purchase of Louisiana a "breach of the federal compact" and had warned as early as 1810 that any decision to wage war against England would compel the New England states to seek a separate peace "by the law of self-preservation," reminded the timid in 1813, "I am not such a slave to my fears of disunion, as to approve of measures which ruin my own part of the country." That portion of their allegiance which the people of Massachusetts had transferred to the Union, added Josiah Quincy, was "not only limited in its nature, but it is, also, conditional." "Union," noted a committee of the Massachusetts House of Representatives, "was only one of the objects of the Constitution," and it deserved Federalist support only "so long as the Union can be made the instrument of these other Constitutional objects."[46]

With this Federalist position so clearly laid out, Republican charges of disloyalty came easily. Even a few embarrassed Federalists saw the hypocrisy of this new Federalist stance. "The old federal doctrine strenuously maintained in 1798, and since, was love of country as a duty enjoined on every citizen—obedience to its laws and respect for its constituted authorities. Shall the arms of the nation now be weakened, at this awful crisis, because those in authority are not of our party? Forbid it patriotism."[47]

Thus criticized from all directions, Federalism was driven into even further disarray. Some of the Federalists' most fundamental principles were turned against them, and perhaps more painfully, the opposition appropriated historical symbols and events that had helped form the party and define its identity. Nor, given the circumstances, were Federalists able to prevent this ideological usurpation. They seem to have recognized that their defense required the reappropriation of their history as the party of the Constitution and order. The *Boston Spectator* thus tried to rally support for the convention by recalling the Federalist tradition of deference and a politics of the general welfare. "If their propositions . . . are wise, (and if they are not, where shall we look among men for wisdom) we are bound to adopt them and carry them into effect; not by any legal, but by that moral obligation, which makes it the duty of every individual in society, to do whatever his own and the common good requires."[48] Other apologists looked beyond the convention and, in traditional Federalist fashion, traced the crisis to democratic flaws within the American system. The short term of the presidential office, for example, was blamed for generating the erroneous belief that it was "the gift of the multitude."

Because ambitious politicians could most easily excite the public through xenophobic manipulation, "there must be, in the very nature of our government, a constant tendency to unnecessary war, as long as the tenure of our highest offices is subject to frequent changes."[49]

But the employment of traditional Federalist arguments to defend their actions was less common than the resort to more general sources of justification. If Federalism's peculiar history could not be reclaimed, the more generic Revolutionary past might be. Joseph Lyman thus called the machinations of Townshend and North "far less aggressive than those we have felt from the Rulers at Washington" and addressed his call to resistance to "the Sons of those who vindicated their rights against the encroachments of Great Britain." Charles Hare appealed to an even more generic source of justification. The Massachusetts resolutions supporting the convention were simply "American in their tone and language."[50]

Once started down this path, it was difficult to stop, and Federalists most commonly, and most ironically, found their strongest defense in a tradition more easily associated with Thomas Jefferson, the social compact theory of John Locke. Hare buttressed his defense via Americanism with a defense of resistance based upon "the inherent right of the people to resist measures fundamentally inconsistent with the principles of just liberty and the Social compact." Artemas Ward quoted Locke directly in arguing "whoever in authority exceeds his powers, acts without authority, and may be opposed, as any other man who invades his rights."[51] The *Boston Spectator,* even while urging patience, acknowledged that "the general government has so violated the principles of the federal compact . . . [that] the people are, both as a nation and as distinct states, in fact absolved from their pledged allegiance."[52] This reliance upon Locke may have formed their most appropriate defense, but it made them no less vulnerable to charges of ideological confusion. Nor did it convince more traditional Federalists that it was the judicious thing to do. This "reversion of authority to the people," admitted Hare, may be the necessary course of action, but it was "dreadful in theory, and may be ruinous in practice."[53]

Politically pummeled and ideologically bewildered, Federalists were whipped closer to complete disarray. Their Republican opponents had all the best weapons, including twenty years of the Federalists' own principles and pronouncements. But at least the Federalists retained the dignity that accrued to their identification as the opposition party. If chastised and vilified, they still garnered the respect that accompanied the fear of what they might be able to do—conclude a separate peace, undermine the war effort, or sabotage the nation's finances. But in the final stages of the war they lost even this.

Perhaps the greatest failure of Federalists lay in their complete misreading of the final events of the war. In addition to their ideological confusion, perhaps because of it, they misread all of the signs by which they might have avoided complete disaster. The first of these critical errors was their misreading of the negotiations at Ghent. Quoting English sources and common military logic, they argued up to the very end that a treaty of peace could never be reached. Consequently when peace did come, the Federalists were caught flat-footed and embarrassed. Unable to take any credit for the treaty and unable to fully celebrate it, the "peace party" could offer little positive response. They thus called it a bad treaty, "proof that our degradation was complete." In their criticism that it achieved none of the objectives that launched America into war, the party of conciliation, the party that had condemned Madison for his "mad adherence" to the absolute position that the United States "must give up no right, or perish in the struggle," now struck the transparently hypocritical stance of hard-line principle.[54]

Even more damaging, Federalists seemed unaware of, or perhaps unable to appreciate, the significance of New Orleans. While the Republican press provided daily reports and endless letters from the front, the Federalist papers questioned the significance of the battle.[55] While the Republican papers caught the nation's imagination with their stories of Andrew Jackson and the heroics of his Tennessee and Kentucky volunteers, Federalists scoffed at the impact of the battle on the peace talks. "No power makes peace in consequence of a reverse in fortune, but one that cannot make another effort."[56] When once again the Federalists were proved wrong, when New Orleans was won in such a nationally ego-inflating fashion, the Federalists were exposed as insatiable cynics, malcontents too jaded and miserable to share in America's triumph.

Their lack of foresight and inability to judge events challenged any claim to their being the party of vision and wisdom. Moreover, their own now pathetic maneuvering, as the war came to its dramatic conclusion, made their previous status enviable. As the nation celebrated Ghent and New Orleans, Harrison Gray Otis carried the demands of the Hartford delegates to Washington, D.C. Vilified before as formidable agents of "civil commotion," their surprisingly tame report was ridiculed as "something like a mouse." Its moderate tone, far from winning them grateful respect, earned only contempt. After they supposedly had labored for years to "weaken and destroy" the Constitution and the nation, the moderate recommendations they now produced were portrayed as the "whining cant of hypocrisy." In the mockery of its Republican opponents and the frontier nationalism of the era of New Orleans, Federalism, already having endured political defeat and ideological disarray, now faced the prospect of political irrelevancy.[57]

The complete realization of these fears was still a few years away. Although ideologically confused by a decade and a half of partisan wrangling and politically embarrassed by the tide of recent events, Federalists still looked for ways to reestablish themselves within national affairs. James Monroe's visit to New England in 1817 seemed to offer just such an opportunity. Amid artillery salutes and lines of flag-waving schoolchildren, local Federalists and the Republican president offered one another exaggerated gestures of reconciliation. Monroe spoke eloquently of the Union, "an object to which I look with the utmost solicitude," while Federalist leaders like Harrison Gray Otis and John Brooks actually competed with local Republicans for Monroe's attention. A dinner party at Otis's home was followed by a carefully scripted tour which accentuated the city's more unambiguously patriotic past. A trip to Bunker Hill and an Independence Day service at the Old South Church set the stage for a presentation before the Society of Cincinnati, where the Federalist governor and Republican president rhetorically embraced one another as "brother of the Cincinnati" and recalled the "common toils and perils" of their Revolutionary experience.[58]

After years of partisan conflict, the consciously conciliatory tone of the events must have been refreshing. But there must also have been something just a little disconcerting in this vision of Federalists vying for the attention of a Republican president. This was the party of Adams and Hamilton; it represented the political and social elite of the nation's most venerable state. Watching it now court the favor of the opposition party's president must have left contemporaries not a little disoriented, if not embarrassed by the ideological disarray it represented. Moreover, all this pandering did not prove effective. Federalist leaders had placed a great deal of hope in Monroe's visit, and in his very character. Perceiving him as weak and vacillating, Federalists believed him susceptible to their influence. But they were much disappointed. Although he did pursue certain Federalist policy objectives, he did not open up many offices to Federalist applicants. When he rejected George Sullivan's request that Daniel Webster be named attorney general as "a pledge to the mass of federalists," Monroe served notice that his own administration would continue Madison's unofficial policy of exclusion.[59]

Similar failure greeted the conciliatory efforts of Harrison Gray Otis, elected to the Senate in 1817. His political realism, concluded Samuel Eliot Morison, made him the perfect "ambassador of peace and goodwill from Massachusetts Federalism to the national administration." While there he made a genuine attempt to adapt to the new political realities. He attended Monroe's inauguration despite having to fight his way through a mob of "Scavengers and wash women of the City" and gave Washington society a try, in 1818 even enduring the "indecorous exhibition" of a waltz. But always somewhat out of place, sensitive to a certain "shyness with which any measure is regarded, that comes from Massachusetts," he completed his term a Senate nonpresence, failing to obtain for Massachusetts compensation for its wartime expenditures, much less to reestablish the state's or the party's national prominence.[60]

Nor was Otis's colleague in the Senate, Elijah Mills, any more successful. Like Otis he made an effort to reassert the presence of Massachusetts Federalism within the Republican capital. But like Otis, his somewhat forced ventures into Washington society served only to confirm for him its distasteful character. He spoke mockingly of Monroe's drawing room where "all classes and conditions of society . . . mingled in ill-assorted and fantastic groups," and irreverently he reduced diplomatic dinners to "the usual insipid interchange of idle questions and needless replies." He took unapologetic comfort in his provincialism, mocking the social efforts of foreign dignitaries, and spoke passionately of his desire to return to Boston and escape Washington and "all the slander, and all the intrigue, political and moral."[61]

Mills's legislative efforts were equally unsuccessful. He complained of a lingering bias against Massachusetts and as time passed spoke of Congress with increasing pessimism and even contempt. He scoffed sarcastically at "the august body" in which "premeditated orations from men of ordinary capacity and less acquirements" had replaced the eloquence and brilliance of Ames, Dexter, and Otis and even more gloomily foresaw on the floors of Congress "scenes of turbulence, of violence, of political rancor and personal abuse."[62]

Within this atmosphere Mills operated with faltering confidence and without a clear sense of political direction. As the party divided over tactics and candidates in the 1824 presidential election, he echoed the general confusion. Crawford was disingenuous, Clay too "rash . . . and inconsiderate." Calhoun was better qualified, "of good talents, well-educated." But he had little chance of success and was "too theorizing, speculative, and metaphysical." Jackson's education was inadequate, and "his modes of thinking and habits of life partake too much of war and military glory." Adams was "unquestionably more learned, better educated, has a more thorough knowledge of our Constitution, our foreign relations, the history, theory, and practice of our government, than either of the other candidates." But there was also about Adams a "cold, repulsive atmosphere . . . that is too chilling for my respiration." In the end he endorsed Jackson, finding him far more "mild and amiable" than the reputation that preceded him. But Mills was far from unequivocal in his support. With an air of detachment that bordered on indifference, he admitted that he lacked "any very strong convictions in favor of either."[63]

The election of a fellow Bay-Stater did not do much to invigorate Mills or Federalism in general. Many criticized Adams's position on tariffs and internal improvements, were disappointed in his use of the patronage powers, and expressed some residual resentment for his betrayal in 1808. Mills, "compelled, by a sense of duty," gained through all of this something of a reputation as "an Administration man." But he was increasingly disheartened by the "total want of talent . . . of energy and political courage, on the part of Mr. Adams's friends." Seeing in their failure the fading of his own vision of government, he fantasized that "if I were ten years younger, and in perfect health, I should like well enough the éclat of placing myself at the head of the feeble band of Administration men." But reflecting his more gloomy and dispirited sense of reality, he concluded he had "neither youth nor health, and have lost something of that ardor that would be necessary to sustain me."[64]

Mills retired from the Senate in 1828 and returned, like Otis, to Boston having failed to reestablish the influence of Boston Federalism. But if in returning to Boston they hoped to find more sympathetic political waters, they were mistaken. In the years following the War of 1812, Republicans built upon their prewar advances and in 1816 captured 50 percent of the state's congressional seats.[65] In addition, the local Federalist Party suffered from dissension within its own ranks. When Otis ran for mayor in 1822, he was defeated by a revolt from the "Middling Interest." The union of elite and public, achieved for so many years through deference, was shattered as the party rank and file first challenged the nomination imposed from above and then forced the naming of a compromise candidate.[66] Recognizing in this rebellion the signs of local, as well as national, political defeat, some tried to impose the comfort of foresight. These "milk and water Federalists," John Lowell pointed out, had never been loyal. "Next to the pleasure of beating the democrats, their greatest is to mortify those whose talents they fear, and whose political probity is an everlasting reproach to themselves."[67] But Otis spoke perhaps more honestly in acknowledging that he and his Federalist friends "did not imagine, when the first war with Britain was over, that the revolution was just begun."[68]

Yet for many old-guard Federalists like Otis, retreat before the advances of this revolution was still unthinkable. Raised to believe that public service was the obligatory burden of their caste, they continued to seek public office despite the frustrations of national and local defeat. Otis, for example, followed his mayoral embarrassment with a race for the governorship in 1823. The Republican opposition responded by attacking, as it had done since 1815, the political sins and miscalculations of the Federalist Party. The failure to support the nation's war effort, the threats of secession, and most importantly, the Hartford Convention, which Otis attended, were placed at the center of their campaign against him.

Otis's supporters defended him with what was by now a rote response.

Question. What was the chief object of the Hartford Convention?
Answer. . . . to consult upon the means of providing an effective defense . . . in concert with the National Government.
Q. Who made the Hartford Convention?
A. The Legislatures of several States.
Q. What said the legislature of Massachusetts to the proceedings of the Convention?
A. . . . well done, good and faithful servants.
Q. What said the people of Massachusetts to the proceedings of the Convention?
A. They testified full approbation of its measures.[69]

But Federalist catechisms like this were not enough to prevent the Republican victory. Once elected, William Eustis, his tactics affirmed by his victory, tried to put the final nail in the Federalist coffin. In his inaugural address he applauded the "change of political sentiment" manifested in his election and beckoned the "rising generation" to the "new era in the history of this commonwealth." Offering no gracious plea for reconciliation, he linked the defeat of the Federalists with the end of the "spirit of party" that had so long prevailed "over the vital interests of the country." With Federalism's defeat, he proclaimed, Massachusetts was "at length restored to the American family."[70]

Federalists were outraged by this attack. But reflecting the malaise into which the party had fallen, Federalists in the state legislature debated their response for days before finally venting not indignation but rather apology. Those were difficult times, they explained; "the whole christian world was involved in the most deplorable warfare; and the constitutional powers, rights and duties, of the National and State governments, were for the first time to be construed, and applied, under circumstances of unprecedented interest, and of the strongest political excitement."[71] The Federalist press denounced Eustis's speech somewhat more aggressively, but it was left to Otis himself to speak out in defense of himself and his party. The decision was a surprising one. In his code of political ethics, the true statesman never sank to such levels. But stung by these criticisms and hoping finally to close the book on the Hartford Convention, he nodded to the new character of politics and published a series of letters in his own defense.[72]

Within these letters Otis first minimized any threats of secession. Similar idle talk had floated around several states for years and represented little more than the angry rhetoric of "family broils." More important, the bitter policy disputes that earlier had divided the parties were a thing of the past as the Republicans adopted Federalist programs as "essentials to the machinery of government." True, partisan attacks still occurred, but on most substantive questions there was "no difference between a member of the Republican family and the persons they persecute." He also defended the reluctance of New Englanders to help finance the war. Their actions were nothing more than the logical expressions of self-preservation and self-interest. That these should be sacrificed to some intangible vision of the national interest was a noble idea. But "unfortunately for mankind, the days of patriotic obligation have gone by; so far . . . as respects silver, and gold, and jewels." Finally Otis addressed the matter of the Hartford Convention itself. Here he argued quite simply that the convention was demanded and subsequently supported by the general public. It was not the creation of some elitist faction, it was not cagily engineered by the wise and the good, but rather it was called into existence, "like peals of incessant thunder," by the people of New England.[73]

This was a remarkable argument. Offered in defense of Federalism, it revealed more just how much Federalism had been unraveled and revised. In minimizing the talk of secession and identifying a new political consensus, Otis closed a chapter of the Federalist past and sounded the end of the first party system. In defending New England's financial pragmatism, he acknowledged the ascendance of a new political morality, one in which private and not public interest legitimately guided political behavior. And finally, in his comments on the origins of the convention, he substituted the directive will of the people for the guiding wisdom of the wise and the good. In defending the Hartford Convention not on its inherent wisdom, or the wisdom of the delegates, but rather on the democratic nature of its origins, he offered an apologetic for the new democracy.

As reflected in Otis's pamphlet, the distance Federalism had traveled since 1800 was indeed great. The once proud party of the wise and the good was now a regional shadow acknowledging the primacy of the popular will. Otis had rallied one more time to defend before the "rising generation" its name and its history, and he may have succeeded in doing so. But he did so at the expense of its ideology. Federalist actions may have been vindicated, but only by announcing the death of the party and its philosophy.

Some historians have argued that Federalism eventually reasserted itself politically. Somewhat modified, considerably subdued, New England's peculiar brand of political conservatism recrystallized, they argue, in the Whig Party of the 1840s.[74] Others have challenged this interpretation, arguing that the Whigs drew more from the moderate or nationalistic wing of the Republican Party.[75] Its future aside, in the short run Federalism struggled politically without direction or confidence. Even those like Otis who had come to accept the new political realities did so more in a spirit of resignation than adaptation. Just as the issues of the earlier era had grown "dry and obsolete," Otis saw himself as something of a relic. "By the perversity of the course of human affairs," he lamented, "I have survived the downfall of the party itself."[76]

But Otis's capitulation represented more a personal failure of imagination than the total defeat of his principles. If he was unable to transcribe the philosophy of the party beyond its immediate failures, there were others more capable. If the Federalists of Otis's generation failed to see beyond the end of the party what was salvable within the broader Federalist tradition, the next generation was far more creative. The young Federalists coming of age during these years of political and ideological upheaval suffered from something of a disadvantage. Their generation lacked the security of status and clarity of direction that had guided their fathers. The political doors were largely shut, the respect and deference of the community could no longer be assumed, and the standard path through Harvard and into law and beyond was not necessarily secure. But in other ways the ideological and occupational disarray was somewhat liberating. It allowed them to reevaluate the political culture of their fathers and rethink their place within society.

The flexibility and creativity of this generation were to prove its most valuable asset. Unlike their fathers, they greeted their more wide-open futures with enthusiasm. They paid homage to their fathers but also criticized that generation's activities and beliefs with the detachment that distance allowed. A few made their way into politics, but more pursued careers in education, art, literature, publishing, commerce, and the law. In the process they transcribed the culture of Federalism to the new social and political realities of America. They worked out a new definition of public service, a new sense of how the wise and the good should serve their communities, and a new ideology of democratic society and their role within it. For a country in the midst of social and institutional development, their innovations were to prove critical. For a country attempting to establish its cultural and national identity, their ideas about literature, history, and the role of the man of letters were to prove of enduring significance.

CHAPTER 3

SONS

➤➤ On most any Sunday evening in 1810, the candles would burn late in the parsonage of the Brattle Street Church as its young pastor, Joseph Stevens Buckminster, indulged himself after a day in the pulpit with an evening of music and conversation. Widely recognized as one of Boston's most brilliant thinkers and affective speakers, Buckminster would lead a discussion that ranged far beyond that day's sermon to questions of literature, art, and science. His guests would include men of established reputation like Samuel Dexter, the eminent lawyer; William Wells, the publisher; and Chief Justice Isaac Parker. But Buckminster also invited younger scholars, men closer to his own age like James Savage and the even younger Edward Everett and John Gorham Palfrey, whose performance at Harvard had brought them early recognition. There, in Buckminster's study, they would discuss the art of Raphael, the poetry of Isaac Watts, and the nature of true virtue and take an occasional recess for Buckminster to perform on his chamber organ.[1] Buckminster's career would be a short one. The victim of epileptic seizures and a frail constitution, he would die in 1813 at the age of twenty-nine. But between 1805 and 1813, his study was the gathering place of Boston's brightest young men and would acquire a reputation, much like his own, as one of the jewels of Boston's intellectual life.

One of Buckminster's frequent guests was the Reverend John Sylvester John Gardiner. The minister of the Trinity Episcopal Church, he was a leader among the Boston literati. A student of Samuel Parr, England's most famous classical scholar, Gardiner enjoyed his status as an urbane man of letters. In his study he wrote literary criticism and prepared a handful of New England's brightest children for admission to Harvard. He also regularly hosted dinners where he introduced his most promising students to Boston's more established scholars. At such a dinner young George Ticknor met Joseph Stevens Buckminster, impressing him so much he became a regular invitee to the latter's Sunday gatherings.

When Buckminster died in 1813, Ticknor's home replaced the Brattle Street parsonage as the gathering place for Boston's young intellectuals. Over the next several years, the circle of friends and scholars would grow. Edward Everett and his brother Alexander, Edward Tyrrel Channing, Nathan Hale, William Powell Mason, William Tudor, and Jacob Bigelow would be joined later by, among others, William Prescott, Joseph Green Cogswell, Francis Calley Gray, Theodore Lyman Jr., Jared Sparks, and William Ellery Channing. As a group they would gain recognition as the aristocracy of Boston literary society, while Ticknor's home with its well-stocked library and erudite host would gain renown as the gathering place of Boston's intellectually gifted and aspiring.

In these years Boston's intellectual life was flourishing. Harvard was proudly championed as the nation's finest college. The Boston Athenæum was generally recognized as among the country's best libraries. But it was these literary circles that lent the city's intellectual life much of its charm and, more importantly, its fraternal character and coherence. The young men coming of age during these years, gathering in the homes of Buckminster, Gardiner, and Ticknor, grew to be intimate and lifelong friends. They traveled together and studied together and maintained a correspondence that expressed a level of affection uncomfortably foreign to contemporary ears. They established business partnerships, founded professional organizations, and in their later years sought refuge from the difficulties of their varied lives in old friendships. The friendships formed in these circles would prove a lifelong resource for these men. Moreover, they reenforced the notion that these circles represented a group set apart, a group with a distinct set of talents and, perhaps, a distinct set of responsibilities.

In cultivating this sense of distinction and exclusivity, these young men acted in a manner consistent with the Federalist ancestry virtually all of them claimed. Not all had fathers as prestigious in Federalist circles as Prescott or Gray, but they all came from established Federalist stock.[2] Born within a culture that drew sharp distinctions between the few and the many and raised to assume that the best bred and most highly educated incurred special responsibilities, they exhibited a corporate sense that suggested the extent to which New England Federalism persisted. Indeed, although the political fortunes of Federalism suffered during these years, much of the Federalist world did remain the same. Harrison Gray Otis may have faced political embarrassment, but he continued to preside over Boston high society, daily breakfasting on pâté de foie gras and setting out a large bowl of punch for his afternoon guests. When the church bells rang on Sunday morning, the Federalist gentry continued to take the most prominent seats, and at Harvard's annual commencement the entire town joined in celebration, as it had for over a century, as the Federalist sons of privilege received their degrees and displayed their talents.

Just as had their parents' generation, these young men also reenforced their communal ties and privileged status through intracaste marriage. Ticknor, Prescott, and Everett would all marry into the families of prominent Federalist merchants. Cogswell would marry the daughter of New Hampshire's Federalist governor. These men also would embark on careers under the tutelage of the leading figures of the Federalist elder generation, in the law offices of William Sullivan, Fisher Ames, and William Prescott and the commercial houses of Thomas Amory and Henry Lee.[3]

The resulting web of loyalties and interests made the Federalist elite a very real and persisting entity within Boston society well into the nineteenth century. As heirs to this tradition, these young men were very aware of the security and status it provided. But it is equally clear that they were not altogether satisfied with the world their parents had made. Although they took the traditional steps to preserve their status—a Harvard education, a well-chosen professional apprenticeship, and judicious marriage—they also sought distance from certain parts of their Federalist past. While they held fast to their privilege, they also took deliberate and sometimes painful steps to liberate themselves from its restrictions and separate themselves from their fathers' errors.

Buckminster's life offers perhaps the most poignant example of this pattern. His election to the Brattle Street pulpit seemed, in many ways, destined from birth. With Jonathan Edwards and Solomon Stoddard on both sides of the family tree, it was a foregone conclusion that he would pursue the ministerial profession his father, the Reverend Joseph Buckminster, called "the most honorable in the world." At four he was taught to read from the Greek Testament and given lessons in Latin grammar.

At five he began holding religious services for the servants, leading them in prayer and preaching to them from the gospel. He entered Exeter at the age of eleven and then Harvard, in 1796, at the precocious but not unprecedented age of twelve.[4]

To this point, Buckminster's progress fulfilled all that his father had hoped. But soon after he reached Harvard, there surfaced some tensions in their correspondence. These years were ones of theological innovation at Harvard. The liberal views that would lead to the selection of Henry Ware to the Hollis Chair in 1805 and the flight of conservatives to Andover were beginning to infiltrate Harvard's divinity department. At the same time student life was increasingly characterized by minor rebellions and student pranks.[5] Amid all this turmoil the response of Buckminster's father is notable for its relative silence on questions of theology and its obsessive attentiveness to issues of discipline and order. He repeatedly urged young Joseph to "cherish a respect for the authorities of the college." Despite the gossip of "dissipated youth," he should remain confident that "they are men of respectability, or they would never have been in the places they are." If he heard the administration criticized or ridiculed, he should "take no part in the ungrateful merriment. . . . Govern yourself, my son, by principles, and attach yourself to them rather than to men."[6]

In contrast to this obsession with Joseph's behavior, this fear that he would "deviate from the paths of virtue, and become an immoral youth," the elder Buckminster had relatively little to say directly about the theological dangers at Harvard.[7] Granted he was not a rigid Calvinist. In Portsmouth he had gone so far as to participate in the Piscataqua Association, an interdenominational group that published a noncreedal magazine.[8] But if not unbending in his theology, he was far from friendly toward religious liberalism and joined other orthodox clergymen in denouncing these "days of great license of practice . . . great prevalence of infidelity." Nevertheless, regarding the doctrinal temptations to which young Joseph was exposed, he offered only the most banal advice. "Hold fast your integrity and your love of God," he said simply in one letter.[9] When Joseph's liberal inclinations came out of the closet altogether, his father's advice was only slightly more animated. "From some remarks you made while you were at home, and the interest they had in your feelings, I feared you were in danger of the fashionable folly of placing reason before revelation. Be on your guard, my son, and let a 'thus saith the

Lord,' or a plain Scripture declamation, silence your objections and satisfy the craving of your mind." Whereas the fear of a disrespectful or unruly son preoccupied Buckminster, theological concerns prompted only the flat reminder, "'Where you can't unriddle, learn to trust.' Take care of your clothes, your health, your morals, your soul!"[10]

His tone changed altogether, however, when Joseph announced his acceptance of a Boston pulpit. For some time Joseph had been in correspondence with James Freeman, the minister of King's Chapel and one of Boston's most liberal clerics. Freeman was one of the first within Boston's nascent Unitarian community to openly proclaim himself a Unitarian and one of the few to move beyond Arianism to Socinianism. The Arian position, more typical of New England Anti-Trinitarians, maintained that although Jesus was created before the world, he was not a part of the Godhead; although he was more than a mere man, he was inferior to God. The Socinian position, represented in England by Joseph Priestley, went a step further and argued that Jesus was only a man, albeit perfectly created and invested with unique authority. This more extreme position advanced more quickly in England than America. In fact, although nurtured in his Unitarianism by Freeman, Buckminster would retain the Arian Christology more typical of this period's Anti-Trinitarianism. Nevertheless, Buckminster's association with Freeman placed him in close contact with a position at the forefront of American liberalism and even further from his father's orthodoxy.[11]

The elder Buckminster was disturbed that Freeman, a relation no less, would encourage Joseph to adopt a set of beliefs not only unorthodox but also contrary to those of his father. But the fact that Freeman had managed "to warp your judgment and seduce your heart respecting some of the important doctrines of our holy religion" was only part of his concern. In addition, and perhaps more importantly, he was disturbed by Joseph's acceptance of the Brattle Street pulpit before he was properly trained. One senses that the toleration he displayed for Joseph's theological drifting was connected to his confidence in the traditional process by which ministers were prepared. Joseph's religious experiments were always far from desirable but could be tolerated as an indiscretion of youth that would be remedied through a patient and deliberate process of ministerial training. But Joseph, in accepting this call, was cutting the process seriously short. "You should resolve to reside with some clergyman whose company, conversation, and ministerial gifts would assist and initiate you

into some of the more private, as well as public, offices of the profession,"
Buckminster urged his son. In this way he would come to more mature
theological conclusions and make himself an acceptable candidate for the
office. But Joseph, although deeply pained by his father's remarks, insisted on taking the position. And consequently the young man, prepared
from birth to be a minister, assumed his first pulpit with his father arguing "you had better be a porter on a wharf than a preacher with such
views."[12]

For Joseph Stevens Buckminster, entry to adulthood was accompanied
by a radical break with his past. As he began his public life at the liberal
Brattle Street Church, he drew a sharp line between himself and the traditional Federalist clerical order his father represented. But this embrace
of Unitarianism, although a shocking decision to the elder Buckminster
and his peers, was far from unusual among the young Federalist intellectuals who surrounded Joseph Stevens. Unitarianism was, in fact, as one
historian described it, the "passion—among the young men of genius,
ambition, and high aims" at Harvard.[13] Edward Everett, Jared Sparks,
John Palfrey, Samuel Gilman, and George Bancroft all followed Buckminster into the Unitarian clergy. Edward Tyrrel Channing, William
Tudor, George Ticknor, Alexander Everett, William Hickling Prescott,
Francis Bowen, Andrew Peabody, Nathan Hale, Joseph Story, Nathaniel Bowditch, Theophilus Parsons, and William Cullen Bryant—in effect, almost every significant member of this rising Boston literati—also
adopted Unitarian beliefs.

Beyond their embrace of Unitarianism, this generation of New England intellectuals broke ranks with their Federalist past in other ways.
Not many made as painful a break as Buckminster, but many of them did
join him in deviating from the career path that their status as privileged
members of the Federalist order prescribed. Edward Everett, like Buckminster, seemed destined for the pulpit. The son of a Boston clergyman
and occasional Federalist candidate, he entered Harvard in 1807 and
graduated four years later at the top of his class. Graduate study at Harvard Divinity School led to a position at the Brattle Street Church in 1813.
But from the start he chafed under the restrictions of clerical life. He later
said it encouraged both facile oratory and passive thinking. When his
Federalist congregation rebuked him for planning a trip to Virginia and
a visit to Thomas Jefferson, Everett concluded that the ministry was not
for him. Seeking freedom from "the prejudices and prepossessions" of the

New England clerical life, he accepted an appointment to Harvard and set off for Europe to prepare.[14]

Many others pursued early careers in law, only to find them similarly unsatisfying. As graduates of Harvard and sons of prominent Federalists, they had access to the most prestigious law offices for training and employment. Nathan Hale thus commenced his professional life in the offices of Peter Oxenbridge Thacher; William Hickling Prescott read law with his father, an eminent judge and statesman; and James Savage prepared in the office of Chief Justice Isaac Parker. But Hale, being neither interested nor particularly skilled in the practice of law, abandoned it for a career in journalism. Prescott, too, found the law tedious and sailed for Europe to pursue an interest in classics. Savage maintained a legal practice longer than the others but also abandoned it when the opportunity arose.[15]

George Ticknor began his professional life by reading law in the office of William Sullivan, the Boston lawyer known as the "high priest of Federalist orthodoxy." Like the others he quickly grew bored with the work and made plans to study in Europe. Before sailing, he made a tour of the United States which at times affirmed and at others challenged his Federalist upbringing. At Quincy he sat quietly, perhaps smugly, while John Adams railed against the Hartford Convention and its chairman, George Cabot, a family friend of the Ticknors. At Philadelphia he met Republican leader John Randolph and found in the "singular deformity of his person" the cretin his Federalist background led him to expect. But at Monticello he had a surprisingly pleasant visit with Thomas Jefferson. At the White House he enjoyed an intimate and no doubt inspiring conversation with James Madison about "education and its prospects, of the progress of improvement among us" and shared in the tension as the president awaited news from New Orleans.[16]

By the time George Ticknor sailed for Europe, the black-and-white world of his Federalist past had begun to take on shades of gray. In Europe his understanding of the world grew even more complex. Arriving in London just as Napoleon was returning from Elba, Ticknor was immediately overwhelmed by the historical magnitude of European affairs and the complexity of the English response. "Having been bred in the strictest school of Federalism," he later confessed, he was surprised to find that English condemnation of Napoleon was not unanimous. Nor was the literary scene as clear-cut as he expected. The paragon of classical scholarship, Samuel Parr, was shockingly ignorant about American affairs, while the bad boy of English letters, Lord Byron, was surprisingly agreeable. It was with "unexpected regret" and a far more open mind that Ticknor left Byron and his wife and continued his travels.[17]

When Ticknor reached Göttingen his Federalist confidence was further shaken. Enrolled in that city's great university, he quickly discovered that Harvard, the pride of New England, was something of a fraud. Its library, compared to Göttingen's, was a mere "closetful of books," and between American and European scholarship lay a "mortifying distance." Although an occasional snub aroused his New England pride, by the time he left Göttingen for a tour of the Continent, he was far more cosmopolitan in his outlook.[18]

Throughout the ensuing tour the confrontation between his provincial biases and his European experiences was played out. In France he ridiculed the shallow and effete character of society, exciting at times but "necessarily transient." Its scholarship was plagued by an obsession with "talking brilliantly." Lacking depth and serious instruction, it had reduced itself to "happy and sparkling phrases . . . an abundance of epigrammatic remarks . . . a kind of amusement." On the other hand, he found French comedy extraordinary, and the French actor Talma was the finest he had seen in Europe or America.[19]

In Rome he was unimpressed by the state of learning and culture. But he was enchanted by the city's ambience and history. "Every fragment" was "full of religion and poetry . . . enough to excite the feelings and fancy, till the present and immediate seemed to disappear in the long glories and recollections of the past." The native Italian society was shallow, but the presence of foreign visitors created a unique and fascinating experience. Even the artistry of the Princess Borghese, that "most consummate coquette," was spared the sanction of his New England morality. It was after all "not a vulgar coquetry, and it is the talent and skill about it which redeem it from ridicule, and make her a curiosity . . . not respectable to be sure, but perfect in its kind." Spain presented the same complexity. The king was vicious, the government officials were corrupt, the police were inept, and the Inquisition, while exaggerated by the foreign press, was still present. But among the general public he found "more originality and poetry . . . more force without barbarism, and civilization without corruption" than he had discovered anywhere else.[20]

By the time Ticknor left Europe, he had not abandoned all his provincial biases. He was relieved to find in England, for example, a people characterized by "activity and improvement and vital strength and power." But he was nonetheless considerably broadened by his travels. The man who had rather self-consciously admitted in 1815 that he had begun fencing lessons after the European fashion was by 1818 dining unapologetically with exiled aristocracy and dancing past midnight.[21] He still claimed to be unswayed in his loyalties. In a letter to Thomas Jefferson, he insisted that "what I saw of Europe only raised my own country in my estimation and attached me to it yet more."[22] He was no doubt genuine in these claims, but his affections and attachments stood on far different ground. His view of Boston and Cambridge was considerably chastened, and his confidence in the political and cultural world in which he had been raised had been seriously challenged.

Nor was Ticknor the only Bostonian of this generation to return from a European sojourn with his New England confidences shaken.[23] Edward Everett, Ticknor's traveling companion, returned similarly jolted by the unexpected complexity of European politics and equally disenchanted with the state of learning in America. Against the depth and variety of German scholarship he contrasted the "unblessed Cartaginian torpor" of American letters.[24] Even Harvard's architectural design, with its "noisy flaring exposure," compared poorly with the "calm seclusion" of European universities.[25] For Joseph Green Cogswell, the third member of this party, European travel revealed not only the immaturity of American letters but also the provincialism and conceit of New England.

For the first twenty-seven years of his life, Cogswell followed the traditional Federalist path.[26] Educated at Exeter and Harvard, he briefly indulged his adventurous spirit with trips to India and the Mediterranean before settling down to his legal studies in the offices of Fisher Ames and William Prescott. Admitted to the bar in 1811, he completed his Federalist development by marrying Mary Gilman, the daughter of New Hampshire's Federalist governor. But her death the following year left him emotionally shattered and ridden with guilt. Shortly before her death he had blamed his absence from her bedside on the demands of business. "You have probably many years to attend to business," she responded, "and probably as few weeks to devote to me." The rebuke haunted him after her death, leading him to see the chastening hand of God in his misery. In grief he turned to Harvard where he hoped to find "a retreat from the bustle of the world."[27]

By 1815, however, his restless temperament led him to seek solace abroad. Drifting aimlessly over the next year, he did not begin to re-collect himself until he joined Ticknor and Everett in Göttingen. But again, personal tragedy cut short his recovery. The death of his mother triggered the same sense of rootlessness he had experienced earlier. "You never knew," he wrote to Charles S. Daveis, "what were the feelings of a man, who has no home in the world, who sees himself cut off, as it were, from all connection with the earth." The sense of drift and alienation became a persistent theme in his letters over the next several months, evolving into romantic schemes of personal sacrifice and African explo-ration. "Nothing remains for me in life, but to prepare for a traveler in some parts hitherto little explored," he wrote to John Farrar of Har-vard, "where Science will be more use to me than Philology, History or Politics." [28]

Over the next two years, however, a rigorous program of study and exercise restored his physical and emotional health. Rising at four, at-tending lectures or tutorials for ten hours, and studying for another eight, he drove himself toward his vision of scholarly excellence. On weekends he hiked through the mountains of Germany discovering an almost reli-gious exhilaration "leaping from cliff to cliff amid German clouds." In those mountains Cogswell recovered his health and sense of purpose; there "I lived 'through that which had been death to many men' . . . there I learnt to admire nature and be enchanted with the 'magic of her mysteries.'" [29]

By the time he returned to America in 1820, he was "a better and a happier man." He also admitted undergoing "some strange revolutions of feeling" while in Europe. His friends recognized in these "revolutions" a continental shifting of loyalties and sensibilities. But Cogswell insisted this was not the case. Boston, he pledged, was still the greatest city in the world, yet "if they would but learn a little modesty there, and not praise themselves quite so highly, I would like them still better." Europe had taught him that "we have so much self-conceit." Not only did this yield an unhealthy defensive response to every piece of foreign criticism, it was not grounded in reality. The institutions and culture of which Bostonians were so proud were not deserving of this conceit. In particular, like Tick-nor and Everett, he now found Harvard a poor excuse for a university. It was little more than a "mere preparatory school," he argued, asking little

Joseph Stevens Buckminster, by Gilbert Stuart, ca. 1810. (Courtesy of the Boston Athenæum)

Joseph Buckminster, by John Trumbull, ca. 1789. (Courtesy of the Yale University Art Gallery, gift of Mrs. Eliza Buckminster Lee)

academic expertise on the part of its instructors and possessing a rather "strange notion . . . against lecturing."[30]

Although Cogswell's path may have been different, the tragedies of his life and the particulars of his recovery led him to many of the same conclusions the others reached. The confident Federalist society in which he had been raised seemed now a bit smug and narrow. The early adulthood of Jared Sparks followed a similar course. Like Cogswell, his path was defined by a somewhat unique set of circumstances. But it ended for this very important member of Ticknor's circle in a similar state of disaffection and liberation. Unlike many of the others, Sparks's life did not begin amid privilege and wealth. He was born in Willington, Connecticut, into a family of moderate means, and his childhood, spent largely in the home of a childless relative, was characterized by erratic schooling and hard work. He did not complete an entire year of school until he was sixteen, and at eighteen he was on his own, teaching in a country school and supplementing his income through carpentry. But a friendship with Willington's Congregationalist pastor, Hubbel Loomis, opened up new opportunities. Recognizing in Sparks a young man of talent and industry, Loomis and Abiel Abbott secured for him a scholarship at Exeter. There he studied under Abbott's cousin Benjamin Abbott, and after two years he matriculated to Harvard, the Abbotts' alma matter, in 1811. There he made impressive, albeit irregular, progress. Forced to alternate terms in school with terms teaching school, he took his degree in 1815 at the age of twenty-six.[31]

The peculiarities of Sparks's first twenty-five years led him to a unique set of loyalties and affections. While his somewhat rootless childhood left him with comparatively few ties of affection or memory, the attention paid him by men like Loomis and Abiel and Benjamin Abbot earned from Sparks effusive affection and gratitude. Moreover, the institutions toward which they steered him were all the more valued for the difficulty it took to reach them. Sparks's biographer, Herbert Adams, commenting on his acceptance at Exeter, noted "the profound impression which admission to that famous academy must have made upon the mind of the country lad from Connecticut. A sense of exalted privilege . . . a consciousness of great personal responsibility."[32]

At Exeter and later at Harvard, Sparks seems to have formed the sense of identity and provincial loyalty that his childhood failed to provide. At the same time his atypical path to these places left him in a peculiar relationship to the rest of the community. His work ethic reflected the familial circumstances that had led him to financial self-reliance at age eighteen. The more privileged student, he complained, failed to appreciate "the inestimable importance of a judicious improvement of his time." Sparks also retained a moralistic suspicion of their wealth. "This overflow of money . . . corrupting their morals, vitiating their tastes, and rendering them wholly incapable of making any valuable progress in study" led Sparks to an "undeniable truth." The students of the greatest privilege and wealth, those "furnished with the most money are the poorest scholars."[33]

This same combination of intense but distanced loyalties characterized his experience as a Unitarian minister. Like many other young men at Harvard, he was caught up in the enthusiasm for religious liberalism inspired by Buckminster and Channing. But characteristically, when his studies were completed, he accepted a call to a pulpit not in friendly Boston but in the more hostile, uncharted religious waters of Baltimore.[34] While in Baltimore, Sparks established a significant reputation. His *Unitarian Miscellany* enjoyed a wider circulation than any of the northern Unitarian magazines, and in 1821 he was selected the chaplain of the House of Representatives. But the trials of his ministry, in what remained essentially unfriendly territory, served to affirm his peculiar relationship to Boston. On the one hand, he was forced to turn in this direction for support. There an established Unitarian community existed. There also remained the friendships most important to him. But the failure of Boston Unitarians to provide him the support he thought they owed him — their failure to contribute articles to his magazine, their failure to send clergy to southern Unitarian ordinations — led him to feel abandoned and poorly understood. "There is nowhere so much refinement and general intelligence in society as in Boston," he wrote Ann Storrow, and yet "nowhere is there so much ignorance of the actual state of things in the southern part of our country." When Boston's neglect turned into criticism of his literary efforts, he grew livid. "I do not write for the wise ones of Boston, nor do I expect they will approve what I write; nor do I care whether they do or do not. . . . I should be much more apt to be swayed by 'Boston notions,' if a little experience in the world had not shown me that these are very often rank prejudices."[35]

His anger on this occasion seems to have hit its mark. Palfrey wrote soon thereafter regarding his magazine, "You have conquered all prejudice." And Everett assured him, "You are our standing boast and delight."[36] But by the time he returned to Boston in 1823, his peculiar attachment to the community was even more peculiar: still devoted to Harvard, still convinced that Boston letters represented the best in the nation, but equally convinced of the town's provincialism and conceit.

By this time, this theme of disaffection had become a familiar refrain. European and domestic travel, personal crises, unsatisfying careers, and family differences had yielded a widespread awareness among these young Boston intellectuals that the world of New England Federalism was far from perfect. Its career options were too narrow, its institutions were overblown, its provincial biases were restrictive, and its conceits were ill founded. As men of letters they were embarrassed by the resulting mediocrity of Boston's cultural institutions. As sons of Federalist activists, they were embarrassed by the resulting myopic partisanship of their fathers' politics.

Joseph Stevens Buckminster, traveling in Europe in 1806, was perhaps the first to admonish his Boston friends for their partisan squabbling. "How mortifying, how disgusting, how low, how infamous, appear the animosities and wicked calumnies, with which our American papers are filled . . . the brutality of our party spirit, the infamy of our political disputes." These not only damaged America's international reputation but led Buckminster to question the legitimacy of its political experiment. "Of what advantage is our boasted freedom, if it is only consistent with such a state of animosity as now exists in New England?"[37] Edward Everett voiced much the same concern in comparing English and American politics: "The prejudice is positively insurmountable! Candor, charity, and justice sink beneath it like grubs under an elephant's tread."[38] William Tudor extended his criticism of this partisan spirit to a gentle critique of one of the institutions of Federalist politics, Fisher Ames. Tudor lavished praise on Ames's public spirit but also cautiously suggested that he had "too much genius and too little worldliness, to make a very successful statesman." His defects, it was true, were rooted in his strengths. Moreover, Tudor generously traced the intellectual indiscretion and partisan excess that he criticized to the "phrensy that was spread over the world by the French Revolution." Yet even in this apologetic there was admonition. The present generation, warned Tudor, must take care to avoid such imbalance. "We may hope," he concluded, "we shall respect ourselves too highly, to endure the license of similar accusations."[39]

Gentle as Tudor's criticisms were, his message, like those of Everett and Buckminster, was painfully clear. This generation must move forward, beyond the errors of their fathers, errors of indiscretion and partisan blindness. They must work to repair the wounds of division and suspicion created by their fathers, knowing that complete political peace would come only at great cost. Mixing admiration with realism, Tudor captured this sense best in looking to the end of partisan division only when "the remaining few of those gallant spirits who achieved our independence . . . [were] gathered to the bones of their fathers."[40]

The critique of partisan politics extended further into a review of their fathers' conduct during the War of 1812. On this question most were respectful and cautious. Tudor was representative in suggesting that their elders erred in criticizing the war for its "wickedness," rather than its "mismanagement."[41] But in 1828 Theodore Lyman Jr. undertook a dispassionate and scholarly review of the war's origins and their fathers' performance. In his *Diplomacy of the United States,* he challenged both the Federalists' role in the war and the pro-British interpretation of its origins laid down by Federalists like John Lowell. In Lyman's careful analysis Great Britain was by no means blameless in its behavior. Its revival of the rule of 1756 "more deeply wounded the rights of this country" than the actions of any other belligerent. Nor did the series of diplomatic conflicts and stalemates point so unambiguously toward Britain's innocence as earlier Federalists had claimed. The British orders that Lowell had defended in 1810 as justifiable counters to the Berlin and Milan Decrees in Lyman's view posed a "much greater grievance to the neutral" than either French measure. Madison's demand for a formal apology after the *Chesapeake* incident, which Lowell criticized for its "lack of delicacy," was to Lyman justifiable in view of the British "assault" upon America's "dignity and sovereignty"; it was a demand, moreover, to which Great Britain had acquiesced on other occasions in response to other "infinitely less important" violations of national sovereignty. The confusion and misunderstanding surrounding the diplomatic missions of David Erskine and Francis Jackson, which Lowell called "an affront to [their] sovereign, and to the whole British nation," Lyman reduced to an "unfortunate business," for which neither side was wholly responsible or to blame. The war that ultimately occurred, which Lowell linked to Republican and French conspiracy, Lyman traced to Britain's great "indifference concerning her relations with America."[42]

This was an impressive work, and coming from the pen of Lyman, whose father had been an ardent partisan, one of the first to consider secession as a viable response to Republican measures, it was an extraordinary testimony to the generation's quest for autonomy. Combined with the critiques of Boston culture and society issued by others of this generation, it completed a multifaceted critique of the established Federalist order.

But in pointing out their elders' faults, in itemizing their political failings, their partisan blindness, the mediocrity of their cultural institutions, and the provincialism and conceit that lay beneath it all, these young Federalist intellectuals had succeeded only in defining themselves by negation. Had they stopped there, this generation would be remembered as just another batch of disaffected youth, a nineteenth-century "lost generation" complete with expatriates and overindulged malcontents. But they did not, for although this generation sought to distance themselves from their parents, they were far from complete rebels. In fact, they still subscribed to many of the basic philosophical premises passed down from their fathers. They still viewed society as a hierarchical and organic entity, and most importantly, they still believed that men of their background and breeding held special responsibilities within this society. To the extent that these young Federalist intellectuals can be labeled rebels, theirs was a rebellion very narrowly contained, a very selective rejection of their fathers' world. To the extent that these men sought to distance themselves from their fathers, they did so more in hopes of clarifying than repudiating their responsibilities as Federalists.

The enthusiasm for Unitarianism among these young Federalist intellectuals epitomizes the nature of their rebellion. On the one hand, their adoption of this particular set of ideas was not an insignificant matter of religious taste. Unitarianism represented more than just the rephrasing of existing religious beliefs, more than just the newest elaboration of religious liberalism. Unitarianism offered, instead, a distinct and coherent system of religious and social thought. This has not always been acknowledged. For years, scholars minimized the intellectual significance of Unitarianism much as they disparaged the intellectual contributions of this period in general. These scholars described Unitarianism as largely imitative, or at best of only transitional significance—a theological stepping-stone between Puritanism and transcendentalism. But since the 1960s there has been a necessary correction of this assessment. Sydney Ahlstrom was among the first to describe Unitarianism as a coherent system of thought. He acknowledged within Unitarianism a certain derivative and transitional character, the persistence of "historic New England doctrines, the Enlightenment, [and] the fervor of Pietism." Nor did he deny in the thought of Unitarians like William Ellery Channing evidence of the "romantic impulse which reached its culminating American expression in the Transcendentalist movement." But he also pointed out the coherence and integrity of Unitarianism itself. Derivative and transitional, it was also "a distinctive, unique, and integrated theological synthesis." Daniel Howe made the argument far more thoroughly in 1970. Within his elaborate study of Harvard Unitarians, he suggested that Unitarianism's importance went beyond its American influences and impact. Within its synthesis of Protestant and Enlightenment thought, he identified, more sweepingly, the "culmination of what may be called 'the Christian Enlightenment.'"[43]

For these young Federalist intellectuals, their adoption of Unitarianism thus represented subscription to a coherent system of thought—acceptance of a detailed and cohesive set of ideas about God and the cosmos, about man and society, about ethics, history, and even aesthetics. To the extent that these young intellectuals were looking for their own intellectual identity, Unitarianism provided the cohesive and systematic system they sought. But at the same time at least part of Unitarianism's attraction lay in its compatibility, on many points, with the culture and ideology from which they sought distance. It is true that in their rejection of Trinitarianism, their refusal to accept what they perceived as the narrow and irrational beliefs of their fathers' orthodoxy, they staked out important new ground. But beyond certain doctrinal principles Unitarianism represented an understanding of man and society perfectly compatible with their Federalist past. Within its dualist view of the universe and its Arminian sense of salvation, Unitarianism offered these young Federalist intellectuals a philosophy that suited their needs for both distinctiveness and continuity, their desire to separate from their parents without denouncing or challenging their basic social philosophy.

Unitarians were identified by their anti-Trinitarian beliefs.[44] In denying the mystery of the Trinity, they broke with one of the most ancient and definitive teachings of orthodox Christianity. But even this act of doctrinal iconoclasm reflected a certain conservative temperament. New England Unitarians rejected the doctrine of three-in-one not so much because it offended their modern sensibilities but because it violated their dualist philosophy. Like many dualist cosmologies of the past, Unitarianism was rooted in the very conservative notion of hierarchy, of higher and lower orders, of distinct realities of spirit and matter. For Unitarians this dualism was reflected in the distinction between God and the world and, within man, between the mind and the body. These were distinct entities, temporarily allied but distinct in their existence. The independence of the spirit was, in fact, the key to its immortality. Whereas the material was temporary, the mind, or spirit, possessed an enduring existence. In addition to being merely temporary, the material was also passive. It had no powers beyond those initiated by the spirit or mind. As a result the material was not so much at war with the spirit as it was a force that needed to be controlled, a reality that was there to be mastered. This was consequently the basic task set before humans—to imitate God in his mastery of the material, to assert their own spiritual character over their material bodies.

From within this view of the universe, the Calvinist teaching of the Incarnation was philosophically absurd—a "relapse into the error of the rudest and earliest ages," according to William Ellery Channing. To suggest that God chose to redeem man through the assumption of flesh, that he sacrificed the beauties of the spirit for the imperfections of the material world, seemed too gross a violation of God's character. Moreover, the doctrine was an insult to man, for implicit within the concept of the Incarnation was the suggestion that man could not appreciate or aspire to the beauties of the spirit, the inference that men lacked the imagination to conceive of an immaterial deity. Granted there was a certain seductive consolation in "an object of worship like themselves . . . A God, clothed in our form, and feeling our wants and sorrows." But according to Unitarians modern men were capable of a more sublime vision, a conception of God divorced of all "material properties," a God of "pure intelligence, an unmixed and infinite Mind." [45]

Although there was a doctrinal radicalism in this most fundamental Unitarian principle, it was far from new and even further from what could be labeled socially liberal. Little within this dualist cosmology would have violated Federalist notions of the social order; nothing within this vision of a hierarchically arranged cosmos would have resonated with the democratic confidence of Jacksonianism. There was little within this, moreover, that was philosophically pretentious or daring. In fact, one suspects that a good deal of Unitarianism's attraction was its refusal to engage in much of the philosophical debate that had characterized the previous century, the refusal to participate in the great theological and philosophical wars that divided the intellectual community during the Enlightenment. Unitarianism was attractive because it avoided polemics—it had no interest in either these questions or the sort of divisive debate they encouraged. In contrast to the existential anxiety of Calvinism, the metaphysical gymnastics of Edwards, the epistemological complexities of Hume, Berkeley, and Locke, Unitarians offered the simplicity of the epistemological and ethical theories of the Scottish Enlightenment.

The thinkers of the Scottish Enlightenment for some time had maintained a particular attraction for American intellectuals. David Hume, Adam Ferguson, Lord Kames, William Robertson, Francis Hutcheson, and Adam Smith were widely read in America during the eighteenth century. But in the nineteenth century a set of contextual similarities caused Scottish thinkers to resonate particularly well with American audiences. The major cities of both countries were simultaneously torn between following English culture and carving out their own intellectual identities. In both countries the upper middle class, led by doctors, lawyers, and clergy, played an important role in sustaining intellectual life. And in both countries the intellectual environment was framed by Calvinism. As Americans of the early nineteenth century struggled to preserve those parts of the Enlightenment suited to their own sensibilities, it was Scottish thinkers who proved most useful. The Scottish spokesmen for common sense philosophy, especially Thomas Reid and Dugald Stewart, offered to American intellectuals, and Unitarians in particular, a set of ideas about the mind and morality that seemed best suited to their thinking and disposition.[46]

For many of the Scots' contemporaries, there was a suspicious lack of mettle to their philosophy, but for most Americans of their generation, and perhaps since, there was a beauty in its simple logic. In response to the great questions regarding knowledge and its certainty, in answer to the dilemma of ascertaining what we know, and how we know what we think we know, the Scots answered with "common sense." They argued, quite simply, that knowledge is rooted in the observations that are processed by our consciousness, and our consciousness orders and processes this information using principles that are independent of our experience. In other words, humans possess an intuitive set of objectively

George Ticknor, by Thomas Sully, 1828. (Courtesy of the Hood Museum of Art, Dartmouth College, Hanover, New Hampshire; gift of Constance V. R. White, Nathaniel T. Dexter, Philip Dexter, and Mary Ann Streeter)

Jared Sparks, by Rembrandt Peale, ca. 1819. (Courtesy of the Harvard University Portrait Collection, bequest of Lizzie Sparks Pickering. Photo: Rick Stafford. © President and Fellows of Harvard College, Harvard University)

true understandings through which they can order and process their observations. The resulting conclusions, or "common sense" truths, can be accepted as objectively true, first, because both our observations and our consciousness possess objective integrity, but even more simply because to believe otherwise would not be commonsensical. It was an argument that was circular to say the least, but also one compatible with their view of God. Our observations must be objectively true, the intuitive understandings by which we evaluate that which we observe must be reliable and true, for had God structured the mind otherwise, he would have acted contrary to his character and the rationality of his creation.

Whether frustratingly circular or beautifully simple, this view of man was a central part of the Unitarian vision. It led quite logically to the emphasis on ethics that suited their genteel inclinations. For among the intuitive understandings all humans possess is a set of moral insights that are both universal and reliable. Drawing primarily upon Thomas Reid, and beyond him upon the Cambridge Platonists, American Unitarians argued that people can intuitively judge fundamental questions of morality. Although these judgments are intuitive, they are also, Unitarians were quick to point out, acts of reason. Reid and the Unitarians took issue with the "sentimentalist" school of moral sense psychology for its assertion that this moral sense lies in the emotions. For Reid and American Unitarians this released individuals from their ethical responsibilities—if moral judgments and actions are involuntary acts of emotion, there is little that individuals can assume responsibility for or take credit for, and equally little for moral philosophers, interested in the didactic possibilities of their work, to offer. Instead, they argued that moral determinations are an act of the reason—a reason that is intuitive, and as immediate as the emotions, but not at all involuntary.

This understanding of man's moral instincts was framed more fully within the Unitarians' understanding of God. In contrast to the Calvinist emphasis upon will, Unitarians argued that God's power is "entirely submitted to his perceptions of rectitude." Men offer up devotion "not because his will is irresistible, but because his will is the perfection of virtue."[47] Morality, moreover, is the key to salvation. Actually, Unitarians rarely spoke in such unpolished terms. They scorned the imagery of radical and immediate transformation inherent in Calvinist doctrines, speaking instead more often in terms of character formation, self-development, or regeneration. Channing's description of "a gradual and rational work, beginning sometimes in sudden impressions, but confirmed by reflection, growing by the regular use of Christian means, and advancing silently to perfection," resonates more fully with Neoplatonism than with Calvinism.[48] So too does Buckminster's suggestion that "your mind is raised to a purer atmosphere; your thoughts reach a more exalted height; you better understand your relation to God and Christ, and the holy duties that result from your new birth." For these Unitarians, Calvinism's understanding of salvation was crude—the linking of salvation to the nailing of a god-man to a tree struck them as the stuff of medieval, even pagan, folklore. In addition, it was immoral; a salvation dependent solely on grace, they argued, relieves man of his ethical and spiritual obligations. Those who believe themselves cleansed through the simple attachment to the person of Christ, as if "by a single act of faith they have got him upon their side, they have no more to fear, and are released from the penalties which their iniquities deserve," warned Buckminster, are sadly mistaken.[49] Not only does this confidence in free grace cheapen the redemptive process, it denies both man's potential for a more authentic regeneration and the logic of God's creation.

For Unitarians ethical questions were the very essence of religion. At a certain level more important than theology or doctrine, morality, or the cultivation of virtue, became the primary objective of religion—"the highest object of Christ's mission."[50] Spiritual progress was equated with moral formation and measured by the acquisition of virtue. This emphasis on behavior resonated with ancient Christian emphases on works and discipline. But significantly, there was nothing ascetic about the Unitarians' interest in self-development. Reflective, no doubt, of the comfort from which most of these men sprang, self-cultivation was never equated with self-renunciation. They aimed not at transcendence of self but rather the cultivation of those qualities and virtues that would lead to the attainment of a fuller and richer life.

Finally, and perhaps of greatest personal significance, their understanding of morality and its importance defined their own place within society. For while the Unitarian understanding of morality began with a belief in a universally held moral sense, the Puritan legacy of moral elitism persisted quite comfortably alongside that belief. Although all persons may possess the ability to resolve basic questions of morality, it is still necessary to leave the more complex questions to men of advanced education—moral philosophers, or "moral scientists," as Levi Frisbie

called them, men whose advanced ethical education left them uniquely
equipped to sort out and subsequently advise society on more difficult
ethical questions. In addition, there are special responsibilities for another
group, persons of "moral taste," distinguished not by their specialized
study as much as by their success at bringing their own faculties into
proper order.[51]

The faculty psychology that informed all of this posited within mankind a series of faculties arranged hierarchically from the "rational" to the
"animal" and the "mechanical." The rational faculties are the most important. They consist of the conscience, or moral sense, and prudence, or
self-interest. The mechanical faculties, involuntary actions over which individuals exercise no control, are the lowest. In between are the animal.
These include "appetites" (hunger, thirst, and sex), "desires" such as curiosity, and "affections." These affections can be benevolent—gratitude,
pity, friendship—or malevolent—envy and resentment. It is these faculties which are responsible for all human behavior. Unlike the materialist
psychologists who believed that much of human action is attributable to
nerve impulses, the Scots believed that all human behavior, even the baser
aspects, is driven by one of the faculties of the mind, or a combination
of them.[52]

It is the primary task of the individual to order his faculties properly,
to make the dictates of the rational faculties direct his behavior. Unfortunately, the strength of the faculties is in inverse proportion to their place
on the ladder. Therefore, what the individual strives to do is to make the
lower serve the higher, to enlist the assistance of emotions on behalf of
the conscience, to manipulate one's affections so that they become servants of the moral sense. Not all persons are successful in doing so. The
careful manipulation of faculties requires time and a certain degree of
education—somewhat predictably the sort of training and leisure only a
few are privileged to possess. But the person who achieves this balance,
the person who not only perceives right but cultivates his affections so
that he takes an emotional pleasure in it, is the person of moral taste. For
this person, moral behavior becomes not just a matter of duty but one of
personal satisfaction and emotional delight.

In "moral science" and "moral taste," Unitarians retained the New
England tradition of moral elitism—they preserved the special role of
the clergyman and the moral philosopher and reasserted the importance
of the individual who by virtue of his own moral development had

reached a higher level of moral authority. The responsibilities of this moral elite are profound. Not only can they sort out the more complex questions of morality, and in so doing provide direction and leadership for those less skilled, they also can work to order the forces of society much as they had ordered their own mental faculties. For society, much like the individuals who form it, consists of a series of conflicting forces—emotion, self-interest, passion, and reason. And much like the faculties in individuals, the strength of these forces is in inverse proportion to their importance. It is the responsibility of men of advanced moral sensibilities, the moral philosopher and the man of moral taste, to order these forces properly, "now by reasonings, then by persuasion; here by removing prejudices, and there by strengthening them; sometimes by appeals to the heart, sometimes to the intellect, sometimes to the hopes, and sometimes to the fears."[53] Through this careful manipulation of the various forces in society, this moral elite can make the lower serve the higher, it can enlist the forces of passion on behalf of the objectives determined through reason and steer those individuals of lesser moral sophistication toward the goals determined by men like themselves.

With this conclusion these young New England intellectuals returned full circle to the most essential premise of their Federalist background— that men of advanced education and breeding possess special responsibilities in the community, that they possess extraordinary abilities to identify the common needs of the community and the unique ability to steer the rest of the community toward their realization. This fundamental premise was differently packaged, it was surrounded by a different set of epistemological and religious understandings, but it left these young Federalists in much the same position as their fathers—with much the same understanding of society and their role within it. Therefore, although they criticized their fathers, although they broke with them on many questions of religion, politics, and profession, they never challenged their most fundamental belief that the health and stability of society depends on the efforts of the wise and the good. Beyond the criticism of their fathers, they thus pursued a vision of how this fundamental premise might be applied to the realities of nineteenth-century America. Leading this effort, giving it direction and a sense of mission was, appropriately enough, Joseph Stevens Buckminster.

In his 1809 Phi Beta Kappa address, Buckminster asked the young scholars in attendance to consider the state of letters in America. With the Revolution safely and successfully behind them, it was time, he said, to advance the literary and intellectual honor of the nation. But where were our men of letters? Where were the men who would "direct our taste, mould our genius, and inspire our emulation; the men, in fact, whose writings are to be the depositories of our national greatness?" The distractions of business and politics in America's dynamic society had turned the attentions of men of talent away from scholarship and learning, he lamented. Equally unfortunate was the tendency of the scholar to study only "to furnish amusement for his imagination . . . to enjoy a certain mild delirium of the mind, regardless of the claims of society." [54] What America needed, Buckminster argued, was a new brand of scholar, one who would provide active leadership through his scholarship—a scholar who would avoid solitary intellectual indulgence, as well as the subordination of his talents to politics.

The impact of Buckminster's address was profound. Everett called it the moment he first "felt all the power of Mr. Buckminster's influence." [55] Ticknor likened it to "the sound of a trumpet," calling young scholars away "from the enthralment and degradation of party politics and party passions." [56] Reverberating through the halls of Cambridge to the backwoods environs of the young William Cullen Bryant, Buckminster's address provided, according to Lewis Simpson, the most important statement about the literary vocation in New England prior to Ralph Waldo Emerson. [57] For the young men coming of age in these years, simultaneously dependent on and disaffected from the society of their parents, this synthesis of new methods and old assumptions would provide a clear and compelling vision of their place and responsibilities. In its call for literary public service and its admonition that the scholar must not prostitute his talents to politics, it would offer an inspiring, somewhat revolutionary role for the man of letters. But its assumption that men of learning and taste must continue to lead and shape the nation would prove consistent with the basic premise of Federalism they still shared.

In putting Buckminster's advice into practice, these men felt themselves well prepared. Men of education and experience, broadened by European travel and instructed by the errors of their fathers, they would succeed in their leadership roles where their fathers had fallen into partisan diatribe and provincial smugness. Even in more practical terms they found themselves well positioned for the challenge placed before them. Most of these young Federalists were born into privilege, and some were introduced into even greater comfort by marriage. George Ticknor, for example, married Anna Eliot, the daughter of Samuel Eliot, Boston merchant and the founder of the professorship of Greek literature at Harvard. William Prescott married Susan Amory, the daughter of Thomas C. Amory, another of Boston's wealthiest merchants. Edward Everett married Charlotte Brooks, whose father, Peter Chardan Brooks, the founder of the New England Marine Insurance Company, was supposedly the wealthiest man in Boston. Comfortably positioned, freed from more practical concerns, the most important members of this circle enjoyed the financial luxury of imagining lives of scholarship.

But in realizing this vision they needed an appropriate vehicle, a journal through which they could fulfill their responsibilities as men of letters. When Buckminster delivered his address, this journal was the *Monthly Anthology*. First published in 1803 by David Phineas Adams and quickly adopted by William Emerson of Boston's First Church, the journal assumed its role as the corporate voice of Boston Federalism with the founding of the Anthology Society in 1805. This collection of Boston's most prominent cultural figures met monthly to assign articles and review submissions over elaborate meals accompanied by wine and cigars.[58]

In the preface to the first volume, Emerson summarized the ambitions of the journal: to "take an exact note of the works of literature . . . the progress of the arts . . . and the state of the publick concerns."[59] Generally consistent with this statement of purpose, the *Anthology* appeared until 1811. But from the start it was troubled by a host of problems—its agenda was too ambitious, its financial support was unreliable, and the society seemed to suffer from a certain confusion rooted in its status as both a social club and a literary journal. Perhaps even more fundamentally, it was burdened by a generational rift that could only temporarily be ignored.

The younger generation of Boston Federalism was well represented in the society. Buckminster (b. 1784) was a charter member, as was William Tudor (b. 1779). George Ticknor (b. 1791), James Savage (b. 1784), and Alexander Everett (b. 1790) also eventually joined the society. But the *Anthology*'s literary and political character was influenced disproportionately by its older members—men like Emerson, born in 1767, and John Sylvester John Gardiner, the society's first president, born in 1763. Although the younger members of the society initially deferred to this older group of Boston intellectuals, the differences between the two generations could not be suppressed indefinitely. Thus when the *Anthology* ceased publication in 1811, it was no accident that the younger members of the society produced its successor, the *North American Review*. Nor was it by chance that the older members of the Anthology Society were not actively involved in the newer journal, for the founding of the *North American Review* represented another step in this younger generation's attempt to separate themselves from their parents—another step in their attempt to define for themselves a new role and a new identity.

The generational character of the *North American Review* is unequivocal. Tudor, at thirty-six, was by far its oldest editor and owner during these early years. When he left the journal in 1817, an even younger group assumed control. All born after 1789, the next five editors assumed their positions at the average age of twenty-eight. Tudor's immediate successor, Jared Sparks, was that age, as was his successor, Edward Tyrrel Channing. Edward Everett was only twenty-six, and Alexander Everett and John Gorham Palfrey were thirty. The ownership of the journal was also drawn from this same generation of Boston Federalists. Tudor sold the magazine in 1817 to the North American Club, a group of seven with an average age under thirty. After 1823 the club relinquished ownership, but it was held by individuals within this circle into the next decade.[60]

In its origins the *North American Review* was, in short, the voice of the rising generation of Boston Federalists. Raised within its privileges and educated at Harvard, intellectually nurtured in the homes of Buckminster and Ticknor, broadened by European travel, given vocational direction by Buckminster and philosophical coherence by Unitarianism, still committed to Federalism's basic ideology but aware of its challenges and shortcomings, this generation of Federalists found its voice with the founding of the *North American Review*. And it is as exactly that—as the collective expression of this generation's reaction and adaptation—that the *North American Review* of these years is most correctly read.

To treat the *North American Review* as the collective voice for this generation is not to ignore the differences between individuals who contributed to its pages. Nor is it to suggest that complete harmony prevailed within the circle that produced the journal during these years. In fact, there were some significant disagreements. In 1819 Richard Henry Dana left the *North American Review* when he did not receive the editorship after Channing's resignation. Perhaps the most militant romanticist in the circle, he had caused some stir among the readership with his review of William Hazlitt's *Lectures on the English Poets,* and the club did not want to alienate its conservative audience. Further controversy surrounded the editorial tenure of Edward Everett. Although Everett privately took pride in being able to help his brother Oliver by means of his position with the *Review,* other members of the circle were uncomfortable when the printing of the journal was transferred to Oliver. Everett also angered the other members with his efforts to revise the editorial process. The journal had previously been edited by a board with roughly equal authority, and his attempt to consolidate editorial authority in his own hands rubbed several members the wrong way. An even more serious rift within the circle was caused by George Ticknor's attempt to reform Harvard. Not only did Ticknor eventually find himself isolated, but the *Review*'s refusal to publish his piece on reform prompted him to never contribute to the journal again.

Like any collective effort, the *North American Review* was not untroubled by disagreement or politics. Yet it is still appropriate to treat the journal as a single voice—the voice of a generation and an ideology. Despite the disagreements, a remarkable consistency in approach and philosophy is expressed in the *Review.* Although minor differences surface over particular books or individual issues, a general uniformity of perspective and philosophy appears throughout the journal.

Even more fundamentally, it is appropriate to treat the *North American Review* as the voice of a culture, an expression of a particular philosophy, because that is the way its owners, editors, and contributors conceived of the magazine. The sense that journalism should be about objective reporting or balanced discussion was not a part of antebellum culture. The notion that journalistic writing should be value-free and characterized by the evenhanded presentation of all sides was not a part of this literary world. The intellectuals of the *North American Review,* like the producers of virtually every other magazine of the period, labored under a different premise—that their journal was the expression of a culture, the voice of a specific view of the world, with a distinct understanding of religion, politics, and culture, written largely for an audience which shared these understandings and recognized its reference points. Consequently, the contributors to the *Review* did not write as individuals, they wrote as dutiful spokespersons for that culture. Their works were published anonymously, generally without compensation, and were subjected to the heavy hand of the editorial board with only rare complaint. Editors, at their end, altered and revised without apology, concerned less with individual egos than with the integrity of the culture they represented.[61]

Just as the *Monthly Anthology* established itself as the voice of Boston Federalism during the first decade of the nineteenth century, the *North American Review* came to speak for the next generation. But the later journal would gain a far more prominent place in the history of New England. Although the target of frequent criticism, it nevertheless would be recognized for much of the century as an important source of literary criticism and social commentary. In the second half of the century, some of America's most distinguished literary figures—Charles Eliot Norton, James Russell Lowell, Henry Adams, Henry Cabot Lodge, Charles Francis Adams, E. L. Godkin, Mark Twain, Henry James, and William Dean Howells—would sit on its editorial board or contribute to its pages. By 1900 it would be recognized as the most popular and provocative journal in the country.

But quite possibly the *North American Review*'s most important work was accomplished during its first decade and a half. Its most important contributions may well have been made not by Lowell, Norton, or Adams but by the group of young Federalists first gathering in the home of George Ticknor. During these years, the thirteen years before the election of Jackson, while older Federalist politicians struggled to establish a viable agenda, while men of the previous generation like Otis and Mills drifted without a candidate or consensus, the young Federalist intellectuals of the *North American Review* drafted a credible conservative blueprint for nineteenth-century America. While older Federalists confronted defeat and the prospect of political impotence, these young men reimagined a future that suggested continued status, influence, and prestige.

CHAPTER 4

LITERATURE:
THE PROSPECTS

➤➤ When the *North American Review* began publication in 1815, there was much in it that no doubt reminded readers of the *Monthly Anthology*. Although its articles were published anonymously, its readers must have recognized many of the same contributors. And although the *Review* changed its format and added some new features, many of its themes should have been familiar. Its calls for the development and support of a national literature and its concern that the practical and activist bent in American society was stifling American letters had been voiced earlier in the *Monthly Anthology*. Long before Edward Everett of the *North American Review*, Joseph Stevens Buckminster had complained that when American talent did surface, it was generally neglected by British critics.[1]

Even so, the differences between the two journals would be great. The diatribe against democratic society so often found in the *Monthly Anthology* would be absent from the *North American Review*. Nowhere in the *North American Review* would be echoed Benjamin Wells's fulminations against the common people of the Republic "who ought to be brightening their plowshares instead of dog-earing their spelling book." The strident partisanship and explicit political commentary found in the older journal would also be absent from the newer. Perhaps most important, the calls in the *North American Review* for the development of a national literature would not be compromised by an underlying deference to British literary opinions. Its pleas for the cultivation and support of native talent would not be undermined by what Van Wyck Brooks described, in reference to the *Monthly Anthology*, as "the self-distrust that marks the colonial mind, a mind that has no centre of its own and clings to the well-tried ways of the mother country after the mother country has thrown them off."[2]

Representative of this new editorial tone was the absence of John Sylvester John Gardiner. A regular contributor to the *Monthly Anthology* and a dominant force in the Anthology Society, he contributed only one article to the *North American Review*. Gardiner, the oldest member of the society when it was founded, was its most powerful link to traditional British literary culture. A student of the English classical scholar Samuel Parr, Gardiner was generally recognized as the most authoritatively credentialed member of the Boston literati. An ardent Federalist and an uncompromising apologist for British behavior and culture, he was also the best example of the odd combination of aristocratic arrogance and cultural provincialism that characterized much of the older Federalist vision. In the *Monthly Anthology* and in Boston pulpits, he railed frequently against the shortcomings of American domestic society—its dissolute youth left in the care of "ignorant and vulgar" house servants, the current modes of female education that taught them only to "dance gracefully and prattle french," and that most "detestable" of all living creatures, an "ill-natured woman," from whom men understandably fly "as from plague, pestilence, and famine."[3] American manners and morals, he complained, were characterized by "vice and irreligion . . . licentious principles and opinions . . . relaxed attention on public worship, loose and latitudinarian sentiments respecting government and religion." With equal vehemence he condemned America's recent attachment to France and urged reconciliation with Britain, "the land of our fathers, whence is derived the best blood of our nation, the country, to which we are chiefly indebted for our laws and knowledge."[4]

But Gardiner was not to play a significant role in the *North American Review*. His partisan excess, antirepublican ranting, and Anglophilic cultural attachments were just the sort of thing the younger Federalists of the *North American Review* wanted to avoid. In founding their own journal, they took pains to separate themselves from the political and cultural orientation Gardiner represented and to carve out a philosophical and cultural identity representative of their own generation.

The differences between the two generations on questions of literary style and philosophy were as profound as those on politics and religion. Just as the younger generation had tired of their parents' political myopia and regional smugness, they grew impatient with the older generation's staid literary tastes. Just as they had abandoned the orthodoxies of Congregationalism, they challenged the literary orthodoxies of neoclassicism. Within the *North American Review* these differences would find full expression, but there had been warning of them in the pages of the *Monthly Anthology*. In an article published in the *Anthology* in 1805, Arthur Maynard Walter challenged the neoclassical orthodoxy of the older generation when he criticized the mainstay of Augustan English poetry, Alexander Pope. Revealing an interest in the romantic poets he shared with many of the younger members of the Anthology Society, he characterized Pope as too mechanical. "Taste, judgment, and sense, predominate in his works," argued Walter, "but in vain do we seek for the creative energies of invention, the sublime soaring of thought, and the audacious struggles of imagination, bursting from the confinement of reason." Gardiner, his education and cultural credentials implicitly attacked, rallied to defend his generation's literary standards. The romantic poets like Thomas Gray were the mechanical ones, he charged, and crude ones at that. Perfection lay not in unpolished genius or raw nature but was the "reward of great labour." Experimenters like Gray and his American followers foolishly pursued originality "at the expense of whatever absurdity." True taste, he lectured them, "admires nature only in her charms, not in the gross."[5]

At this point the leader of the younger scholars, Buckminster, joined the debate. "There is a higher species of poetry than the mere language of reason," he wrote in an essay directed at Gardiner. Gray's poetry was indeed irregular, yet "I take as much delight in contemplating the rich hues that succeed one another without order in a deep cloud in the west, which has no prescribed shape, as in viewing the seven colours of the rainbow disposed in a form exactly semi-circular." But Gardiner was far from swayed. What Buckminster thought sublime, argued Gardiner, was actually "perpetually obscure." Buckminster and his friends, he closed, should employ their talents "more usefully, than in the defence of absurdity."[6]

With the controversy reaching uncomfortably personal levels, Gardiner wrote one final attack on Gray and his supporters in the society. But after reading it at the monthly dinner, he tore it up and threw it in the fire. This ended the dispute in an appropriately gentlemanly manner. However, the rift between the two literary camps, and essentially the two generations, was never fully repaired. A decade later William Tudor would rather generously trace the cultural dependence of his elders to the youthfulness of America and the political passion of their times. These had warped their literary as well as their political judgment and yielded an "unlimited deference to the great standards of English learning." But hindsight had not disproved the earlier conclusion reached by Tudor and his young colleagues on the *North American Review* that this excessive deference was ultimately "highly injurious."[7]

It was thus with a different set of tastes and standards and a different sense of its literary mission that the *North American Review* began publication. The traditional, neoclassical literary tastes of the *Monthly Anthology* were replaced by ones considerably more flexible and modern. Pope would still have a following, and few would embrace romanticism as passionately as Richard Henry Dana. But there was a fixed determination on the part of these young intellectuals to free themselves from the stale tastes of the previous generation and the dictates of British literary opinion. The editors of the *North American Review* were intent that American critics establish their own literary standards, and along with this identify and promote American writers and encourage the development of an authentically American national literature.

It was therefore portentous that Tudor featured in the first number of the *North American Review* a response to an article in London's *Quarterly Review* that had lambasted America. This was not the first attack in the English press. For some time the dailies had provided a steady stream of anti-American rhetoric, and seemingly every English traveler to America returned home only to publish a catalog of the country's cultural and political shortcomings.[8] But the periodic lampoons in the *Quarterly Review* were particularly infuriating. One of England's more respected literary periodicals, closely linked to the British government, the journal had featured anti-American ranting since its founding. In 1809, the *Quarterly's* first year of publication, the release of Abiel Holmes's *American Annals* had offered the journal its first opportunity to attack American life.[9] Its reaction in 1814 to the publication of C. Jared Ingersoll's *Inchiquin Letters* provoked Tudor's response.[10] Ingersoll had hoped in his book to defend American culture and society and to beg for fairer treatment from the European press. But if anything, his book had the opposite effect. The *Quarterly* responded with a blistering attack on American culture, society, and government. Labeling the courts biased and Congress decadent, the people immoral and the religion gloomy, the *Quarterly* included in its harangue everything from America's political institutions to its misuse of the English language.[11]

At a certain level it might seem odd that Americans would pay heed to these attacks, much less react so defensively. Received as they were by a nation caught up in the heroics of Andrew Jackson and excited by the prospects of westward expansion, one might expect Old World castigations of American culture and manners to strike Americans as comically irrelevant. But despite their budding frontier ethos, Americans were far from indifferent to matters of culture and the details of refinement. As Richard Bushman has pointed out, during the eighteenth century a new style and form of affluence emerged in America, one more concerned with the draperies and symbols of gentility. By the late eighteenth century this new style, with its more refined forms of architecture, amusement, and speech, was being appropriated by the middle class. Farmers, artisans, and shopkeepers of middling prosperity might not be able to afford a brick house with an entry hall, formal parlors for entertaining, or a grand staircase, but they could acquire the smaller ornaments of genteel culture—a punch bowl or a wine decanter, a bookcase or a mirror. In short, despite America's burgeoning egalitarian ethic, there was a huge interest in the forms and symbols of refinement. Andrew Jackson may have captured the nation's political imagination, but Chesterfield's letters defined the standards and forms of social behavior.[12]

Within a society so absorbed, it is therefore far from surprising that these British attacks on American culture would produce so strong and so widespread a response. From Yale, Timothy Dwight launched a counterattack that rebutted the *Quarterly* piece point by point and labeled another antagonist, the *Edinburgh Review,* "a nuisance to the world." In New York, James Paulding wrote another in his series of defenses of America, while in Philadelphia, Robert Walsh eventually published his own "appeal."[13] But William Tudor's reaction is perhaps most significant. The centerpiece of the first edition of the *North American Review,* his response to the *Quarterly* formed something of a cultural declaration of independence for his Federalist peers and a statement of purpose for the newly born journal. Labeling the *Quarterly* piece typical of the "systematick" abuse that sought to "blacken and degrade our moral character," he suggested these attacks had "poisoned" British opinion against America. Arguing that they had jeopardized British-American relations, he suggested that "some punishment should be devised by common consent." He threatened that if American overtures were not met and the British took no measures to "remove prejudice, and to cultivate esteem and good will toward us . . . we may at once apprehend, and prepare for a constant succession of future wars, founded not in policy, but in passion."[14]

Few went so far as Tudor to see war at the end of these literary attacks. But the jibes at American society, government, and most poignantly, culture that were to persist well into the 1830s provided a continuing rallying point for the *North American Review,* and their rebuttal became one of the journal's defining features. In 1828 Alexander Everett was still complaining of the "continual sneers of a set of heartless and senseless foreigners upon our want of literary talent." His brother Edward Everett perhaps best summed up the consequences. The ties of language and literature between the United States and England had always been great, and there had always existed great "partiality for the English name and character." But after years of this abuse, "this feeling has been declining."[15]

This reorientation of affection, this alienation of cultural sympathies, was to provide yet another critical piece within the formation of these young Federalists' social and cultural ideology. Already removed from the partisanship and parochialism of their fathers, having rejected the previous generation's stuffy and imported literary tastes as well, their attempt to redefine themselves was given a nationalistic edge by these attacks in the British press. The resulting ideological hybrid was both new and somewhat ironic. Having rejected their fathers' provincialism, many of them through their travels abroad, they were now repatriated by the barbs of foreign writers. But no longer narrowly New Englanders, they were now both more cosmopolitan and more American—cosmopolitan in their training and judgment, American in their identity and loyalties.

The most persistent expression of this new sensibility lay in their calls for a national literature. This was not a new ambition. American scholars for some time had lamented the deficiencies in American letters and looked for an explanation. Most often the fault was traced to the democratic focus of American education and the pragmatic, commercial character of American society. John Sylvester John Gardiner made the argument against American education most pointedly. As a result of seeking to educate too many, "everything smells of the shop." Robert H. Gardiner was more tactful and balanced. The abundance of schools allowed for a useful diffusion of general knowledge, but "the multiplicity . . . tends to disperse the rays." If they were "collected into one focus," American scholarship and letters might improve. Buckminster laid the blame more on the character of American society—pragmatic and commercial—and the abundance of opportunity. American writers were distracted by the "extraordinary opportunities we have had of making money." Two decades later Alexander Everett was making much the same argument in blaming the "continual demand for talent in the various walks of active life." Those attracted to poetry and prose soon were distracted by the opportunities for profit or, more nobly, the demands of public service. American audiences consequently were left only with the "unripe fruits of their youth."[16]

But in the decade and a half following the War of 1812, most contributors to the *North American Review* detected considerable change. Increased literacy, improved education, the rising demand for journals and books, all suggested that the time was ripe for the cultivation of American letters. Moreover, many of the long-accepted excuses for the absence of a native literature were dismissed. The suggestion that America lacked the material for good literature was challenged by numerous critics who found the American past rich in materials for both poetry and romantic fiction.[17] To those who argued that political affairs still required Americans' undivided attention, Francis Gray responded with the new consensus: "Our political institutions, they have resisted adversity . . . the foundations of the temple are deeply laid, its superstructure firmly established . . . it is now time to decorate it with the labours of the muses and, kindle the flame of science on its altar."[18]

A few remained unconvinced that America was well suited to the cultivation of fine literature. Edward Channing continued to argue that an American setting was too familiar to perk the interest of the reader of romantic fiction.[19] Others found a deterrent in the egalitarian structure of American society. A successful novel, it was argued, depended on a certain "generalizing principle." Characters must be representative of classes so that the audience will feel a degree of "familiarity with the feelings and passions pourtrayed."[20] In addition, it was doubtful, the argument continued, that the daily life of a republican society contained enough romance, intrigue, and adventure to sustain the reader's interest. The romance novel must revolve around a leisured class whose lives were more exotic and exciting.[21]

John Sylvester John Gardiner, by Gilbert Stuart, ca. 1815. (Courtesy of the Boston Athenæum)

William Tudor, by Thomas Sully after Gilbert Stuart, 1831.
(Courtesy of the Boston Athenæum)

But most contributors to the *North American Review* disagreed. Although America lacked rigidly stratified social classes, there were numerous distinctions of region, religion, and ethnicity that could be exploited. Moreover, those distinctions had the advantage of being naturally maintained. The "artificial and arbitrary distinctions" of Europe actually interfered with the proper development of the novel's characters and warped their construction "into constrained and formal fashions." American society allowed for the more natural and satisfying development of characters "unshackled by forms, unfashioned by governments."[22] As to the argument that only a leisured class led lives fitted for the novel, one critic responded that while American life might lack intrigue, it was filled with "enterprise." American writers had neither use nor need for a class of idlers "whose only employment is to glitter at places of public resort . . . and to form plans to outshine, thwart, and vex each other." Among the active classes, "where the passions and affections have their most salutary and natural play," writers would find their best material. Nowhere would they find "the great objects that worthily interest the passions, and call forth the exertions of men, pursued with more devotion and perseverance."[23]

Furthermore, just as American letters were being fed by improved conditions, British literature seemed on the decline. Alexander Everett outlined a theory of literary evolution that placed Shakespeare at one end and Schiller at the other. Shakespeare represented the dawning of the present literary age—"the exuberant fulness, the fresh and joyous flow of thought and feeling" unfettered by prescribed forms or literary conventions. At the other end of the spectrum was Schiller, a fine writer but one in whom "the form predominates over the substance."[24] Everett was not a literary rebel. He believed Pope to be the "point of perfection" within this literary era. But he noted that since Pope, subsequent poets had faced the choice of either imitating his perfection or awkwardly pursuing originality. While the former "look like affectation in the copy," the latter "run into extravagance."[25] Neither was desirable. Romantics like Byron could hardly be endorsed; their style was too irregular, and their works were far from moral. But equally to be regretted was the "established empire of taste" against which "genius itself . . . does not venture to rebel." Standards must be maintained, but at the same time he doubted that "the fresh impression of nature, and . . . the same impression of power" could ever be reconciled with "a strict observance of all the formal rules of taste."[26]

In discussing the state of English drama, William Hickling Prescott noted a similar sterility. It had not always been so vapid. The Elizabethan stage, he argued much like Everett, had been inspirited by its unique historical context. The last residues of feudal heroism and the remnants of medieval superstition lent the age "a rich illusive coloring of poetry." The resulting drama, uninhibited by ceremony or convention and energized by its popular focus, was a "faithful transcript of nature;—nature in all her nakedness and variety of passion." But during the reign of Queen Anne, the French theater, and more specifically Racine and Boileau, had corrupted English drama. "Reason took place of imagination, and cold correctness of free and lofty enthusiasm." Pope was the most notable example of this perversion. Mimicking the French, he abandoned nature for the "rules" and enslaved the Muse "who had before sported in the capricious and unreproved liberty of a mountain nymph, into the circle of fashion . . . instructing her to move there, with the brilliant decorum of a studied and heartless formality."[27]

Prescott argued in a similar fashion that not only English literature but also the English language were in a state of decline on the other side of the Atlantic. In the late eighteenth century, the language was characterized by its "precision, perspicuity, copiousness, grace and vigor." But in recent years it had suffered at the hands of careless writers and abstract thinkers. The printing press had encouraged "the ignorant to write and the learned to write rapidly." Among others there was an unhealthy tendency to substitute the "complex abstract phraseology of science, for the simple intelligible dialect." Still others had weakened the quality of English prose through an "indiscriminate passion for notoriety," while others had cluttered the language with their "excessive refinement." Prescott was concerned that this stream which fed the American language would soon corrupt American letters, but he was pleased to note that to date American expression was still marked by its "unvarnished style." He even had hopes that American social and cultural conditions might inspire the English language to "put forth its energies with new spirit and freedom."[28] If this happened, not only would American letters be protected, but British letters might be redeemed.

This was a hope expressed by others in the *North American Review*.

William Tudor was even more explicit than Prescott in placing the calls for American literature within the broader goal of reinvigorating the literature and language of the mother country. But not all took so smug and condescending a tone. America was not yet, wrote Richard Henry Dana, the "home of the intellectual greatness of man." Nor had England yet become an intellectual "prison-house." American literature must continue to acknowledge its dependence on British literature, argued Willard Phillips, and begin by "imitating judiciously." The language community in which Americans wrote, agreed John Chipman Gray, still offered "numerous striking and chaste models." Although excessive deference to English critics should be avoided, American literature would benefit from the "coolness of foreigners." Even though American writers should not pander to British tastes, they could benefit from the existence of two distinct but sympathetic markets.[29]

These sorts of concessions to British literature were not very common, but neither was the position staked out by the linguistic revolutionaries at the other end of the spectrum. For men like Walter Channing, American prose was stifled by the language in which it was written. A colonial people could never generate an authentic national literature until it freed itself from the language that implied provincialism and could never capture the peculiarities of American life. Jared Sparks agreed. The English language was as "copious and pliable" as any of the modern languages, and it would permit the American genius to exert itself in numerous intellectual arenas. But it could never "supply those strong motives to intellectual exertion, which it would, if it were growing up with our growth, and receiving on its very front the deep marks of our national character and peculiarities." America would contribute much to science, history, and political theory, but Sparks feared "the literature of the imagination and the heart, will be cramped by the language . . . it will creep too servilely in the track, which thousands have trod, and be too long a slave to foreign models and foreign caprice."[30]

While Gray and Sparks represented the two poles on these questions, most contributors stood somewhere in the middle, acknowledging some continuing dependence on English literature but taking a certain smug satisfaction in the prospect of eclipsing British letters in the future. Most seem to have followed Edward Everett who argued that the benefits inherent in the existence of only one language in America were more significant than its foreign origins.[31] And far more welcomed the emergence of a national literature for what it offered America than for what it might do for England.

In the development of a national literature the *North American Review* saw tremendous benefits. Most immediately it would provide a response to the critics of American culture. A national literature was the repository of a people's best thoughts, its highest ideals. Until this was developed, America could not take its place as the literary, as well as political, leader of the world. In addition, only a natively produced literature could properly portray the American people. Left to foreign interpretation, the American mind and character were subject to misinterpretation and ridicule. Only the American writer raised within the particularity of American society could fully capture the "thousand delicate shades of manner." Only an American could portray the true character of the American people, reveal the "ennobling and elevated," and "transform it from mere buffoonery."[32]

But their interest in a national literature went beyond the redemption of their cultural pride and international reputation. In addition, these young Federalists suggested that such a literature could do much to complete the forming of America—much to help construct a truly national identity and mold the American people into a moral and cohesive people.

Central to this vision was the romantic belief in the particularity of national languages and the literature they produced. George Ticknor and Edward Everett brought home from Europe a belief in the peculiar character and vigor of national languages. There they were exposed to the literary theories of Madame de Staël and A. W. von Schlegel who argued that beauty depended upon its particular representations mediated by local customs and styles. Ticknor in particular was moved by these theories and his own observations to the conclusion that beauty did not assume universal forms but lay "concealed in those idiomatic phrases, those unobtrusive particles, those racy combinations" essentially unobserved and unappreciated by the nonnative speaker. Edward Tyrrel Channing, informed more by British literary journals than by travel, reached many of the same conclusions. A veneration for the classics was important, he wrote in the *North American Review* in 1816, but the writer should avoid making what is "foreign, artificial, and uncongenial, the foundation of a man's literary habits, ambitions, and prejudices." The literature of a country should be as "domestick and individual, as its character or political institutions." Its charm lay in its "nativeness," and thus it should be written for the native audience uniquely capable of appreciating it. "It has, or should have," he concluded emphatically, "nothing to do with strangers."[33]

This emphasis on the particularity of a national literature had several implications. It meant that only the native writer could accurately capture the native character. Only the native writer could paint a true picture of America for a foreign audience. But perhaps more important, only a natively produced literature could fully speak to American readers. Only a national literature, produced within the particularity of American society, written from within and to its peculiar sensibilities, could fully resonate within the American audience.

This being the case, there were some very practical benefits in the generation of a national literature. Most fundamentally, a national literature could be a powerful tool in shaping the character of the reading public. Exposure to more modern, romantic theories of language did not unseat this basic premise of their neoclassical training. The idea that literature had social responsibilities, that it ought to uphold the existing order and could actually further the causes of religion and morality, was part of the canon of literary criticism derived from neoclassical sources like Addison and Boileau and the Scottish rhetoricians Kames and Blair. Works of art, argued Alexander Everett, have a "powerful moral influence." A work like Schiller's *The Robber*, which inverted the proper order of things and made a sympathetic hero out of an outlaw, not only "sins against the rules of taste," but it also "saps, at the same time, in proportion to the power with which it is executed, the foundations of good conduct." Even Byron, who may have been the best English poet since Pope, ought to be removed "forever from the public view," as his works were irreparably "tainted with immorality" and were bound to produce "an unfortunate effect upon the reader's mind." Edward Channing believed public morality was similarly imperiled by Thomas Moore's confusing of the moral order, by his mingling of the coarse and the pure, his casting of all reality under "luxurious twilights, which shall dim or soften whatever is holy or disgusting." Willard Phillips criticized Godwin for similarly failing to respect literature's obligations to uphold the moral order. Writing "with the spirit of a conspirator against the moral government of the world," he equated decorum with tyranny and institutional restraint with slavery, thus leaving the reader "sickened and disgusted with the world, as a scene of misery and guilt . . . ready to exclaim against Providence and reprobate the constitution of nature."[34]

Literature's ability to influence morality gave it more than trifling responsibilities, and in America these were sharpened by the nature of the political institutions. Dependent as these institutions were on a sober and virtuous electorate, writers possessed "political as well as social duties." The moral character of their work influenced not just the moral condition of the public but also the stability and health of the political order. As Alexander Everett explained, civil institutions could do only so much, at best provide only the machinery of government. It was up to a nation's literature to "touch the secret springs, that regulate the whole complicated movement of the political machine."[35]

This confidence in the importance and power of literature can seem somewhat naive to modern readers. But in antebellum America this belief that language had power, that the written and the spoken word could move people and influence behavior, permeated cultural and political life. This was, after all, the golden age of American oratory—citizens gathered by the thousands to hear the great stump speakers like Daniel Webster declaim for hours on the legacy of Plymouth Rock, and for days to hear Lincoln and Douglas debate the intricacies of slave law. During these years the American Bible Society believed national redemption lay in the placement of a Bible in every home, and the American Tract Society was convinced that religious tracts—readable, concise packets of spiritual and behavioral prescription—could reform public morality.[36]

Nineteenth-century American culture began with a belief in language and its power, and for intellectuals from New England this belief had perhaps its deepest roots. Despite the fatalistic implications of Calvinist theology, Puritan ministers had long before carved out a role for the spoken word. It may not actually effect salvation, but it could soften the heart and prepare the congregation for the call that must be answered. By the nineteenth century Puritan theology had lost much of its rigor, but the popularity of the pulpit performer remained. Boston's most prestigious churches pursued promising young preachers with an amazing disregard for age and experience—Buckminster was twenty when summoned by the Brattle Street Church, Everett was nineteen—so long as they demonstrated gifts of eloquence.[37]

Although New England's religious background underlay this confi-

Edward Everett, by Gilbert Stuart, 1820. (Courtesy of the Harvard University Portrait Collection, gift of Henry W. Miller, Class of 1897, 1947. © President and Fellows of Harvard College, Harvard University)

William Hickling Prescott, artist unknown, 1815. (Courtesy of the Massachusetts Historical Society)

dence in language, a second source of this faith, one more frequently referred to in the pages of the *North American Review*, was the tradition of classical oratory. Contributors to the *Review* repeatedly cited the works of Cicero and Demosthenes, not just as examples of perfect speech but as viable models for contemporary oratory. For John Chipman Gray, Demosthenes provided an example of passionate yet reasoned discourse that could still serve in the nineteenth century. Challenging those who suggested that classical oratory was too crude or emotional for the present, more rational age, he argued that Demosthenes' power lay in his ability to weave together passion and reason. His eloquence flowed "from his heart, as well as his intellect. . . . Logic and rhetoric are blended together." The result was discourse of irresistible power. "We feel ourselves in the grasp of a giant, and are hurried along in the course of his argument with unceasing and breathless interest."[38]

In Demosthenes' recognition that public influence required an element of eloquence but also a respect for reason—in his willingness to "inflame our passions" but not "till he has overpowered our understanding"—Gray identified a model for statesmen of the present day. Edward Tyrrel Channing was far more ambivalent about the suitability and safety of these forms of public discourse, but he was as certain as Gray of their persisting power. Channing would have preferred dispassionate appeals to men's conscience and the independent exercise of reason. He would have preferred that truth be left to "its own power, to lay by the drapery of speech, and maintain a sturdy good sense and homely simplicity of manner." But the world had not yet reached "this ethereal purity and susceptibility." Men still needed to be "quickened." Reason and logic might be the most noble of human attributes, but "it is in their hearts or imaginations that we are to find principles which shall lend energy to their convictions." Contemplation and study might carry men to great thoughts, but it was through the vehicle of language that these thoughts took on effective meaning; it was "by the terrours or persuasions of eloquence, that we can best give a presence and reality to danger, guilt, and virtue."[39]

Both Gray and Channing were quick to point out that the American public was far different from the "wild rabble" of the ancient democracies. Americans were far more deliberative and careful. Their educational and republican institutions presupposed and helped form a community

of "thinking, reflecting individuals." But this community was not impervious to the appeals and power of language. It only demanded, said Gray,
that oratory be styled appropriately, that it be "manly, argumentative eloquence . . . which seeks to convince and persuade, not to entertain; which
speaks to the reason and the heart, rather than to the fancy." Oratory of
this type, oratory which sought not just "to speak, but to speak true,"
added Channing, could still produce in its audience "a deep and inextin-
guishable energy."[40]

If these young intellectuals drew upon their Puritan past and their classical education in explaining their faith in the power of language, it was
also repackaged somewhat within the more modern premises of faculty
psychology. When Gray encouraged oratory that spoke to the "reason
and the heart," or when Channing conceded that the emotions needed to
be quickened before the mind could be moved, they also drew upon the
hierarchical understanding of human nature and society advanced by the
Scottish theorists Lord Kames, Thomas Reid, and Dugald Stewart. From
these thinkers American intellectuals drew the belief that appeals to the
highest faculties—prudence and moral sense—might be the most sublime but, given the makeup of men individually and collectively, not
the most effective. Because the lower faculties—the emotions or "affections"—possessed greater strength in society, just as they did within individuals, the orator must make some concessions to this reality. He must
appeal to these emotions and appetites, men's sense of pity and filial love,
their feelings of resentment and envy. He must not concede too much.
These Federalist intellectuals condemned the evangelism of the camp
meeting and its raucous enthusiasm. But it was not so much the emotion-
alism of the revivals that disturbed them as the lack of balance. Appeals
to the heart were necessary, but the emotion aroused must be placed in
the service of the higher faculties. As Daniel Howe explained, the orator
must strike a delicate balance, one which "gave concrete application to
the abstractions of faculty psychology, addressing and stimulating the
various elements in complex human nature . . . to arouse the emotions
enough to motivate action but not so much as to destroy the primacy of
rationality."[41]

That these New England intellectuals should thus retain a belief in the
power of language—that these heirs of the Puritan and classical traditions and students of faculty psychology should place so much confidence
in the spoken word—should not be a surprise. But that they should so

easily transfer this confidence to the written word is highly significant. Some of these men, Alexander Everett for example, believed that despite speakers like Webster and Ames, contemporary oratory had lost much of its power. More often read than recited, generally lifeless and banal, contemporary oratory, Everett complained, failed to build the "natural sympathetic chain" that previously linked together speaker and audience. Without it, without the interactive "electrical communication of hearts and minds," the great and living oratory of the past could never be re-created. But this did not mean that language had lost its power. Everett still believed that it possessed unique powers to move men, only now that power was exercised through the printed word.[42]

On this final point John Chipman Gray was in agreement. Although he was more confident than Everett that oratory could be revived, he agreed that it was no longer the eloquent speaker but rather the eloquent writer who holds the "keys of our knowledge." Concomitantly, language retained more, not less, power. No longer addressing a small forum, no longer writing for a limited circle, the modern writer was addressing the "whole people." He was addressing both the scholar and the commonly educated; he was the instructor "of an immense empire."[43]

It was this increased importance of language, this even more exalted power of the printed word, that gave these contributors to the *North American Review* their most excited sense of themselves and their role. For what else was there in America that could match their reach or equal the range of their influence? The American continent was huge, its population was sparsely and widely settled. How else might this population be reached and, more importantly, linked together? During these years Americans of all sorts questioned what would or ever could tie America's increasingly distant and disparate people together as a nation. Although their revolution had accomplished independence, it had left unfinished the task of nation building. Perry Miller several decades ago argued that the revivals of the Second Great Awakening should be understood in this context—as exercises in national identification, as collective statements of community purpose by Americans aware of and disturbed by the distended conditions of the growing country. George Forgie has identified the early nineteenth-century anxieties surrounding nation building as the defining feature of the "post-heroic generation"—a generation inspired by the heroics of their fathers but plagued by fears of inability, a generation tormented by evidence of in-

creasing materialism and political indifference, convinced that no contemporary leader matched up to the standards of their fathers, and
haunted by the fear that amid these conditions the great experiment in
republicanism would dissolve.[44]

In many ways the intellectuals of the *North American Review* were representative of this post-Revolutionary generation. Like those Forgie described they were preoccupied with the next step in the work begun by
their ancestors, intent on completing the grand political experiment so
nobly begun. But unlike those Forgie emphasized, and characteristic of
the optimism that separated them from their Federalist fathers, these
young Federalists placed hope in the power of the culture they shepherded. Convinced that language retained power, they saw in their literary efforts the answer to all the concerns about morality and virtue. Certain that literature and literary criticism could influence behavior, they
believed that the national literature they promoted would shape Americans' moral and political character. In addition, they believed this literature could provide the most effective means of forming national identity
and cultivating national feeling. A critical tool in the formation of the
public morality, a necessary ingredient for the viability of republican institutions, a national literature, they argued, could provide the glue of
nationalism so badly needed.

Willard Phillips argued, for example, that Americans were disappoint-
ingly nonchalant about the political principles that ought to form the basis of the national identity. "Quite as ready to calculate as to feel," they
demonstrated a "commonplace, hackneyed" attitude toward the subject
of liberty, rather than the sort of vibrant enthusiasm it deserved. But
certain forms of literature, he noted, seemed capable of stirring Americans' national pride. Cooper's novel *The Pilot,* for example, had managed
to touch a "string to which the national feeling vibrates certainly and
deeply," and in so doing it had succeeded where political ideology had
failed.[45]

William Prescott expressed a similar confidence in the power of literature when he argued that nothing operated "more strongly in infusing a
love of country into the mass of the people, than the union of a national
music with popular poetry." Jared Sparks suggested that amid the faction
and discord of national politics, histories that recorded the origins of the
country's political institutions and the heroic deeds of Americans' ancestors would provide the "polestar to which all may look for safety." But it

was John Chipman Gray who made the argument most explicitly. Seriously tested in every decade, most recently during the Missouri controversy of 1820, the bonds of national identity were tenuous at best. But a national literature, Gray argued, could unite the disparate elements of the Union. "In literature, more than in any thing else of equal moment," he announced, "we may hope for universal similarity of opinion, and cordiality of feeling." It was up to the poet, the historian, and the essayist to stoke the fires of patriotism and forge the ties of nationhood. Institutions and laws would prove insufficient. Political allegiances and even religion, that which we might hope would provide the necessary bonds of sentiment and commitment, had instead exacerbated a tendency toward sectarianism and discord. When all these failed, "our national literature may be the only subject of harmonious interest left us." [46]

It is in this belief that these young Federalists appeared the most ambitious, this striking belief that literature could form the nation, that books could build ties of sentiment and feeling across distances created by geography and the divisions engendered by religion, ethnicity, and politics. Yet the conclusions of students of nationalism suggest these hopes were far from absurd. Benedict Anderson has argued, for example, that a nation is essentially an "imagined community"—a collection of individuals united primarily by intellectual abstraction, a community of citizens linked less significantly by commercial or political or social contact than by the fact that "in the minds of each lives the image of their communion." It is less dependent on the actual resolution of all differences or the elimination of inequities than on the formation of "a deep, horizontal comradeship." [47] For America this understanding of nationhood seems particularly useful, for in the early nineteenth century it was a nation of only vaguely defined boundaries and immense distances, not united by a national church or long-established institutions or untroubled by differences of region, economics, and politics. America in 1820 was a nation in possession of only the briefest of histories, and that a history of separation and local prerogative. For the intellectuals of the *North American Review* to conclude that literature offered the best, and perhaps only, means of building national identity was not only sensible but possibly correct.

Nor were they the only members of this generation to suggest that nationalism and nation building would be best achieved through literary means. The belief of James Madison that the American republic would be best served by the isolating and intellectually fragmenting effects of the American space was not widely shared. More seem to have been aware that these distances could and should be closed, that America would be better served by the narrowing of distances and the sharing of information and ideas—the construction, in effect, of an intellectual and ideological infrastructure.

This belief would inspire the efforts of revivalists, tract societies, and Sunday school and public school reformers. But it was most practically expressed in the Postal Act of 1792 and the elaboration of the American postal system. With routes penetrating deeper and deeper into rural areas, with postal administrative positions increasingly prestigious and desirable, the growth and perceived importance of the system were reflected in the elevation of the postmaster general to a cabinet position in 1829. Surpassing the British and French systems in coverage and efficiency by the 1840s, the American system's history is truly an impressive story of institutional and bureaucratic development. Yet to reduce the story of the postal system to one of bureaucratic elaboration is to miss the theoretical and ideological premises implicit in its development. As Richard John has pointed out, the postal system from its inception was conceived not just as a utilitarian apparatus but as a powerful "agent of change." Within their promotion of the system and its expansion, the visionaries behind it advanced "the deceptively simple proposition that communication could create culture, that the movement of information could spark the movement of ideas."[48]

The driving importance of this philosophy was evident throughout the expansion of the system. It was revealed in the demand that new routes be opened regardless of their fiscal viability, and even more clearly in the special privileges awarded newspapers. While personal and business correspondence was charged between six and twenty-five cents a page, the 1792 Postal Act granted newspapers equal access to the mails at the bargain rate of one cent for less than 100 miles and $1^{1}/_{2}$ cents for longer distances. Exchange copies—copies to be distributed to interior newspapers or papers along the postal routes—were delivered at no charge.[49] This pricing disparity did not go unchallenged. Throughout the first half century, critics complained that Congress seemed to believe newspapers had a "divine right to some exclusive privilege at the post-office."[50] Nor were they very far from the mark in their sense of the underlying philosophy of the postal system. As its purpose was not just to deliver the mail but to link a nation, newspapers, as carriers of community information, were entitled to special rates. As the more sublime purpose of the postal system was the reconstruction of the public sphere, these literary repositories of the collective conscience deserved privileged status.

Although business and personal correspondents complained, congressmen were quick to adapt to this new print-based polity. Speeches were recorded and posted verbatim; British critics noted that speeches were published that had no real bearing on the workings of Congress. But such was the nature of this imagined community. Not defined by walls and borders or held together by institutions or even laws, it was "disembodied," less a place than a process, an arena in which Americans could exchange information and ideas and join themselves to the whole regardless of location. As a result, the actual political arena in Washington, D.C., was, in certain ways, less important than its perception within the broader literary public sphere created by the postal system. Realizing this, congressmen added their speeches and congressional transcripts to the postal pouches filled with newspapers and thus helped create "a national community that existed in the collective imagination of the citizenry."[51]

The intellectuals of the *North American Review* were thus participating in a far more general process of defining the new public sphere. With traditional avenues of public action not only cut off but also increasingly extended, they joined a broad and diverse effort to unite Americans together through literary channels—to create a nation through words, to negate the significance of time and space, and to reconstruct the "electric chain" of sympathy through the written word. The confidence that their literature and their criticism could influence public morality and civic behavior was thus not unusual but rather symptomatic of the age. And their even more ambitious hope that this same literature might forge the bonds of nationhood was an elaboration of a more general ambition.

Reinforced by the broader ambitions of the society in which they lived, their particular slant on this goal nevertheless served their journal and themselves particularly well. This belief in the power of language and literature, this belief that the cultivation of a national literature would both answer foreign critics and moralize and unite the American people, provided the *North American Review* with a clear sense of purpose. Drawing upon both romantic and neoclassical influences, its contributors defined a literary agenda that focused the journal's efforts and found expression in everything from Tudor's regular review of books on North

America to the frequent responses to foreign critics written by Edward Everett, from the repeated calls for the support of American institutions that would foster the fine arts to the regular reviews of American literary works. The romantic-neoclassical hybrid, and the sense of mission it produced, provided the *North American Review* with a sense of purpose that the *Monthly Anthology* always lacked. In addition, it served the contributors and editors of the *North American Review* in more personal ways. In identifying a purpose for themselves that was agreeable to their own cultural pretensions, it offered them a prestigious role that suited their sensibilities. In identifying a purpose that held national implications, they were offered a place within the national culture that promised continued influence and status.

CHAPTER 5

LITERATURE:
THE PROBLEMS

➤➤ During the first years of the *North American Review*'s existence, the journal advanced a vision for American literature that was indeed promising. Weaving together the old and the new, neoclassical principles and romantic theories, the journal's young Federalist intellectuals constructed a theory of literature that offered a great deal to the American character and polity, an understanding of literature that emphasized its powers to strengthen individual morality, shape the public conscience, and form the bonds of nationhood. It was a vision that was both promising and timely. British letters were on the decline, but America's republican society was generating those conditions best suited to the production of a new literature, an authentically American literature that would complement the county's political contributions to the march of progress.

The prospects for American literature were great indeed, not only for the nation and the public but also for the young Federalist editors and contributors to the *Review,* for this literary vision offered to its architects promises of continued status and influence that were especially compelling. For some of the intellectuals contributing to the *North American Review,* their role as editors and critics took on a significance greater than even the literature they were called to promote. For Prescott this exaggerated importance lay in the peculiar vitality and immaturity of American letters. Within a society so "buoyant" and "young," the need for the literary institutions that could "regulate it" was all the greater. American letters would be fueled by this youthful energy, but it was imperative that scholars like himself and his friends "set an example of pure, perspicuous, classical composition." For Jared Sparks the need for, and even superiority of, the critic lay in the formulaic nature of the modern novel. The example set by Scott could be reduced to a handful of ingredients—a historical plot, rich scenery, rapid plot transitions, diverse characters, and provincial quirks like accents and peculiar customs. As these were easy to reproduce, the critic was all the more needed to "exercise a strict surveillance over this department of literature."[1]

John Gray reached a similar conclusion. He approached the problem from within a more broadly focused aesthetic theory, but his conclusions regarding the importance of the critic and editor were equally sublime. For Gray, beyond the endless opportunities for artistic treatment offered by nature, there were equally endless opportunities in "transposing, in expanding, in illustrating, in adorning the leading thoughts." Knowledge and culture were progressive and cumulative. "The march of genius" was consequently as dependent upon the refining pen of the editor as the creative spark of the poet. "He who improves and perfects, is often preferred, and justly, to him who first produces." In fact, American literature suffered less from the absence of creative talent than from a dearth of good criticism. "Nothing would tend more to accelerate our progress in letters," he concluded, "than the encouragement among ourselves, of a spirit of enlightened and liberal yet exact and fearless criticism."[2]

For the *North American Review* the sense of direction provided by its literary mission thus carried an equally profound sense of the importance of its contributors. In not only identifying and promoting but also screening and selecting, they would shape, not just trumpet, American literature; they would form and not just preserve American culture. Their sense of purpose was thus in place. But inhibiting their efforts was the actual state of American literature; inhibiting their crusade was their sense of the literature and the writers they sought to promote.

The problem began with their sense of the women writers who became such frequent contributors to the nation's literary efforts during the first half of the nineteenth century. By 1850 fully one-half of the popular works produced were written by women, and even before 1830 roughly one-third of all those publishing fiction were women. The publishing industry was far from gender-blind in its practices and attitudes. The acerbic responses of Houghton's female writers to the publishing company's male-only anniversary celebration in 1870 speaks to the persistence of traditional gender attitudes throughout the century. But there was nevertheless a great deal of opportunity for women as writers, perhaps largely

because writing offered a vocation which did not seem to challenge existing perceptions of womanhood. The sense that writing was an occupa-
tion of leisure, pursued, in Lawrence Buell's phrase, in the spirit of "genteel amateurism," was easily reconciled to the perceptions of appropriate
female activity. The belief that literature should be didactic and moral, as
well as the sense that most writers, while talented with words, were naive
commercially, also squared well with nineteenth-century attitudes toward
women.[3]

This convergence provided a unique opportunity for women in early
nineteenth-century America, and it also explains the conservative nature
of most of the work they produced. Written from within, not in defiance
of, existing gender attitudes, little of the period's literature provided female models that were too far afield of existing prescriptions. Highly
sentimental, often timid, dependent on the men who surrounded them,
generally finding fulfillment in traditional marriage and family choices,
antebellum heroines and their creators were so conservative as to be considered "traitors to their sex" by some later critics. But as Nina Baym has
pointed out, this criticism is rooted in an unfair decontextualization of
these writers' efforts and a too narrow conception of "domesticity." Later
perceived as the ideology of imprisonment, domesticity meant something
different for these women writers—not the mythology of co-optation
but rather a prescription for human happiness, an understanding of human relationships rooted in love and mutual responsibility. Although it
may have served ultimately to encourage subordination and dependence
and may have contributed to the sequestration of women in the home, it
was not conceived so calculatingly for this purpose but rather as an alternative to commercial capitalism, an ethic of love and support to challenge
the rising spirit of competition. The home within this context was perceived not as a prison but as the arena in which all people found true
fulfillment, an arena over which, Baym added, women presided.[4]

However interpreted, the essential fact is that there was little inherently
radical in the works of women writers or in the very act of their writing.
The reaction of the *North American Review* to women writers, or more
precisely their invisibility within the journal, thus at first seems surprising.
Even though women were finding all sorts of new opportunities as writers during these years, as novelists, poets, and essayists, and even though
their contributions largely reenforced traditional cultural standards, virtually none contributed to the *North American Review*. In the first fifteen

years of the journal's existence, only three women contributed to its pages—a few pieces of poetry, some scenery sketches, and an essay on beekeeping. Over the next seventy years, fewer than thirty women were among the more than seven hundred writers contributing to the *Review*. There was a corresponding muted response to the literary works produced by women during the early years. Even though women were responsible for roughly a third of all the works published, the Federalist intellectuals behind the *North American Review* had relatively little to say about them.

The most comprehensive commentary on the women writers of the period was offered by Jared Sparks in 1825. In a review of recent American novels, he discussed five written by women: *Hobomok*, by Lydia Maria Child; *A Peep at the Pilgrims*, by Harriet Vaughan Foster; *The Witch of New England*, attributed to Eliza Buckminster Lee; *Saratoga, a Tale*, by Eliza Lansford Cushing; and *A Winter in Washington*, by Margaret Bayard Smith.[5] Somewhat disdainful of novel writing in general—"works of this sort are easily written"—he was even more unimpressed by this particular body of recent work.[6]

Sparks praised Foster's novel for its skillful description of scenery, but otherwise he found it uninspiring. It was cluttered with too many characters, the dialogue was forced, and in too many places it offered little more than historical narrative. The author should forget about a writing career, he concluded, unless "satisfied with the praise of mediocrity." He reviewed *The Witch of New England* even more severely. It too included some decent handling of scenery and character, but its treatment of the history in which the book was placed was "ridiculous." The author, Sparks concluded, seemed to be at least aware of the sources but proved herself surprisingly "ignorant of the early history of the country." Smith's *Winter in Washington*, Sparks said, was laborious reading. He conceded that the author undertook a very difficult task: "describing and rendering picturesque, things that are common." But he was unequivocal in concluding that she failed in the attempt. He described Cushing's *Saratoga* more favorably. Despite its "crowding of persons and plots," Sparks called it a "respectable novel" with decently drawn characters and good dialogue. He praised Child's *Hobomok* for its well-drawn characters. The qualities of America's Puritan founders were portrayed with "great ingenuity and power," and the Indian characters in the book were drawn with particular beauty. But even this praise was tempered by Sparks's criticism of the plot, which was in "very bad taste," and in the end he could go no further than commend the novel as the best among a rather poor bunch.[7]

Sparks could think of worse pursuits for these authors and their readers. "Those persons who waste their time in reading poor novels, or, if our readers please, any novels, would probably waste it in some other way not more innocent, if novels were not to be had." Therefore, he concluded by suggesting that these writers might just as well continue to write. He reminded them that they must not transgress the standards of morality or decorum, and they should not expect any more favorable a response. But so long as they did not mind "laboring sometimes in vain," they might as well proceed with their efforts.[8]

The other critics of the *Review* were considerably more encouraging. Although no other contributor offered a similar comprehensive review of female literary work, within more limited assessments they spoke far more positively about novel writing and female contributions to the genre. Alvan Lamson went so far as to credit women writers with rescuing the literary form. Not only were their contributions distinguished by their volume and quality, they had succeeded in "rescuing fiction from the service of corruption and profligacy." Francis Greenwood suggested that the cultural significance of these women writers was even more far-reaching. Their success in this field "has vindicated for her sex that equality with the other, which has been both doubted and denied." It had inspired among women more generally a "disposition to read, to study, to think; making something desirable beside personal attraction." This demonstration of female intellectual equality would, moreover, have a positive effect on men, reminding them that a woman was neither "the queen nor the plaything for an hour." Instead men would find greater satisfaction in sharing life "with an accomplished fellow creature, than with a brainless idol." In short, women writers had done more than merely save the novel; "the successful literary efforts of a few females, have a direct tendency to raise the whole mass of human intellect."[9]

Greenwood's comments were offered in a review of Catherine Maria Sedgwick's *Hope Leslie*. Among the American female writers, Sedgwick received by far the most thorough and positive response in the *North American Review*. Quite plausibly her intimacy with this intellectual circle contributed to this receptivity. The daughter of Theodore Sedgwick, High Federalist statesman and jurist, and the sister of *Review* contributors Theodore Jr. and Henry Dwight Sedgwick, she was raised within the same Federalist culture and was intimate with the same social circle that spawned the journal. Never marrying, she lived in her brothers' homes, embraced Unitarianism, and like her brothers' friends seems to have recognized the new opportunities for cultural influence opening in the wake of political disappointment.[10]

William H. Gardiner offered the first mention of Sedgwick's work in a review of Cooper's novel *The Spy.* In a somewhat curious footnote, Gardiner acknowledged her *New England Tale* as a "beautiful little picture of native scenery and manner" and proof of the "abundance of original character we can supply to the domestic tale." Pleased both by the book and what it seemed to say about the potential for a native literature, Gardiner closed with a backhanded slap at Cooper. "We may with far greater confidence boast of a religious Edgeworth in our land, than of a wonder-working Scott." William Cullen Bryant was equally impressed with Sedgwick's second novel, *Redwood,* and similarly inspired by what the book suggested about the potential in America for the novel. Her work revealed "a rich and varied field" for the American writer. This field was, moreover, inaccessible to the foreign observer, and therefore it was left up to the American writer to explore the "copious and valuable materials the private lives and daily habits our countrymen offer." George Hillard placed a similar national spin on his review of Sedgwick's fourth novel, *Clarence.* Her works, he argued, offered important contributions to the "neglected vineyard of American fiction" and brought "honor to our land."[11]

Clearly, Sedgwick's work was appreciated in large part by these critics for what it offered to their nationalist agenda. But they were not indifferent to its intrinsic merits. Gardiner believed she wrote with "exquisite delicacy of taste, and great strength of talent." Bryant was most impressed by the skill with which her characters were drawn. "They are made to look and act like people in the world around us," he wrote, and her moral was "well wrought into the texture of the work." Greenwood thought *Hope Leslie* was Sedgwick's best book to date and praised its "purity and delicacy," its "lofty sentiment" and "solemn breathings of religion," as well as its "wit and playful satire." Hillard waxed that there was a "beautiful tenderness and sensibility breathing out from her writings, like the fragrance from a rose."[12]

But there was also a great deal of qualification in their praise. Bryant found the unraveling of the plot in *Redwood* somewhat heavy-handed, and Hillard criticized *Clarence* in similar terms. "A most cumbrous mass of machinery is employed to disengage and bring to a point the tangled threads of her story." But more problematic for these critics, and more significant in explaining their general neglect of women writers, was the repeated reminder that although Sedgwick was a talented writer, she was only a writer of fiction and limited to this genre and, even in this genre, by her sensibilities as a woman. Greenwood, despite his elaborate pontificating regarding the influence of female writers, could not deny that female literature had its "proper walks . . . peculiar in its nature and distinct in its influence." The moral and religious temperament of women and their "natural sympathies . . . even such of them as have never been mothers themselves" left women perfectly suited for the production of children's books and the other "lighter kinds of literature." But beyond these literary forms they could not successfully aspire. "Into the paths of abstruse learning, few of the sex will bend their steps. Their situation, habits, and feelings leading them not there." A few had tried, Greenwood noted reproachfully, but "she cannot be false to her nature." [13]

George Hillard was even more thorough in making the argument. To the appropriate genre the woman writer brought unparalleled abilities — a sense of morality and style, elegance and purity, that few men shared and powers of observation "far higher than the cold forms of mere learning." But she was equally limited by her nature. Sedgwick, for example, could not draw a villain; "she has no idea of the spasms and convulsions of the mind." In fact, where her works suffered most was in those places she attempted to write outside of her gender, where she attempted to move beyond the wholesome narrative or the sentimental tale, those places where she "attempted to give a tragic grandeur to the workings of dark passions, and to thrill us with the fearful collision of guilty minds." This required insights and intuitions, a character and sensibility beyond her nature, "a peculiar and masculine talent," as well as "a familiarity with all the dark corners of the human heart . . . [which] no respectable woman has ever an opportunity of remarking." The tragic and the heroic must be left to men. Women writers like Sedgwick must content themselves with the "lesser foibles of life, and the unostentatious homebred virtues." [14]

No other female American writer received as much attention during these years. Only Lydia Maria Child was mentioned more than once. John Chipman Gray was more complimentary than Sparks in discussing her *Hobomok*. In its descriptions of scenery, development of character, and "genuine pathos," he thought it the equal of any piece of American fiction. But her second effort, *The Rebels*, was a disappointment. It strayed little from the historical narrative and, significantly, offered little that was not expressed "with far more force and eloquence in the writings of Adams and of Quincy."[15]

The other female American writers of the period were never mentioned. Susanna Rowson and Hannah Foster, whose works, although published earlier, were still popular in these years, were ignored. Sara Josepha Hale, whose *Northwood* was first published in 1827, was not recognized until 1849. Nor, if we look forward a bit, did the female writer of the 1830s and 1840s receive any better response. Susan Fenimore Cooper, Eliza Leslie, Eliza Lee Buckminster, and Caroline Howard Gilman did garner a bit of attention. But Emily Judson and Sara Jane Lippincott (or "Fanny Forester" and "Grace Greenwood"), Hannah Farnham Sawyer Lee, Emma Catherine Embury, Eliza Lee Cabot Follen, Mrs. A. J. Graves, Louisa C. Tuthill, and Almira Hart Phelps, all of whom published novels or collections of some popularity and/or significance, were not reviewed in the *North American Review* through at least 1877.[16]

It is worth noting that the female giants of British literature fared a bit better in the *North American Review*. Anna Barbauld was reviewed at length by Alvan Lamson, and Marie Edgeworth was reviewed and discussed on several occasions. But the young Federalist response to these more established writers differed little from that offered their American colleagues. Lamson believed Barbauld's contributions were profound; her works offered a "powerful agent in correcting the moral judgments, and refining and exalting the moral feelings of the community." But her genius was of a lesser type. Her works might offer a "moral and devotional character," but they were also "somewhat deficient in sensibility and ardor"; she might possess a "calm and chastened manner," but she offered "little depth of feeling and little pathos." Edgeworth was held in greater esteem. But even her reputation was qualified. Phillips found her a refreshing alternative to the "fantastical splendour" and "seductive fancies" of most fiction, an "antidote to the poisons" abundant in contemporary work. Yet he acknowledged her not as a great novelist but a "great reformer." William Peabody argued that she drew characters that were vivid and memorable, but unlike those of Scott, they did not merit a second reading. Edward Everett suggested that in certain ways she did deserve to be ranked right alongside Scott. In her "qualities of invention, observation of manners, familiarity with life, both elegant and common, of wit and sense," she was Scott's equal. But betraying the same sense of gender sensibilities that colored these reviewers' appreciation of American female writers, Everett argued that she could not compare with Scott in those areas that raised the novel to a higher literary form. "Where she is inferior, it is not so much in that which properly belongs to the novelist, as in those higher and more splendid qualities, which are rather the portion of the orator and the poet." [17]

To Everett's credit he pursued an explanation for these differing abilities. He rejected the suggestion of the phrenologist William Lawrence that there was a "sex to the mind." Instead he noted the differences of education and upbringing that inhibited any inclinations toward originality or independence. [18] But the other critics seem to have been little troubled by these questions. If any shared Everett's curiosity or his conclusions, it was secondary to their more pressing concern of identifying and promoting a native literature. In this crusade they were convinced that the contributions of the rapidly expanding corps of women writers were of limited significance; they strengthened the field of children's literature, they offered a great deal in the way of "lighter" reading—light poetry, simple essays, and short stories. But they did not offer, nor according to most were they capable of offering, much more. The sort of literary production that would significantly raise the reputation of American letters, that would seriously elevate the status of American culture and silence the foreign critics, was for these Federalist critics a task only men could pursue.

But upon turning to the male writers of the period, the intellectuals of the *North American Review* were only slightly more impressed. There was a talented young poet to celebrate in William Cullen Bryant, and three American authors—Charles Brockden Brown, James Fenimore Cooper, and Washington Irving—had managed to achieve some international recognition. But the intellectuals of the *North American Review* were not entirely convinced of the value of their contributions.

Of these, Bryant drew the most enthusiastic reviews in the *North American Review*. There was no doubt an element of local ownership informing their assessment, for Bryant was a native of Massachusetts and the son of a Federalist state legislator. His first published work, in fact, was a satiric attack on Jefferson entitled "The Embargo." In addition, the *North American Review* could claim the honor of first publishing his "Thanatopsis" in 1817. Inasmuch as Bryant became, as Richard Ruland and Malcolm Bradbury have argued, "the cosmopolitan writer America had needed," these New England cultural advocates no doubt were pleased.[19]

But there was more than regional pride behind the *Review*'s approval of Bryant. He shared the journal's commitment to the development of a national literature, while at the same time agreeing that this should not deteriorate into a quest for originality at the expense of all established standards. Praised by Willard Phillips as able "to express fine thoughts, in true and obvious English," Bryant offered the mix of national origi- nality and literary conventionality they preferred. Celebrated more elabo- rately by Alvan Lamson as "always faithful to nature . . . alive to the beautiful forms of the outward world" but at the same time respectful of "genuine classical English," Bryant expressed the combination of roman- ticism and neoclassicism many of these critics sought.[20]

The other major American writers of the period, however, drew far more equivocal responses. Although anxious to celebrate American works and identify the forerunners of a new era in American letters, the literary missionaries of the *North American Review* were unable to offer these American writers unqualified praise. One of these, Charles Brockden Brown, was actually of an earlier era, dying in 1810. But he was the only American novelist to gain significant attention abroad prior to Cooper and the only writer able to challenge Cooper's and Irving's claims as foun- ders of American fiction. Prescott eventually would confer upon him this distinction, but for the most part the critics of the *North American Review* were as divided as twentieth-century critics in their assessment of him.[21] In particular, they were not willing to accept Brown's own claim that he had successfully transferred a European genre to the American soil. An- ticipating the *North American Review*'s nationalist agenda, he noted in his preface to *Edgar Huntly* that "America has opened new views to the naturalist and politician, but has seldom furnished themes to the moral painter." Arguing that America was rich in material, he stated his inten- tion to "exhibit a series of adventures growing out of the condition of our country."[22] But the critics of the *North American Review* were not con- vinced of his success. They found his Gothic style neither appealing nor quintessentially American. William Gardiner, in fact, found little pecu- liarly American about him. His novels were placed in America, it was true, but his characters, "those dark monsters of the imagination," were "not beings of this world," much less America. Edward Channing traced Brown's morbid tastes to his misanthropic temperament. A recluse, childless and socially inept, he was happiest when alone with his thoughts and seemed to write more for himself than for the world outside. Although the detailed character studies this temperament produced were at times intriguing, Channing more often found them "excessively irksome." Too introspective, maddeningly "hunting for materials of thought rather than motives to action," Brown's characters exhibited a "perverse love of perplexity and doubt" that wearied even the scholarly Channing. [23]

Cooper drew an entirely different but no less equivocal response. There was no denying the American flavor of his works. Rich in American history, set vividly within the American landscape, and filled with skillfully drawn, authentically American characters, Cooper's books offered proof of the romantic potential lying in the American scene.[24] Phillips argued his work would remain a "permanent part of our literature," while Gardiner labeled him "the first who has deserved the appellation of a distinguished American novel writer." [25]

However, this praise was loaded with qualifications. Cooper's narratives possessed energy, but his stories often lacked subtlety. His characters were colorful, but they also lacked depth. Gardiner praised his skills at engaging the reader in "the flight, the hot pursuit, the charge, the victory," but complained that he seemed incapable of moving the "softer affections." His descriptions of nature were at times vivid, but he never fully captured its power—"that deep moral feeling which weds the soul to beauty wherever it exists, and breathes its own freshness and fragrance over all that it creates."[26] Finally, while Cooper's work was "thoroughly American," Phillips found in it certain "national characteristics" of the country's literature that were best abandoned. The colorful and the vivid often degenerated into the too graphic and natural. Some passages were "too harsh," some scenes were "more shocking than interesting."[27] Throughout there was too much haste and imprecision. Phillips concluded that a work did not need to be perfect to garner praise, and Gardiner decided that there was really no one else who could challenge Cooper for the "palm as an American novelist," but they were far from unambiguous in their support. Gardiner looked forward to Cooper's future efforts but pleaded that he "write his book before he prints it; and . . . read it over once into the bargain."[28]

Washington Irving's reception was similarly mixed. Richard Henry

Dana labeled him "the most popular writer in this country" and predicted he would "always be a standard author amongst us." Alexander Everett credited him with helping to establish a "purely American literary reputation of the first order" and labeled him the "harbinger and founder of the American school of polite learning." Both found much to praise in *Salmagundi* and the Knickerbocker tales, and Everett placed his *Life of Columbus* among "the very best histories of any age." [29]

But there was also a shared sense that Irving's works were intellectually thin. As Martin Green wrote in 1973, Irving combined "what was harmless in the new Romanticism with a cautiously genteel sensibility" within a bland formula designed to make the American reader "feel culturally reassured." To their credit the critics of the *North American Review* did not reward his caution. Dana called his work humorous and skillfully written, "exceedingly pleasant morning or after-dinner reading," but his praise went no deeper than that. Always light, never taxing or intellectually challenging, Irving's work, said Dana, succeeded best when he did not wander from his comic formulas. Everett thought that with his humor he "proves himself substantially a poet" but noted that "he does not attempt the sublime." Similarly, his historical work was of the less ambitious, "purely narrative" type. Although a first-rate example of this type, it was inferior to "philosophical history," which analyzed cause and effect and sought to identify general principles. Irving's work reflected "diligence" and "perseverance," whereas philosophical history called upon "the most glorious exercises of the intellect." [30]

Irving also had made the cardinal error of not only moving to England but also, according to the critics of the *North American Review,* altering his style to suit English audiences. Although Irving claimed that *The Sketch Book,* written in 1819, served the nationalist ambition of establishing a legendary past for America, his American critics were struck more by the compromises apparently made to foreign sensibilities.[31] His original vitality and clarity were replaced by a "more studied, periphrasitical mode of expression," said Dana. What before had been "masculine— good bone and muscle" was now "feminine, dressy, elegant and languid."[32] Everett suggested that Irving's residence abroad not only had inhibited his language but also had weakened his inventive powers.

That Irving might pander to European audiences would not be surprising. Until 1891 the United States failed to participate in any international copyright agreements. Arguing that such agreements served only to restrict access to higher learning, men like Henry C. Carey and William Leggett framed their opposition in terms of republican education and the democratization of knowledge. The public may indeed have benefited. As American publishers were free in the absence of these agreements to reprint foreign literary works without compensation to the authors, the American reading public was provided with multiple inexpensive editions of books published in Europe. But while the public may have benefited, American authors did not. Unable to compete with writers who could not demand compensation, they were largely neglected by American publishing houses and forced to look abroad for publishers and an audience.[33]

The critics writing in the *North American Review* were fully aware of the problems resulting from the absence of copyright protection, and they supported reform. But this made them no more accepting of Irving and his apparent truckling before European audiences. Edward Everett saw in Irving's transformation an insulting acquiescence to British ridicule. His brother Alexander was more generous. He did not think Irving was merely "hankering" after aristocratic recognition. He was willing to read into it instead a courteous act of deference to his host nation. Nevertheless, he was disturbed by Irving's bootlicking portrayal of English society. In particular, he found Irving's flattering treatment of the British aristocracy—a class Everett found distinguished by its "foppish dress . . . the grossest and most profane language; an ignorant and contemptuous disregard for religion and morality"—not only inaccurate but also from "a republican . . . somewhat ungraceful."[34]

Some twentieth-century critics have echoed this assessment of Irving. Russell Blankenship was similarly offended by Irving's sympathetic portrayal of the English gentry. "So lovingly does Irving describe the landlord class of England," Blankenship wrote, "one is tempted to wonder if he regretted the disappearance of the patroons from New York."[35] For the critics of the *North American Review,* however, their disappointment with Irving and the other American writers was more problematic. Called to be literary advocates, as well as literary critics, they did not enjoy the historical detachment of later analysts. And as British criticism of American letters continued throughout the decade, the challenges inherent in their dual responsibilities grew even more great. That they refused to give in to their nationalistic instincts, that they refused to indulge in unqualified support for American writers, deserves some recognition.

Of course, not every contributor to the *Review* managed to balance the demands of patriotism and literature so successfully. Francis Greenwood was unapologetic in reviewing "with infinitely more delight" a good piece of American writing than one produced abroad. He minced no words in stating a preference for American literature simply because "we are Americans ourselves." But Greenwood was not representative. Most took pains to assert their critical objectivity and argued that obligations to both literature and the nation could be maintained. Alvan Lamson, for example, admitted he looked for works that were "strictly American," but he insisted that he refused to settle for "a low measure of excellence."[36]

Most seem to have had little trouble pursuing what Prescott labeled the "science of literary criticism." They recognized that the essence of their new roles and their credibility as spokesmen for a national literature lay in their ability to set aside "petty national prejudices." In order to celebrate American literature credibly, they must examine the literature of all nations for the "general principles of beauty applicable to all." William Cullen Bryant voiced this responsibility succinctly. "It is only the productions of genius, taste, and diligence that can find favour at the bar of criticism."[37]

But if generally able to balance the demands of patriotism and literature, they found it more difficult to balance their obligations to society and to aesthetics. Their commitment to cultivate a moralizing, nation-building, and implicitly popular literature found itself at odds with their commitment to the artist and the work of true genius.

Some reviewers were unambiguous in their enthusiasm for the new popularly directed literature and its moralistic exploration of common themes and daily life. John Gorham Palfrey found it among the "distinguishing glories of the age" that some of its greatest minds had "not disdained to employ themselves . . . in making the homely rules of ordinary duty intelligible and interesting to the least improved." But others, even while noting the benefits for public morality in this popularly accessible literature, were disturbed by the corresponding compromise of quality. Franklin Dexter concluded that "we cannot reasonably complain, while so much is effected by it for religion, and morals, and civil liberty," but he had to concede that because this literature must accommodate itself to "the taste of the lowest capacity," this wide distribution of literature was "unfavorable to its eminence."[38]

Nor were all the others so accommodating. Men like Prescott, Channing, Theophilus Parsons, and Dana were far less ready to accept the sort of literature that their social obligations seemed to require. They were far less willing to embrace the notion that accessibility was a criterion for approval or that an unambiguous moral quality was essential to a work of art. Thus although Maria Edgeworth's work was celebrated by many for its moral clarity—Willard Phillips called her a modern Hermes refining the Republic with her prose just as the god had civilized Egypt with his lyre—others recoiled at her excessive moralism and clumsy style. Prescott believed her relentless moralizing warped the flow of her plots and consequently was "revolting both to the taste and conviction of the reader." Richard Dana found her heavy-handed guidebook to poetry for children even more disturbing. It was typical of the "dull tranquility" of the age, the insistence that passion and energy be subjected to the heartless formalism of reason and rigid morality. Poetry could not be explained or dissected; it must be experienced on its own terms and illuminated not by a glossary but by numerous "untold associations" originating in its readers' feelings and affections.[39]

In the end most probably agreed with Phillips, who sat down to his review with the intention of finding fault with Edgeworth—he had to agree with those who complained that she forced her lessons "with too relentless a perseverance." But in realizing that "she does not write for a select few . . . but for the mass of story-readers," he was reconciled to her aesthetic imperfections.[40] Nevertheless there persisted certain troubling questions about the responsibilities of the artist and the work of art. The assumption these young Federalists inherited was that writers held well-defined responsibilities to the community—a certain set of obligations to which their craft and education must be employed. The preservation of the community and social order required that writers, like all the community's members, recognize and act their part, accept the social character of existence and employ their talents accordingly. But increasingly, contributors to the *North American Review* suggested that the artist or the genius was a person of peculiar talents who lay beyond the dictates of convention, beyond both the censure and the obligations of normal people.

Edward Channing, for example, lamented the "motley race" of critics who had fallen into the "bad habit of dictating to great minds." A respect for convention was necessary among the more common sort, but to impose restrictions on the artist was "to destroy the whole worth and character of genius." His very distinction and ultimate worth lay in his peculiarity. Working alone, "leaving friends unconsulted, enemies neglected," the artist could only realize his genius through unfettered action. Those who succumbed to the dictates of literary convention, the recommendations of critics, or the whims of the public traded their genius for mediocrity. This was the way to turn "great men into confectioners, and second-hand caterers."[41]

Theophilus Parsons was similarly troubled by the inhibiting effects of criticism. On the one hand, the printing press and the increase in literacy had created a stimulus to literary production that made criticism all the more necessary. But on the other, the resulting combination of critics and public had produced a "formidable and despotic body" which stifled the "boldness and independence of commanding genius." Parsons may have sought to establish some sort of balance, but in his recommendation that American writers follow the example set by Jeremy Taylor, Francis Bacon, and Richard Hooker—men who had produced a literature that was "rough and rude, but gigantic in its strength"—he seems to have fallen on the side of genius. From these writers American authors should adopt "the consciousness of an intellectual supremacy . . . a consciousness of inexhaustible resources and boundless affluence . . . boldness, independence, and self-reliance."[42]

These conclusions flew sharply in the face of the social obligations ascribed to the writer. Not only was he beyond the censure of common men, but his works need not apologize for their esoteric qualities. In making this argument, Francis Greenwood suggested that Wordsworth was victimized by the injustices of the modern literary market—the tyranny of criticism, in this case the *Edinburgh Review,* and the demands of accessibility. Neither was just; both did a disservice to the character of genius. An artist like Wordsworth, he argued, lay beyond the appreciation of "the common mass of readers." Richard Henry Dana agreed. Despite being the most gifted poet of the age, Wordsworth was accessible to only "a small class of society." In comparison, Greenwood traced the inferiority of the poets of Queen Anne's age to their writing for too large an audience rather than "the man of sentiment and genius alone in his study."[43]

Some of these same critics seem to have carved out a similar type of social isolation and even irresponsibility for the discriminating reader. In Wordsworth, Greenwood argued, this select readership found "an intimate and intelligent friend, who could draw forth capacities, and excite reflections, which received but little exercise, and met with little sympathy, in the ordinary intercourse of life; who could address feelings, which had never been spoken to before, but had sat silently in his heart, musing, and solitary, and ignorant of companionship." Horace Holley similarly suggested that literature provided a pleasant escape from common responsibilities. The primary pleasure of reading lay in the emotional freedom it allowed—the freedom to observe and respond without any obligation to act. It enabled the mind of the reader to "indulge its feelings and its tears without the check which the task of business or relief would impose." Prescott expressed appreciation for the meager demands of contemporary fiction. He was thankful it was freed from the "polemics and politics" of an earlier era, and he celebrated the "agreeable fictions; which so sweetly soothe the dull ear of sickness . . . 'cheer but not inebriate,' brighten the horrors of a rainy day; dispel the tedium of a winter's evening." [44]

Dana made this case for a literature of escape even more forcefully. The power of the poet lay in his ability not only to see uniquely but also to transform reality. Through creative powers that seemed to rival God's, the poet "formed another creation, but it is one within ourselves." Through this creative power the reader was exposed to a self he never knew and transported to this new world where he became lost. "It is we and the pleasures, the business and desires of life that have been a delusion; we are made to feel a serious concern in what we find in him, and reality itself becomes idle and unimportant." [45]

This was a significant conclusion—a significant departure from the literary mission originally adopted by the founders of the *North American Review* and from the role and responsibilities of the man of letters outlined by Buckminster. A literature that sought not to educate or improve but only to entertain was not what Buckminster had in mind. His early criticism of study that served as an indulgent amusement for the solitary mind clashed sharply with this approval of poetic and intellectual isolation. But it was representative of the sort of confusion toward which many of these critics moved. Called to reform public morals and build a national identity, they felt obliged to reward uplifting efforts, even if the writing was mediocre. But also anxious to establish literary standards, they were moved to acknowledge genius and carve out a space for its operation. Interested in the formation of the new public sphere, believing that their efforts as critics and essayists would solidify the national community, they pursued an agenda of a deeply social nature. At the same time interested in setting the highest standards and encouraging the efforts of the truly gifted, eager to encourage men of genius to pursue literary and artistic lives rather than be lured away by politics or commerce, they made concessions to a sphere more interior and indulgent.

To be fair, this drift toward the aesthetic, toward indulgence and personal amusement, was perhaps inherent in the nature of this new literary infrastructure. This drift toward artistic isolation and literary escape—toward the private—may have been the inevitable result of the disembodiment of the public sphere, for in substituting the written for the spoken word, the autonomy of the writer was enhanced. At the same time, this new literary sphere offered fewer of the ancillary tools of influence and control offered by the public meeting hall. Just as the writer and his message gained autonomy, the reader acquired the power inherent in privacy to accept or reject, to translate and transform its content. As the line between the private and the public grew blurred, as the home became the town hall and the easy chair replaced the pew, the writer and reader were left opportunities to explore and experiment, to indulge and escape.

Thus if the members of the *North American Review* found themselves making a greater concession to the private sphere, they were driven partially by the logic of the infrastructure. If implicit in their concession to genius was the danger of atomization, it was a danger inhering to processes outside their control. But even if they were not wholly to blame, it was not what these young Federalists had anticipated. What had distinguished their efforts was the belief that the social and the private could be simultaneously sustained, that public morality and the more personal and private worlds of aesthetics and beauty could be reconciled. They had, in fact, been trained to believe that the public and the private were one, that the moral and the beautiful coincided, that there was a logic and an order to creation which were reflected in all its expressions.

Alexander Everett took issue with both Madame de Staël and Joseph Druz, the former for believing that benevolence must be an exercise in self-sacrifice and the latter for arguing that happiness, rather than moral perfection, should be the purpose of life. In Everett's roseate view "the sublime and beautiful order of the universe" made the benevolent and the moral coincide with the useful and the pleasurable. Moral perfection brought happiness, the pursuit of benevolence dovetailed with personal interests, the needs of the individual and society were one.[46] The artist, Everett continued, was acutely in tune with the benevolent rationality of the natural order and found in this sensitivity an uncommon sense of peace. Although his heightened sensibilities made him more aware of the vicissitudes of life, these same sensibilities brought him more fully in tune with the "'divine philosophy,' which cures the wounds they inflict."[47] Willard Phillips expressed this same confidence in the logic of the universe and the artist's relation to it in identifying a "natural alliance between genius and purity." William Peabody voiced similar complacency when he linked the popular and the aesthetically correct—"What is exclusive, is almost always wrong."[48]

But as their ideas unfolded, as their tastes responded to the works of the age, they found these confidences undermined. They found beauty alongside immorality, creativity amid misanthropy, and egoism, rather than benevolence, driving genius. Nowhere was this more evident than in their troubled response to Byron. Here was a poet of undeniable genius and power. Phillips praised the boldness with which he described setting and the "keen sagacity" with which he analyzed and presented character. Alexander Everett labeled him a genius of "the first order," the greatest English poet since Pope and actually superior to Pope in his versatility. But here also was man whose life and works were filled with immorality. Norton sensed in his work a "pestilential atmosphere," and Phillips decried his "wanton contempt of all the common notions of propriety." Everett argued that the philosophy which pervaded his work tended to "degrade human nature and destroy the belief in virtue."[49]

Not only did brilliance and immorality coincide in Byron, they seemed to stem from the same source. Not incongruous and in conflict, they seemed instead to be inextricably linked. The misanthropy and egoism that scarred his work were also the source of its power and brilliance. It was not Byron's "mild and tender" passages that formed his "master strokes," noted Phillips, but rather those evoking the "terrible and ferocious," those mired in "relentless despair." Norton argued quite plainly that it was "his passions, and his intense egotism," that made him an exceptional poet. Not in sync with the beauties of nature or the sublimity of the moral order, he in fact seemed incapable of describing noble or virtuous subjects with any power. But with subjects more decadent and morbid, "where the aspects of nature corresponded to the gloom and storminess of his own mind," Norton conceded to Byron "a burst of poetry, which will never be excelled."[50]

Phillips closed the book on Byron by regretting that one who "has written so well . . . has also written so ill," while Norton condemned him for enlisting "without shame in the cause of evil." Everett went even further in suggesting that for all their beauties his works should be removed from the shelves.[51] But there lingered the challenge implicit in Byron's brilliance—a writer in whom their sense of balance, this inextricable meshing of morality and beauty, seemed proven false, a writer who challenged not only the relationship between their moral and their aesthetic standards but also their conceptions of nature—their sense of order and logic, the relation between good and bad, truth and beauty—and on a more personal level the nature and responsibilities of genius.

Most fundamentally, Byron thus raised questions concerning their own roles. Their responsibilities to both literature and the public, to both aesthetics and morality, their obligation to be men of erudition and scholarship while also serving the public and the nation—these now all seemed part of an unworkable mix. Byron's lack of balance and their recognition that it was this lack of balance that made him great, that fed his poetry, that drove his genius, suggested that there was not necessarily a balance and a harmonious logic to the world and its parts. In Byron there was the suggestion that genius was defined by its eccentricity and not its balance, that the genius was a man set apart, not a man fully integrated, and that neither he nor those who hoped to appreciate and judge him could be limited by the conventions of the common man and his morality.

In 1819 Richard Henry Dana, the most militant romantic and most outspoken apologist for the privilege of genius, left the *North American Review*. His departure left the more conservative voices within the *Review* the more prominent ones.[52] But it did not eliminate the tension between these conflicting visions of art and the artist, for it was a tension that existed within individuals as much as between them. Throughout this period the neoclassical and the romantic, the moralist and the aesthete, the socially oriented and the escapist, appeared as conflicting tensions within individuals on both ends of the spectrum.

Edward Tyrrel Channing, for example, was among the most eloquent and frequent spokesmen for the peculiarity and privilege of genius. A person thus gifted, he argued, possessed a "distinct being, another nature," and consequently should be sheltered from the conventions and obligations that restrict common men.[53] The genius was something of a work of art himself, a subject for research and analysis. The student would be interested in not just his productions but also his "judgments, purposes, and feelings," not just his poetry or novels but "the history of his mind."[54] And his work, correspondingly, was valued not just for its objective merits but as an expression of his individual genius.

But Channing was not entirely free of the traditional notions regarding literature, the artist, and their obligations. He criticized the publication of Cowper's memoirs because they described the indiscretions of his youth. These revelations only served, Channing complained, to weaken the "living intimacy" between Cowper and his readers that was so essential to the moral power of his work. He suggested that the moral purposes of art and the publicly perceived character of the artist transcended both the artist's confessional rights and the literary historian's obligations to objectivity. "We would not have our remembrance of such a man disturbed. . . . we are unwilling to hear, even from himself, that he was once a profligate, and all but a self murderer."[55] Quite in contrast to his usual deference to genius and its autonomy, in this instance Channing suggested that the social obligations of a piece of art conferred ownership on the public and made the character and even the claims of the creator unimportant.

If there was ultimately a persisting conservatism to Channing's thought, a certain tension between his celebration of the artist and the social obligations of art, he was not alone. Francis Greenwood was similarly outspoken in his defense of the rights of genius, but he too expressed a certain residual respect for art's social obligations. Wordsworth may have been a poet for the few, a spiritual consort for the most sensitive of readers, but there were certain limits he must respect. Greenwood took issue with Wordsworth's romanticizing of the commonplace, his swelling "out into a vast importance those circumstances, which . . . should have been treated with a brevity and indifference suited to their station." He also criticized the liberties Wordsworth took with language. Words, Greenwood argued more in the spirit of the custodian of culture than the protector of genius, "are the property of the public, and not of an individual poet . . . he has no power over those whose uses are definitely settled."[56] Wordsworth may have been a genius of unique talents, but he still must respect the proper relation between high and low, the noble and the common. He may have possessed the privilege of speaking to man's inner heart, but in doing so he must respect the social and the linguistic order.

Even Dana, despite his elaborate defense of the privileges of genius, recognized some limitations. When his advocacy of this cause carried him to the realization that America's egalitarian social framework—its inheritance laws and generally accessible commercial opportunities—provided a perhaps impenetrable barrier to the cultivation of native literature, he shied away from any recommendations of reform. "We would hardly forego the substantial good which our political equality has given us, for the mere luxuries of the mind."[57]

At the other end of the spectrum—among those who seem to have been most concerned with the social obligations of literature—there was similar ambiguity. Phillips, despite his moralism, was willing to concede that the artist must be judged "from the position assumed by himself or that occupied by the generality of his readers," that the biases and tastes of the critic must be set aside in evaluating the work of genius. Alexander Everett, despite his staunch defense of standards and preference for the classical, had to admit that genius "ennobles and beautifies every form." Andrews Norton, whose morality demanded Byron be condemned, had to admit that the times required "something more exciting and passionate," and that the age of which Byron was a part had left mankind with "wider views, of higher principles of action, more consistent and intrepid in his reasoning, more energetic in his will, more tender, generous, and sincere in his affections."[58]

As Jackson's election approached, the *North American Review* concluded its first thirteen years with a considerable sense of promise but also some serious challenges—some significant achievements but also some underlying confusion. In its literary mission the editors defined a purpose which focused the journal's efforts and provided the editors with both status and broader public influence. Within the literary philosophy they formulated, they envisioned a literature that would advance morality, undergird the social and political order, forge the national identity, and in so doing unite the nation. In their embrace of romantic as well as neoclassical principles, in calling for a more open and independent set of literary standards, they advanced a more authentic national culture and opened the door for future literary efforts. But as their ideas unfolded, there appeared a set of views that threatened to undermine many of their efforts, views that could threaten the social and moral order as well as their own status and influence. They voiced a conception of literature that was more elitist than popular, a sense of the writer that was more egoistic than social, and described a sphere of creative isolation that was impervious to both the demands of the public and the dictates of even their own journal. Somewhat ironically, while working to strengthen their own position and compensate for the loss of political influence enjoyed by their fathers, they elaborated a vision of the artist and his audience that could in time undercut this same position and leave them to their fathers' fate. In fact, as the century progressed it appears that this mixed record—this combination of success and potential failure, this combination of messianic clarity and philosophical confusion—produced a set of consequences that was equally mixed, a set of results that was equally ironic.

In very practical terms their contributions to the elaboration of the growing intellectual infrastructure seem to be large. In adding a layer to the growing web of literature—prescriptive, didactic, critical, and inspirational—they helped to form the ideological structure necessary to the formation of America's "imagined community." But in relying as they did on the written word, in contributing to the belief that the social and national ties could be built upon words, they reenforced a set of tendencies that were as much centripetal as centrifugal. Not only did this privatization of the public sphere allow room for indulgence and escape; even more dangerously, from the standpoint of these conservative intellectuals, it allowed individuals and groups the opportunity to construct alternative spheres, alternative circles of meaning, identity, and interaction.

Carroll Smith-Rosenberg, for example, has described the separate sphere created by women during these years. Excluded from public life, often confined within unsatisfying marital relationships, at best inhibited by the "formality and stiffness" characteristic of Victorian male-female relationships, women turned to one another for support, friendship, and even intimacy. The separate sphere they created was built upon a web of familial and extrafamilial relationships and strengthened by the thousands of hours spent in sharing domestic duties, visiting one another, caring for the local sick, and attending to one another in childbirth and illness. These relationships crossed generations; through family visits and shared activities, mothers initiated their daughters into these "single-sex or homosocial networks."[59]

Although these networks, this alternative sphere of interaction and self-identification, did possess a spatial element, they were maintained across distance by the steady stream of letters that followed separation due to marriage or migration. Intimate relationships were sustained for years over great distances by letters exchanged and saved; circles of friends would gather and remember a distant comrade by collectively reading her missives home. Grieving women would even console themselves within the context of this female world by copying the letters of condolence sent by friends into their diaries.[60]

Mary Kelley has more fully explained how literary activities became the means through which women not only built a distinctive culture but also pushed the edges of gender prescription. Books provided "the ground on which women readers built a dense and diversified mental life." They provided the lens through which women could privately explore the prescriptions of the dominant culture and "a site for experiments in personal transformation." Significantly, although this was in one sense a private process, it was also a public one; although reading may have been a private activity, it was also a "collective practice." Books were shared, reading clubs were formed, and literary opinions were exchanged. As a result books became not just a vehicle for personal exploration but also "the medium of exchange" through which women "constructed a common intellectual and cultural world."[61]

The opportunities for self-discovery and cultural schism provided by this new literary sphere left hopes that the written word would prove a source of cultural cohesion largely unfulfilled. Although the contributors to the *North American Review* may have succeeded in adding a layer to the national culture, the decentralized nature of the national community prevented their maintaining any hegemony over its prescriptive content.

In similar fashion the philosophical content of the literary culture they promoted served only some of their goals. Just as the infrastructure they hope to establish was inherently flawed, the literary culture they advanced was filled with ironies. On the one hand, their interest in advancing American letters, in promoting American writers and books, provided a significant contribution to the cause of a national culture. In particular, the synthesis of neoclassical and romantic principles they forged appears crucial to the advancement of a national literature. From neoclassicism the editors of the *Review* drew their sense of the social responsibilities of literature—the sense that literature was essentially social, that it had moral and political obligations, and that they as critics had responsibilities that corresponded to the importance of literature. From this tradition they drew their sense of self-importance as cultural custodians—men specially responsible for the development of American letters and the defense of American culture against foreign criticism. It was this sense of art and of themselves that defined their mission, called them to action, determined their responsibilities. From romanticism these same intellectuals drew their understanding of the particularity of language, the unique ability of a national language and literature to speak to a particular people. It was from romanticism that they drew their sense of the unique character of the American experience and its peculiar suitability to literary presentation. And it was from romanticism that they drew their sense of the importance of the artist as the talent uniquely capable of presenting the special character of America to the American people and to the rest of the world.

It was the synthesis of these two literary philosophies that defined their contribution; this combination of neoclassicism and romanticism was essential to their cultural vision. Concomitantly, it is doubtful that either by itself could have had the same impact on American culture. Left to itself, neoclassicism would have encouraged a literature that was purely imitative. Given neoclassicism's belief in the universality of expression, it would have been satisfied with the imitation of established forms. It would not have placed the same emphasis on the need for and support of native talents; it would have reduced the *North American Review* to just another version of the *Monthly Anthology*. Similarly, left to itself, romanticism might have stimulated an interest in national works, but there would have been nothing of the same sense of mission about these efforts. The *North American Review* would have lacked the sense of responsibility to defend American culture and to inspire a literature that could speak to and help form the American people. Romanticism might have inspired the energies of individual genius, but they would not have been placed within the broader context of national crusade.

Given all this, it would seem that it was the philosophical hybrid forged at the *North American Review* that distinguished its literary efforts and gave clarity to its purpose. It defined for its contributors their approach to literature and American culture, gave direction to their work, and placed huge demands upon them. Moreover, this same hybrid enabled these young intellectuals to recast for the public an understanding of national culture that was far more compelling. This synthesis of neoclassicism and romanticism made this ambition as much social as it was aesthetic. It gave the cause of literature and art national implications. It suggested that as a country's literature both reflects and shapes its political and moral character and its very identity as a nation, it mattered not just to some cultural elite but to America as a whole.

The broader impact of their thought is difficult to gauge; the extent to which American writers and readers adopted this particular take on national culture is hard to measure. But if Benjamin Spencer is correct in arguing that in antebellum America virtually every writer and magazine was inspired to think in terms of a national literature, to "reflect upon their relation as writers to the national culture. . . . and to expound some version of a national literature," then the particular slant given the cause of a national culture by the *North American Review* would seem crucial.[62] If numerous historians are correct in arguing that by 1850 the literary establishment had grown far more receptive to American authors—whereas in 1820 only one-third of all books published in America were written by Americans, by midcentury the number had risen to two out of three—the importance of this more compelling reconceptualization of national literature would seem considerable.[63] And in these possibilities, the broader contributions of the *North American Review* begin to appear. In preparing the American audience, redirecting American authors, and prodding the literary establishment, these young New England intellectuals helped prepare the ground for the next generation of American romantic writers. If American letters "flowered" during the 1840s, if American literature enjoyed a "renaissance," it was largely because the cultural stage had been so carefully set.

Just as these intellectuals helped to wean Americans from English tastes and dictates and prepared both the literary establishment and American audiences for a new style of literature, these same critics helped redefine the artist in a manner necessary for his survival in the new literary marketplace. Michael Gilmore has argued that success within this new market required a recasting of the artist—in the absence of more traditional forms of aristocratic patronage, success within the literary marketplace required that writers rethink themselves. The "communal and self-negating accents" of the republican culture of the eighteenth century had to be "inflected in the direction of an individualist aesthetics." The neoclassical sense of the artist as a servant to social order had to be replaced by a vision of the artist as a person of unique sensibilities. And the neoclassical sense of art as the property of the greater good had to be replaced with a conception of art as the "personal inspiration and . . . property" of the artist.[64]

Gilmore concluded that this recasting of art and the artist depended on the redirection of the social and economic order. An "individualized regimen in social and economic relations," he argued, "was the necessary complement to the rise of Romantic art in the United States."[65] But the willingness of the contributors to the *North American Review* to rethink the artist while pursuing a broader vision that was more traditional and communal in nature suggests that this recasting of the artist was more a philosophical and aesthetic creation than a by-product of social and economic transformation. Although the emerging social and economic ethic of individualism may have reenforced this new identification of the artist as an autonomous individual, the more finely nuanced position that the artist was not only autonomous but also privileged, appears more derivative of the principles within romanticism itself. The idea that the artist was somewhat absolved of the social obligations of more common men— an idea central to American literary culture of the mid- to late nineteenth century—seems less the concomitant of social and economic change than a consequence, albeit ironic, of these Federalist intellectuals' efforts to establish a position of influence for literary persons within the new American order.

The contributions of these writers and this journal would thus seem huge. Moreover, they do not seem matched by any other journal of the period. In particular, the contribution effected by the philosophical synthesis constructed in the *North American Review* seems to have been unmatched by any journal of comparable stature or permanence. Other journals of the period were inspired by the new literary theories of European romanticism. Some, such as the *United States Literary Gazette*, even reflected a more thorough and militant embrace of its principles, just as others, like the *Port Folio*, remained more inflexibly attached to neoclassical principles. But no journal of significance seems to have offered this same synthesis of the two literary schools. No journal combined the two within so complete and so authoritative a vision of the potential and benefits of a national literature. Consequently, no journal of the period was able to offer so significant a contribution to the cause of national culture.

There is a certain degree of risk in making so broad a comparative statement. The American literary scene was filled with journals during these same years. Moreover, editorial positions changed frequently, and contributors overlapped. To argue too emphatically the uniqueness of any particular journal requires some qualification. But a cursory comparison suggests that in many ways the *North American Review,* as measured by its stature, its critical position, and its contributions, was unique in the first three decades of the nineteenth century.[66]

The journal with the most comparable profile in terms of circulation and respectability at the time of the founding of the *North American Review* was the *Port Folio,* published in Philadelphia by Joseph Dennie. Dennie, a Harvard graduate and New England transplant, carried his old New England political and cultural biases with him to Philadelphia. Staunchly Federalist and Anglophilic, Dennie had a vehement distaste for democracy and explicit contempt for the common people. "Their praise," he grumbled, "is often to be dreaded, and their censure is generally proof of the merit of the object." Like many of his Federalist peers, he feared Jefferson and mocked his philosophical and literary pretensions. Even the Declaration of Independence he labeled a "false, and flatulent, and foolish paper."[67]

Under Dennie's management the journal was far closer to the *Monthly Anthology* than the *North American Review.* Making no concessions to the new America, its literary and cultural loyalties were closer to those of fellow Anglophile John Sylvester John Gardiner than to those of William Tudor, Edward Everett, or any of the other young Federalists. He considered the Revolution a mistake and democracy doomed. He emphatically criticized Webster's attempts to Americanize the English language; and rather than defend American culture against the attacks of European journals and travelers, Dennie, like Gardiner, who in fact contributed to the *Port Folio,* was more apt to join in the harangue. *Bulow's Interesting Travels in America*—the sort of travelogue that drew strident response from the *North American Review*—was labeled a "frightful caricature" by Dennie, but also "eminently useful." Its reproaches, however painful, might "interest some, and instruct others."[68] By 1809 Dennie's alienation from the new America was complete. Renouncing politics altogether, he took refuge in the "republic of letters"—a community of like-minded thinkers that knew no national boundaries and sought solace in classical literature, a literary world of superior virtue that stood outside of time.[69]

The *Port Folio,* a reflection of Dennie's character from its inception in

1801 until 1806, grew more balanced after poor health forced him to assume a lesser role. Shortly after his death in 1812, the journal took on an entirely new character after its acquisition by two brothers, Harrison and John Ewing Hall. Like the *North American Review,* the new *Port Folio* assumed a more national tone. Its "principal object," the new editors announced, was "to vindicate the character of American literature and manners from the aspersions of ignorant and illiterate foreigners."[70] But Dennie's death also deprived the journal of its most capable essayist and critic. If the new magazine was more patriotic, it was also duller; although the journal became more modern, more in step with American affairs, it also lost much of its authority. William Charvat identified a few pieces of solid literary criticism in the years between Dennie's death in 1812 and 1820, but Frank Luther Mott did not acknowledge even these. It "never regained," he concluded, "the verve, insouciance, and savoir-vivre" of Dennie's years.[71]

Many of the other journals founded during these years cannot really be compared to the *North American Review* because of their narrow focus. The *Journal of the Franklin Institute* (Philadelphia, 1826), the *American Journal of Pharmacy* (Philadelphia, 1825), the *New England Farmer* (Boston, 1822), even the *American Journal of Science* (New York and New Haven, 1818), had no interest in literary questions. Others were narrowly theological in focus—the voices of a particular denomination interested more in doctrinal presentation and institutional news. The *Christian Spectator* (New Haven, 1819) was the voice of orthodox Calvinism. The *Christian Advocate* (Philadelphia, 1823), edited by Asabel Green, the former president of Princeton, was the voice of Presbyterianism. Both included a few literary reviews, but these were far fewer in number than their religious articles and clearly of secondary importance. The *Panoplist* (Boston, 1805), founded by Jedidiah Morse during his crusade against Unitarianism, reached a large audience after merging with the *Missionary Magazine* in 1808. But its emphasis was doctrinal and polemic; it rarely discussed nonreligious issues. The *Biblical Repertory* acquired an impressive reputation from its inception in 1825 to its cessation in 1888 as the *New Princeton Review.* But even though its name changed many times, it remained primarily theological in its focus until Charles Hodge retired in 1871. The Quaker journal, the *Friend,* included a fair amount of literary commentary in its first volumes but thereafter was filled more with scientific news and memoirs.

Even among the other Unitarian journals the *North American Review* was unusual.[72] Its immediate predecessor, the *General Repository and Review* (Boston, 1812–13), was too short-lived to be labeled anything more than transitional. The *Unitarian Miscellany and Christian Monitor,* published in Baltimore and edited by Jared Sparks and Francis Greenwood between 1821 and 1826, was more self-consciously denominational in character. Its primary aim was the elaboration and defense of the Unitarian position, and it was consequently more theological and combative than the *North American Review.* The *Christian Disciple,* or what eventually became the *Christian Examiner,* was far closer to the *North American Review* in terms of its overall character and prestige. Orestes Brownson labeled it "second to no periodical in the country," while Mott praised its "distinctive work in literary criticism."[73] Published in Boston, the journal shared the *North American Review*'s Unitarian character and even drew upon many of the same contributors. But founded initially to gently advance the cause of liberal religion amid the controversies perpetually stirred by Jedidiah Morse, the journal focused almost exclusively on theological questions until 1829. Charvat concluded that it made its greatest contributions between 1830 and 1835.[74] Mott argued that its most impressive critical work was not accomplished until after the formation of the Examiner Club in 1839.

Many prominent and enduring journals shared the *North American Review*'s interest in the advancement of a national culture. The *Niles' Weekly Register* and *Niles' National Register* (Baltimore, 1811) were nationalistic, even Anglophobic, in their tone and lent their voice to the cause of national literature. But they were more noteworthy for their balanced presentation of documents and speeches than their literary criticism. The *American Quarterly Review* arrived on the literary scene later (1827) and was far less enduring (1837) than the *North American Review.* It was similarly broadly focused, was committed to the development of a national literature, devoted considerable space to literary criticism, and drew from an impressive list of contributors (James Kirke Paulding, George Bancroft, Caleb Cushing). But, at least according to Mott, its criticism was inferior in quality, especially its poetry reviews, and tainted by its "uncritical national pride."[75] And, according to Charvat, it remained neoclassical in its literary tastes far longer than the reading public. Except for a series of uncharacteristically positive reviews of romantic literature in 1836, the *American Quarterly* achieved little of the balance and thus influence of the

North American Review.[76] The *Analectic* (New York, 1813), edited for a time by Washington Irving, lasted several years and included some significant literary commentary. But the magazine also drew heavily from British periodicals. Its tone was clearly nationalistic, but this was set primarily by James Kirke Paulding's naval histories and biographies. It is memorable less for its contributions to American letters than, according to Mott, as "a service journal of the navy."[77]

Some journals made distinctive contributions, but they were very short-lived—perhaps too much so to be credited with having any sort of significant impact on the American audience or literary establishment. The *Portico* was nationalistic in temperament and literary in focus, but it was published for only two years, 1816–18. The *United States Literary Gazette* out of Boston and the *New York Review* were, according to William Charvat, modern, romantic, and intelligent. They contributed to the assault on neoclassicism and provided a vehicle for some of New England's most talented intellectuals—Richard Henry Dana, William Cullen Bryant, Theophilus Parsons. But the life span of the journals was only three years; founded in 1824, they merged in 1826 to form the *United States Review and Literary Gazette,* which lasted only a year.

Still other journals developed an entirely different profile and audience. The *New York Mirror* and its descendant the *American Literary Gazette* were long-lasting (1823–57) and reached a wide audience. They included both literary reviews and original American writing. But their focus was more popular, their fiction tended to be sentimental, and their lasting significance lay more in their commentary on popular culture than any contribution to the shaping of American literature. *Graham's Magazine,* and its ancestor the *Casket,* maintained a similar profile. They boasted an impressive list of contributors—Bryant, Paulding, Dana, Poe, Cooper, Longfellow, Lowell—but were more interested in entertaining than influencing American readers. As Mott concluded, *Graham's* aimed to be "amusing rather than profound."[78]

Thus it would seem that its American tone and orientation, the quality and philosophical character of its criticism, and its endurance made the *North American Review* unique in these years. The young Federalist intellectuals who founded and shaped the journal in its first decades made both a significant and a singular contribution to the emerging national culture. Yet despite the significance of their efforts and the uniqueness of their contribution, their achievements were laced with irony, for the constellation of literary principles that made the development of an American culture possible also contained a set of contradictions that made this hybrid eventually unsustainable. Romanticism, with its emphasis on particularity, could not long remain reconciled with the neoclassical confidence in universal and timeless standards. Nor would its tendency toward individualism and emotional freedom, its antagonism toward tradition and institutions, remain long reconciled with moral absolutism and social convention. The differences between the two philosophical schools were just too great, and a rift was inevitable. Moreover, the peculiar bias within the American cultural experience toward romanticism created the further irony that as these Federalist intellectuals succeeded in advancing the cause of a national culture, they undermined their own status as cultural architects and custodians.

Numerous literary historians have argued that romanticism was peculiarly well suited to America. Richard Chase framed the debate even more narrowly in arguing that American literature has always been essentially romantic. Unlike the English novel, which sought to weave the "wide ranges of experience into a moral centrality and equability of judgment," the American novel has always been moved by the "aesthetic possibilities of radical forms of alienation, contradiction, and disorder." Nor has it usually seemed necessary for the American novel to reconcile these contradictions. Uninspired by the British literary "high purpose" of bringing order out of chaos, the American novel has been content to "explore, rather than appropriate. . . . It has not wanted to build an imperium but merely to discover a new place and a new state of mind."[79]

In explaining this preference for the romantic, Chase drew upon the insights of Tocqueville. The American, he argued, was defined by his solitary condition. Lacking traditions, established patterns of thought, and political institutions to mediate between himself and the state, as well as ecclesiastical institutions to mediate between himself and God, the American was "habitually engaged in the contemplation of a very puny object, namely himself." As a result, neither the American audience nor the American writer was able, argued Chase, to appreciate or generate a literature which depended on a subtle understanding of the nuances of social behavior. Instead, Americans' literature was characterized by melodrama and larger-than-life experiences, by flat characters, epic plots, and supernatural resolutions.

Other twentieth-century scholars of American literature have reached similar conclusions. G. Harrison Orians did not see romanticism as endemic to the American experience, but he agreed that a variety of factors—America's democratic ideology, the interest in antiquarianism and Indian history, a fascination with the American landscape, and the instinct toward anti-traditionalism—fostered a predisposition toward romanticism within American culture after 1805 that all but eliminated the earlier neoclassical traditions. Lawrence Buell, although critical of those who would argue that the influence of neoclassicism was negligible, conceded that romanticism was peculiarly well suited to nineteenth-century America. Its emphasis on particularity encouraged cultural independence and implicitly challenged European traditions. Its interest in landscape transformed America's primitive conditions into a "national treasure." In romanticism's celebration of individuality of style, the American penchant for antiauthoritarianism was affirmed. And its emphasis on the individual conscience echoed the Puritan tradition of introspective piety.[80]

Given this predisposition, if not instinct, for romanticism, it would appear that the wider the literary critics of the *North American Review* opened the doors to its acceptance, the more inevitably they unsettled the careful balance of neoclassicism and romanticism they had hoped to maintain. And, as their own status as cultural arbiters and literary critics rested on neoclassical principles, the more thoroughly American literature came to be defined by romanticism, the more rapidly their own status was subverted. By midcentury, as Benjamin Spencer has pointed out, American romanticism had shed itself of vestigial neoclassical formulas and was more thoroughly focused on the "popular tastes and issues of the day." Romanticism had come to mean not just the affirmation of national particularity but also the celebration of "democratic sources of power." No longer tied tenuously to a belief in the necessity of standards and professional criticism, romanticism linked the further advancement of a national literature to the "elimination of the professional literary class."[81]

For these young intellectuals, seeking from within this hybrid not only to advance an American culture but to secure their place within it, their efforts and their achievements were indeed ironic. The more they succeeded, the more they failed; the further they advanced the cause of national culture and the further they opened the door to a form of literature more suited to the American experience and temperament, the more quickly they hastened their own displacement as cultural spokesmen. Having set out to adapt to the new cultural and social realities, to separate themselves from their fathers' literary provincialism, to advance American literature, they succeeded on all fronts; but in so doing, they facilitated the emergence of a literary and cultural style that eventually would have little use for them.

CHAPTER 6

INSTITUTIONS

➻➻ Not all of the young Federalist intellectuals coming of age during these years, traveling in the same social circles and contributing to the *North American Review,* rested all their hope in the power of culture. To rely solely on the influence of literature and literary criticism would deny the range and power of the faculties that animated individuals and communities. Their fathers at least had realized that social order depended on the construction and careful maintenance of institutions, even though they had been shortsighted in their management. But what institutions would ensure social stability now that the political institutions were so uncertain, and what role would these young men play within these new institutions? To a certain extent young Federalists found an answer in the extrapolitical associations that had proliferated since the turn of the century. In a process that was more evolutionary than revolutionary, they embraced the web of charitable and extragovernmental associations founded by their fathers and shaped them into social institutions that offered both social cohesion and class status.

Boston's ruling class had never rested its hegemony on just the political order. The city's Puritan founders had established the precedent in making the civil institutions only one source of authority, and a subordinate one at that, within the overall social framework. Over the next two centuries Boston's social and political order had continued to draw upon the church and an assortment of extragovernmental institutions for support. Among these were included the ad hoc committees that were formed to address periodic concerns ranging from education to epidemics to imperial harassment. These committees, on the most immediate level, served humanitarian or utilitarian needs, but on another level they provided an important social function. They helped identify the ruling members of Boston society, they provided forums for the modeling of public service and civic responsibility, and they linked Boston across class in civic endeavors.

As tools for the preservation of social order, the value of these committees was clear, and in the first part of the nineteenth century, as their political hegemony was challenged, Boston Federalists rebuttressed their social position through the formation of even more charitable organizations. By the end of the war in 1815, there were separate associations addressing the needs of female orphans, indigent boys, stranded sailors, fire victims, widows, the sick, the insane, the improvident, and perhaps most importantly, the intemperate. Boston's Federalist community abounded in good works, and it would be unfair to dismiss as disingenuous the religious and humanitarian rhetoric that surrounded them. God, said John Sylvester John Gardiner, called them to "universal benevolence. . . . private interest must always yield to public welfare." Philanthropy was also a natural expression of the human condition. Man, said John Kirkland, was a social being; charity was the necessary expression of his social character. Even the "mere epicure," he noted, "is unwilling to sit down to his table, without a companion." Yet these men were also quite open in acknowledging the broader sociological benefits of these organizations. While philanthropic and useful, they also strengthened the social order. When critics questioned their altruism, mocking the ostentation of their activities, Eliphalet Porter offered a very honest and prescient explanation of their sociological utility. "The anniversaries, the processions, the public appearances and discourses of societies, instituted for benevolent and useful purposes, are not so vain and trifling as some may be ready to imagine. They are public acknowledgments and memorials of our obligations to be useful to our fellow men. They are regular invitations and excitements to the duties of humanity."[1]

At times these "invitations" took on a decidedly mercenary air. The Humane Society offered cash rewards for acts of public service, one amount for aiding a drowning child, another for assisting a stranded sailor. The specificity of their instructions suggests that the public responded more in kind than in the spirit of Christian charity. Not every effort would earn a cash award, reminded the society, for heroic public service represented "more than barely reaching out of the hand, or throwing a rope from a wharf, or a boat, or even wading into the water to half a man's depth."[2] But if more pecuniary in their inducements, their aims differed little from earlier calls to good behavior on the part of the church. As institutions of social cohesion, models of good behavior, and forums for the identification of Boston's leading citizens, the broader utility of these associations was clear.

No charitable organization better represented the multiple purposes of its members than did the Massachusetts Society for the Suppression of Intemperance, founded in 1813. Its membership overlapped that of several other charitable organizations and represented the leading members of Boston's Federalist upper class. Calling upon all citizens "of a fair moral reputation," the society sought through "example and influence" to promote "temperance and general morality." As its agenda unfolded, the society settled upon the tactic of encouraging employers to discontinue the furnishing of spirits on the job. The Boston chapter joined those of neighboring counties in adopting resolutions that emphasized abuse among day laborers and urged the substitution of "good and wholesome drinks in the place of pernicious liquors."[3]

There were no doubt many practical benefits in this strategy for the employer. But it would be inaccurate to see in these tactics merely an attempt to secure a more compliant and regular workforce. Although this was a benefit they no doubt recognized, addressing intemperance through the workplace was rooted also in the recognition that the society could not appropriately "interfere with the manners of private life, or the intercourse of persons at their own houses."[4] Moreover, society members acknowledged the ubiquitous nature of the problem in urging members of all classes to discontinue the serving of ardent spirits in the home. In fact, the society's second annual report located the blame for intemperance in the behavior of the upper class, not the workers, in the "flattering guise of hospitality to friends and of generosity to dependents."[5]

Thus although they adopted tactics that served their business needs, their analysis was more complex, and their goals were far broader. For the MSSI the problem of intemperance was at heart a social problem. It, in fact, represented the very antithesis of those qualities necessary for good order. In preventing the exercise of sound reason and good judgment, in discouraging self-restraint, intemperance threatened the good conduct and self-government essential to social harmony. Intemperance, at bottom, was thus less a personal vice, or a sin against God, than a threat to the fabric of society. As Jesse Appleton explained, "By corrupting the publick morals, it relaxes or dissolves the only bond, which can retain, in one compact, well organized mass, the discordant materials, of which society is composed."[6]

The temperance society thus served ultimately to advance the same objectives as the other associations. Humanitarian and utilitarian on one level, more basically it pursued the more traditional and fundamental vision of social cohesion. In all these efforts there was quite clearly the recognition that times had changed and new methods had to be applied. The Humane Society thus attempted to buy civic courage, and the Provident Institution, a savings bank for Boston's poor, substituted financial for eternal security as the reward for practicing the traditional Protestant virtues of industry and thrift.[7] In their adaptation there was an occasional nostalgic lament. Kirkland asked what signified the failure of "our accumulated moral means, and especially Christianity," to curb intemperance. Had the church become too much "a theory of articles of faith" and too little "a code of laws and a guide to virtue"? Had the direction of American life toward greater liberty and prosperity increased the "means and incentives of excess . . . [and] served to furnish ingenious apologies for vice"? To their credit men like Kirkland moved beyond this nostalgia and conceded that if the traditional means were failing, they must find an "additional instrument of publick morals."[8]

By 1815 Boston Federalists had gone far to create compensatory organizations amid political defeat. The extent to which these men formed these associations as conscious attempts to maintain influence and prestige amid waning political fortunes is not altogether clear. There is at least a hint in the records that this was the case. The Washington Benevolent Association of Massachusetts, for example, was chartered in 1812 for the ostensible purpose of inspiring "a patriotic interest in public affairs." Joined and supported almost exclusively by Federalists, in practice it operated more as an adjunct to the party—a forum for the dissemination of Federalist information and an instrument for political organization. There was in its constitution a clause which provided for the "disposal of any surplus money . . . for any benevolent or useful purpose." But the financial records of the group suggest this rarely occurred. In 1813, for example, the Massachusetts chapter contributed a mere $10 to charity organizations, out of a total budget of close to $2,000.[9]

Its public activities also illustrated the essentially political and partisan nature of the organization. Anniversary addresses could be counted on to promote the Federalist agenda and, during the intense partisan quarrels of the Jefferson and Madison era, recount the history of Republican Party calumny and anticommercial conspiracy.[10] But in 1813 Thaddeus Mason Harris tried to establish a different tone and direction for the organization. In an address commemorating Washington's birth, he explicitly resisted the expectation to comment on current affairs. Instead he reminded his audience that "the object of the Society . . . is not to cherish, but to heal party animosities . . . to conciliate every discordant opinion in one sentiment of enlightened patriotism; to combine the talents and influence of all in the most honourable exertions, to maintain the independence, strengthen the union, and contribute to the welfare of our common country." The means of doing all this, he argued, was charity. Reminding his audience that the organization's constitution contained a clause recommending benevolent activities, he suggested a redirection of the society's efforts, "with PATRIOTISM for the motive, BENEFICENCE for the practice, PEACE for the pursuit, and WASHINGTON for the model."[11]

The number of Federalists sharing these views is not clear. Clifford Griffin has argued that political frustration led directly and consciously to expanded charitable efforts: "If the stewards could no longer make men behave through political action, they might persuade them to be good through reform societies." Historians looking more narrowly at individual philanthropic efforts and reform movements have come to the same conclusion. Joseph Gusfield argued that the temperance movement of the early nineteenth century was "the reaction of the old Federalist aristocracy to loss of political, social, and religious dominance in American society." Ian Tyrrell agreed that the Federalists of the Massachusetts Society for the Suppression of Intemperance "sought to reassert social control." "So close in time and temperament" to traditional Federalist elites, the MSSI reflected the objectives, premises, and social outlook of the eighteenth century. Encouraging moderation rather than abstinence and regulation rather than elimination of the liquor traffic, they sought to restore the legal controls of the last century. Appealing to the public spirit of shop owners and employers, they pursued reform from within the traditional Federalist understanding of disinterested public service. And hinging their efforts upon the example and prestige of prominent citizens, they relied upon traditional notions of a socially responsible elite and deferential public.[12]

But if Federalists did indeed turn to philanthropy in the wake of political disappointment, their efforts should not be confused with those of other philanthropists and reformers of the early nineteenth century. Tyrrell drew a sharp distinction between the MSSI and the American Temperance Society that emerged a bit later. The MSSI was a short-lived effort, inspired and made possible by events and conditions surrounding the War of 1812. The economic dislocation resulting from the Embargo and war exacerbated older concerns about poverty and the dangerous tendencies of alcohol. The destruction of the war itself fed clerical concerns about the decline of public morality, made even more acute by their own sense of diminishing influence. Within this context many liberal and orthodox Protestants were able to put aside doctrinal differences to form the MSSI. But always only a "makeshift response to temporary circumstances," the MSSI could not sustain its efforts once this crisis had passed.[13]

Its greatest weakness, argued Tyrrell, was its narrow composition. Lower-class workers were suspicious of its intentions. Methodists and Baptists, despite their similar moral views, were not about to ally with Congregationalists who had resisted disestablishment. Republicans detected a Federalist plot. These "moral societies," suggested William Bentley, were "formed under the garb of religion for political purposes."[14] But the American Temperance Society that succeeded it was far different in its composition and methods. Believing the MSSI too equivocating, it called for abstinence, not just moderation—the complete elimination of all hard liquor. Closely connected to the Second Great Awakening and its message of free will and personal responsibility, it was dominated by evangelicals who carried the message of abstinence directly to the middle and lower classes. Drawing upon a far different constituency, the American Temperance Society attracted very few members of the MSSI—only three of the Temperance Society's twenty-seven honorary members and only two of its fifteen Massachusetts branch officials had been members of the older organization.[15]

The distinction Tyrrell has drawn and the transition he described are important ones. Most recent scholars of antebellum reform have tended to affirm his conclusions regarding its evangelical, post-Federalist character. Paul Boyer, for example, acknowledged that traditional Federalist elites, "members of the upper class whose status was rooted in a preurban order," did contribute to urban reform efforts in the early nineteenth century. But it was their combining with members of "an emerging urban commercial class" that gave their efforts breadth and power. This latter group, he pointed out, became the more significant reformers. Less connected with the old Federalist class and culture, the leaders of the new reform associations—the American Tract Society, the American Bible Society, and the American Sunday School Society—were "evangelical in religion, conservative in politics . . . men of recent wealth who were also comparative newcomers to the cities where they were forging their careers." In addition, more significant than their initial partnership with old Federalist elites was the alliance these new reformers formed with rural and urban middle and lower classes. This yielded "a vast second tier of volunteers who provided the sinews" of the voluntary associations, teaching Sunday school, distributing tracts, and directly confronting the evils of alcohol and urban poverty.[16]

Not all students of antebellum American society have reached these same conclusions. Edward Pessen argued that traditional patrician elites "dominated and shaped the policies of the army of voluntary associations," just as they continued to control the urban governments these associations were meant to augment. But Pessen utilized a rather broad definition of these reform associations in reaching this conclusion, including cultural associations as well as those directed against vice and irreligion. From the involvement of Federalist patricians in the Boston Athenæum, the Massachusetts Historical Society, the Massachusetts Peace Society, and the Boston Society of Natural History, he concluded that democratic voluntary associations were as mythical as the age of democracy itself.[17]

Even though Pessen overstated his case and employed a somewhat loose set of definitions, his research does point to some useful conclusions. Although Federalist elites may not have made the transition to many of the new reform and philanthropic associations, as Tyrrell and Boyer convincingly argue, they did continue to play dominant roles in other civic associations. They may not have joined the American Tract Society or the American Temperance Society, but they did involve themselves in numerous cultural associations, and they did continue to support many of the older philanthropic organizations and a select few of the newer civic organizations.

The activities of the young Federalists of the *North American Review* are representative of this selective participation in philanthropy and reform. Although their names do not show up on the membership lists of the Tract, Bible, or Sunday School Societies, they did staff the boards and contribute to the coffers of numerous other associations. William Tudor, for example, sat on the board of the Boston Dispensary and spoke before the Humane Society. George Ticknor was on the boards of the Boston Provident Institution for Savings, the Massachusetts Congregational Charitable Society, and the Farm School for Boys. James Savage was an officer of the Provident Institution and was also a founding member of the Boston Athenæum. Their selectivity raises some interesting questions. No doubt the evangelical character of the new reform associations was unattractive to these young Federalist Unitarians. But a closer look at their activities and their writings suggests that their choices were dictated by more than sectarian differences. These young Federalists did not just reject the new reform associations, they attempted to move beyond them. They were not indifferent to reform, nor did evangelical advances force them to retreat into only cultural associations. Instead, these young Federalists attempted to transform the ad hoc philanthropic organizations of their fathers into more permanent institutions, ones which depended less on the efforts of well-meaning amateurs than on the skills of highly educated professionals, institutions which through centralization and professionalization would better serve society and simultaneously preserve the Federalists' status and influence as a class.

The history of Boston health care is illustrative of these efforts. Long mindful of the health needs of the disadvantaged, Boston's leading citizens in 1796 formed the Boston Dispensary to serve them. Arguing that the ill among the poor could be cared for more effectively, compassionately, and frugally in their own homes, the dispensary offered a drop-in clinic for the ambulatory and home visitation services for the confined. Reminding Bostonians that "benevolence is an attribute of Heaven, bestowed on man to lessen the ills of this life," the dispensary board funded these efforts solely through private donations.[18] Staffed by uncompensated local physicians, the Boston Dispensary became in the first decade of the nineteenth century one of the boasts of the Federalist philanthropic community. It also offered a perfect example of their approach—voluntary physicians, decentralized care, and private funding, all exercised within the philosophical framework of Christian benevolence.

But by 1810 a new set of ideas was gaining support. John C. Warren and James Jackson, young physicians and friends of Tudor and Ticknor, suggested that these charitable efforts, although laudable, were inadequate. The needs of the poor were greater than could be addressed through the dispensary and were beyond the proper function of the Alms-house. What was needed was a "well-regulated" hospital, where diet could be monitored, surroundings could be controlled, and patients could receive the constant attentions of a qualified physician and a "skilful" nurse. In addition, the creation of a hospital would offer certain "collateral advantages." It would prove a useful adjunct to the medical college and ensure that Boston's students would receive a practical and professional education.[19]

William Tudor made a similar argument in speaking before the Humane Society in 1817. In addressing this charitable organization, he, in effect, spoke of the need to transcend charity. In the past these efforts had accomplished a great deal, but "the wants of society are progressive in a compound ratio." A more thorough, systematic approach was needed in the present age. Moreover, he too emphasized the secondary benefits of a hospital. It would provide not just relief for the sick but also "a school for instruction." Within such a hospital the medical community would be centralized, and its irregular and haphazard techniques could be improved. The surgeon would find more "frequent practice," and the most serious medical conditions would be "brought under the inspection of medical men." Nathan Hale's *Boston Weekly Messenger* made a similar argument in soliciting contributions. The proposed hospital would regularize medical care. The sick from all over the state would be brought under one roof, and the opportunities for study and medical advancement would increase in proportion to the number and variety of patients. Treatments would become standardized, medical knowledge would be centralized, and the current hodgepodge of well-meaning but inefficient medical charities would become obsolete.[20]

For men like Warren, Jackson, Tudor, and Hale, the general hospital project offered an opportunity to move a step beyond the humane and useful but somewhat amateurish efforts of Boston's philanthropic community. Substituting centralized for decentralized care and public funding for private, they built the case for the modern public hospital. In their vision one can see the movement from the charitable association to the professionally maintained institution, a transition that offered to the rising generation not just new methods of promoting social cohesion but also a clearer sense of their role within this society. The community at large, however, seemed slow to grasp their vision. The private contributions, which the state required in return for matching funds, fell far short of the trustees' expectations. At one point they angrily announced to the public that perhaps the hospital "must be left for times, when a higher cast of character predominates, and to a more enlightened and sympathetic race of men."[21]

When the funding did materialize, however, and the hospital began construction, it announced a new era in public services. Vestiges of the older approach to these charitable associations persisted. When Josiah Quincy applauded the efforts of "all classes of their citizens, combining and concentrating their efforts . . . not, as has happened in other countries, to destroy, but to found and erect institutions," he recalled the unifying role of older charitable associations. When a speaker at the groundbreaking ceremonies applauded the "munificence of opulent individuals," many of them conspicuously displayed on the stage, he drew upon the older vision of the voluntary association as a means of identifying social leaders. Responding to those who mocked the elaborate ceremony presided over by the Grand Master of the Free Masons, a Masonic editor recalled the social value of public ritual. "This is an idle ceremony to him only who believes God requires no homage from the heart of man, and that man needs no sacred rites, no holy seasons to enliven and invigorate his sense of duty."[22]

But the very existence of the hospital spoke to the ascension of a new vision of public service and a new understanding of professionalism—a vision that placed the systematic and the institutionalized over the voluntary and the ad hoc, a vision which substituted the specialist for the amateur and measured efforts by their effectiveness rather than their benevolence. Over the next several years, other professions and other public institutions would be reformed along similar lines, and young Boston Brahmins would play prominent roles in their development.[23] Samuel Gridley Howe would work toward the professionalization and institutionalization of education for the handicapped. Under his direction the irregular and privately funded efforts of various philanthropic groups would be replaced by publicly funded institutions staffed by trained specialists.[24] Howe would also join Horace Mann in his efforts to professionalize Boston's system of public education. The controversy sparked in 1843 by Mann's *Seventh Annual Report of the Board of Education* would culminate in the appointment of Nathan Bishop as Boston's first city superintendent of public schools in 1851. Henceforth the administration and inspection of public schools would be transferred from lay boards to a public bureaucracy managed by a professional educational administrator.[25] Josiah Quincy would work during his tenure as mayor toward the professionalization of municipal services. Street cleaning and sewer maintenance would be transferred from private hands to public agencies managed by professional engineers. Concerns regarding housing conditions and water quality would lead to the creation of a short-lived but farsighted Board of Health Commissioners, and the police and fire departments would be removed from the supervision of community boards and placed under the jurisdiction of professional public officials.[26]

The young Federalists contributing to the *North American Review* in its first fifteen years of existence similarly advanced the cause of professionalization. Within its pages, for example, the benefits of systemization and specialization were argued in their calls for penal reform. Striking something of a middle ground on the question of rehabilitation versus punishment, they argued that the primary objective of the penal institution should be the protection of society. Sentencing and punishment should not be guided by a vindictive thirst for retribution or a naive faith in rehabilitation. It should be determined by a calculated and studied analysis of the deterrent effect of a particular punishment weighed against the possibility of public sympathy engendered by excessive punishment. In their eyes the well-intentioned but amateurish efforts of local prison societies needed to yield to the more calculating and studied efforts of penal experts.[27]

But most commonly the contributors to the *North American Review* preferred to focus on the institution that they saw underlying the new institutional order. Although clearly supportive of the new emphasis on professionalization, they emphasized more the institution upon which the professions would depend. Combining their experiences abroad, their new commitment to professionalism, and New England's historic commitment to education, the conservative social planners of the *North American Review* articulated a distinctively American conception of the university and placed it at the center of their social order.

New Englanders, especially those from Massachusetts, had long prided themselves on their commitment to education. They liked to remind the rest of the nation that among the first measures taken by their Puritan ancestors was a provision for the support of schools. They still claimed the greatest number of educational institutions, and Harvard continued to be the nation's preeminent institution of higher learning. But during the late eighteenth and early nineteenth centuries, New England's reputation was challenged by educational reformers from other parts of the Union—theorists who challenged the traditional structure and content of education and state legislatures that threatened to surpass even Massachusetts in supporting the cause of education.

The challenge had begun as early as 1749 when Benjamin Franklin published his views on the type of education most suited to America.[28] His *Proposal Relating to the Education of Youth* reflected his own distaste for formal schooling, especially as practiced in colonial America. Rote recitation, Greek and Latin, the memorization of classical texts, were explicitly rejected in Franklin's scheme. Instead, he called for a more practical and scientific approach to education. English, math, history, geography, modern languages, natural science, agriculture, and even carpentry and gardening would replace the traditional disciplines. Classical languages would still have a place, but only for those students who would need them in their careers—physicians and the clergy. The purpose of education, argued Franklin, was not the stashing of useless pieces of information in the heads of a pedantic elite. Instead it should serve to prepare people for their places in society as useful and contributing members.

The teaching methodologies Franklin prescribed placed this same accent on the practical and the experiential. The six-year course of study, open to children over the age of eight, emphasized the active participation of the students in their education. Students would teach one another spelling and vocabulary, they would discuss among themselves the moral implications of the stories they read, and in order to develop writing skills they would exchange letters discussing common occurrences.

Franklin's distaste for classical education was echoed in part by another of Philadelphia's educational innovators, Benjamin Rush. His theories, published in a series of works during the late eighteenth century, included the argument that classical study actually hampered scientific progress.[29] The study of ancient languages not only distracted students from more important educational pursuits, it fostered attitudes hostile to the study of science. Freed from the educational burden of these dead languages, American students would inaugurate a scientific revolution.

Rush's ideas went beyond this iconoclasm. He argued most consistently that education in the new Republic should aim at the formation of cultural nationalism. Within a nation so young, the greatest educational need was the cultivation of patriotism and national identity. At times this emphasis produced a chilling rhetoric. American students should be reminded, he argued, that they do not belong to themselves, they are "public property." Although family was important, the true American must "forsake, and even forget them, when the welfare of his country requires it."[30] But these tendencies were tempered by a commitment to the values of both the Enlightenment and Christianity. American students must be taught not only to serve their nation but also to ensure its fidelity to the values of liberty and progress. They must be instructed in the imperative of national loyalty, but this loyalty must be framed within a more compelling commitment to the truths of revealed religion.

The means of doing all this were outlined in a 1787 letter *To the Citizens of Philadelphia: A Plan for Free Schools.* In this essay Rush argued that the state should assume responsibility for the education of its citizens, especially those unable to provide one for themselves. Avoiding the unsettling threat of direct taxation, he suggested that the state should charter private corporations for the purpose of generating funds for these free schools. But consistent with his sense of the importance of religious and moral training, he suggested that these schools be church affiliated. Within these publicly supported but also church-affiliated schools, American children of all classes would uniformly and systematically develop those religious, moral, and civic values essential to the health of the young Republic.

The most visible educational reformer of the period was the Federalists' nemesis, Thomas Jefferson. In his plan for universal general education, his efforts to reform the College of William and Mary, and his founding of the University of Virginia, Jefferson laid out a far-reaching and thorough challenge to New England Federalists anxious to preserve their reputation as educational leaders. Jefferson's achievements should not be overstated. The Virginia legislature did not pass the plan he placed before them in 1779 in his "Bill for the More General Diffusion of Knowledge." Similarly, one should not overstate the universality of the educational opportunities Jefferson's plan offered. Within it all children were to be guaranteed three years of elementary education to study reading, writing, history, and arithmetic. But beyond this only the most talented or the more affluent would find access to schooling. The secondary schools, which taught Latin and Greek, higher mathematics, geography, and English grammar, would be funded by tuition. Only the most capable students from among the poorer classes would be allowed to attend on state scholarship. And an even smaller number would enjoy access to the College of William and Mary at the public expense.[31]

Yet for all its shortcomings, when it was proposed Jefferson's plan offered more in the way of universal education than existed anywhere else. For New Englanders, proud of their own commitment to education, his vision proved a serious challenge. Of course, New Englanders had their own educational theorists—Noah Webster introduced important innovations regarding language. Arguing that the language of the United States must be as free as its political institutions, he developed an American dictionary and grammar as the first step toward cultural independence. His legacy to the school systems was a set of readers, texts, spellers, and grammars that sought to correct the Anglophilic biases of older materials.

Despite Webster's contributions, there persisted the suggestion during these last decades of the eighteenth century that the mantle as education leader had passed from Massachusetts.[32] When the nation turned its attention to the task of education after the Revolution, it was the Philadelphia-based American Philosophical Society that offered a prize for the best plan for a "system of liberal education and literary instruction adapted to the genius of the government of the United States." More practical legislative efforts further challenged Massachusetts's claim to educational preeminence. Although Massachusetts's state constitution of 1780 emphasized the dependence of liberty upon education, it made no concrete provisions for the establishment or funding of schools. The constitutions of Pennsylvania, Vermont, and North Carolina not only called for the creation of schools but provided for some degree of public support. Pennsylvania's constitution even provided for teachers' salaries. In New York, DeWitt Clinton lobbied, eventually successfully, for improved teacher training and tax-supported common schools. In 1812 he led the state in its efforts to establish the first state superintendent of schools.

By the 1820s George Ticknor was complaining that Massachusetts's commitment to education compared poorly not just to that of other states but to that of the commonwealth's founders. Whereas an act of 1647 had required towns with more than fifty families to provide reading and writing schools and towns with more than one hundred families to establish grammar schools that would prepare students for admission to Harvard, the educational act of 1789 allowed smaller towns to reduce their school year to six months and required only towns with more than two hundred families to maintain grammar schools. An 1824 act reenforced this misdirection; in requiring that only towns with more than five thousand persons establish grammar schools, the state legislature in effect excluded all but five or six towns in Massachusetts from the responsibility of preparing students for advanced education.[33]

Ticknor was relieved that most towns had demonstrated a commitment to free primary schools, and he believed that the Boston public system provided the sort of complete model the state needed. Rooted in a 1789 city measure offering free public education to all children, male and female, between the ages of seven and fourteen, the system had grown by 1824 to include four tiers, educating six thousand students. In addition, foreshadowing later reforms in the direction of professionalization and bureaucratization, the curriculum within these schools was standardized, as were the school calendar and teaching schedule, and oversight was placed in the hands of an elected school committee.[34] But few cities followed Boston's example, and perhaps more ominously, the state legislature provided little support, much less leadership, to the current reform efforts.

Therefore, as the people of Massachusetts joined Ticknor in evaluating their school system, they did so with an awareness that other parts of the nation were at least catching up, if not passing them by in terms of educational innovation and leadership. Moreover, they did so within an intellectual climate filled with the ideas of European reformers such as Jean-Jacques Rousseau, Johann Heinrich Pestalozzi, and his disciple Phillip Emanuel von Fellenberg. As the young Federalists of the *North American Review* joined Ticknor in this discussion and debated the form and responsibilities of public education, they knew that European reformers were challenging both the structure and content of education even more aggressively.

Rousseau's most significant contributions to this discussion revolved around his recognition that childhood was not static, that instead it consisted of various stages of growth and that the disciplines studied and the instructional methods employed should be determined by the developmental status of the child.[35] Within a child's educational development, the family served as the most basic educator, and the role of the mother was particularly essential. Rousseau suggested further that as experience was the best educator, and as the ultimate goal of education was to cultivate the interest and skills necessary for self-education, the most critical component of any educational system was intellectual and emotional freedom. Consequently, teachers should neither coerce nor buy their students' efforts through a system of punishments or rewards. Instead, they should treat their students respectfully and provide them the security and freedom they needed to navigate through the process of self-education.

Pestalozzi drew heavily upon Rousseau, in particular, in his appreciation of the role of the family and the developmental stages of the child. Like Rousseau he emphasized the organic nature of education—its natural progression from the simple to the complex and the importance of the senses within this process. It was the teacher's responsibility to cultivate the child's natural interests and abilities, leaving the child's own natural instinct for learning to provide the necessary incentive for education. In addition, the teacher should address the moral and physical character of the child. The goal of education, as institutionalized at schools in Neuhof, Burgdorf, and Yverdun, was the full development of the child— intellectual, moral, and physical.

Of perhaps greatest interest to Americans was the work of Fellenberg—both his writings and the school he established at Hofwyl. On one level a set of antiegalitarian premises underlying his school made it an unlikely subject of interest for American educational reformers. It was actually a complex of schools offering vocational-type training for the lower-class students and a more rigorous academic training for the children of the more wealthy, and Fellenberg's pedagogical theories were rooted in a vision of rigidly and appropriately stratified social classes. He sought in his school to prepare students of all classes for the purposes for which they, as determined by their social station, were best suited. But, unlike other academies, his school was to educate the rich and the poor, those receiving a liberal arts education and those receiving vocational training, in close proximity to one another. In this way reciprocal feelings of sympathy, kindness, and respect would be cultivated. The rich would come to appreciate the character of the poor, while the poor would see the generosity of the rich. As an American visitor, William Woodbridge, rather charitably observed, the poor "become accustomed to living in view of splendour and luxury, without desiring or hoping to partake them, they learn to recognize the inferiority of their rank without being degraded by it; while the pupils of the higher classes acquire by this connection the habit of treating their inferiors with kindness and deference."[36]

Although Fellenberg's elitist philosophy disturbed many American reformers, the other elements of his system were better received. Like the other reformers, he encouraged a revision of the traditional authoritarian teacher-student relationship. Recognizing the primary role of the family in education, he suggested that the classroom teacher cultivate a more paternal and affectionate relationship with the students. Fellenberg also emphasized the development of the whole child, the improvement of the body as well as the mind, and the cultivation of all the faculties, intellectual and moral. Rooted in the faculty psychology so fundamental to American thought, the diverse and holistic curriculum Fellenberg established at Hofwyl—an academic regimen of both ancient and modern languages, history, philosophy, chemistry, mechanics, mathematics, music, and art, as well as instruction in gardening, fencing, gymnastics, and hiking—offered a program which suited Americans' own sense of the self.[37]

New Englanders interested in education were aware of the new ideas coming from Europe, just as they knew of the ideas and efforts from other parts of the Union. The *Monthly Anthology* reviewed Rousseau's *Emile* and discussed, generally negatively, its ideas on education. The journal also unfavorably reviewed Joseph Neef's repackaging of Pestalozzi's ideas in 1809.[38] In particular, the reviewer criticized Neef's repudiation of classical studies and his instructional system's overdependence on self-education. Even so, there was a considerable softening of the Federalist position on education over these years. Faced with these intellectual and institutional challenges from neighboring states and abroad, Federalists, especially those from the younger generation, moved toward a more flexible position on the questions of curriculum and pedagogy.

By 1820, for example, Boston Federalists had grown far more supportive of the "general diffusion" of knowledge; they even took the lead in increasing the accessibility of Boston's school system for the city's youth. When Boston's ad hoc committee revealed that a significant number of the city's children did not attend the public schools because they did not meet the entry requirement of literacy at the age of seven, it was Federalists Elisha Ticknor and James Savage who lobbied for reform.

Demanding that all children "have an equal chance to understand the nature and principles of our Republican Government," they successfully worked for the creation of primary schools for these children.[39]

By 1820 Federalists were also receptive to the reformers' suggestion that education become better connected to the "active business of life." Alpheus Packard in the *North American Review* singled out a school in Gardiner, Maine, as a useful model for curricular reform. There, practical education was raised to the level of science as mechanics, farmers, and manufacturers were given scientific training. Orville Dewey applauded these same tendencies. Ridiculing the "idiotic vociferation" of incomprehensible and ultimately meaningless rules of grammar and logic, he too called for the "application of science to the business of life." Arguing that education should give to man's daily activities "a more intellectual character," he encouraged a revision of school curriculum to serve the students' most immediate needs as farmers and craftsmen and make their day-to-day economic decisions less "an affair of barter" than a "subject of science."[40]

By the 1820s Federalists could thus agree with the reformers on many questions. Where they parted company was over the question of classical studies within this reformed curriculum. Jared Sparks, for example, was able to accept the fact that "utility is the watchword of American genius." If America's refined literature and scholarship did lag behind Europe's, at least its "domestic literature is adequate to our immediate wants." But when Republican reformer C. J. Ingersoll suggested that classical studies were thus completely obsolete, that they ought "perish under the mass of knowledge destined to occupy entirely the limited powers of the human understanding," Sparks asserted the hope that "a remnant may be spared to visit the groves and cull the flowers of antiquity." Although Packard acknowledged the benefits of Amherst's new two-track program, one pursuing traditional classical studies and the other substituting modern languages, he feared for the effects on liberal education. Granted, persons intending a career in commerce did not require the same preparation as those anticipating professional study. But he was afraid that this practice would lead to the complete neglect of the more rigorous classical program, and he did not approve of Amherst awarding the same degree to both courses of study.[41]

In this defense of classical education and differentiated degrees, there was more than just pedantry and ego. As Richard Hofstadter and

C. DeWitt Hardy have suggested, a particular curriculum represents not just a body of knowledge deemed worthy of passing on but also "what kind of mind and character an education is expected to produce."[42] For these young Federalists a classical education offered more than a particular set of facts, more than a timely call to civic virtue; it offered mental discipline and unmatched standards of intellectual greatness. Herodotus had illuminated the cycles of history to perfection, just as Xenophon had provided a timeless analysis of the flaws of democracy. In Cicero they saw unequaled eloquence, and in Homer a poet of unmatched brilliance. The preservation of these studies and the degrees that traditionally were awarded for their mastery represented thus a defense not just of tradition but also of time-honored standards—a defense of literary and intellectual excellence and the hierarchical view of culture it implied.[43]

Mental discipline, order, and hierarchy continued to be central within even these young Federalists' vision of education. As they sorted through the ideas advanced by American and European reformers, they retained a peculiarly Federalist vision of education—although they accepted a more flexible curriculum and supported greater access to it, they retained a vision that was still elitist and on many questions conservative, that valued inherited tradition and sought the preservation of an established canon, that retained a respect for cultural hierarchy and educational authority.

Representative of the position toward which Federalists moved was Joseph Green Cogswell. While touring Europe, he visited both Pestalozzi's school at Yverdun and Fellenberg's Hofwyl.[44] He was disappointed with the former; by 1818 when Cogswell visited, Pestalozzi was senile, and his school was in disarray. At Hofwyl, however, Cogswell found a curricular theory and an approach to teaching that suited both his philosophy of the mind and his personal experience.

In particular, Cogswell was impressed at Hofwyl by the relationship between the teachers and their students. Unlike the formal, authoritarian, and often adversarial relationship that existed in American schools, at Hofwyl he observed "the greatest equality and at the same time the greatest respect, a respect of the heart I mean, not of fear . . . how delightful it must be to govern, where love is the principle of obedience."[45] He also observed the sort of broad-based curriculum that appealed to his own sense of a person's educational needs. He well understood the premises of faculty psychology, and they had been reenforced by his own experience. Having found solace and rejuvenation through a combination of rigorous study and physical exercise, Cogswell embraced Fellenberg's holistic approach to education and incorporated it within the blueprint for the new school he and George Bancroft would eventually found.

The school that Cogswell and Bancroft established in 1823 at Round Hill—a rural setting near Northhampton, Massachusetts—drew heavily upon the model at Hofwyl.[46] The students at Round Hill rose at six and followed a tightly regulated schedule of classes, private study, structured exercise, and free play similar to the holistic curriculum at Fellenberg's school. The course of study drew heavily upon the classics, but there was also instruction in modern languages, science, history, and geography. At Round Hill, as at Hofwyl, the attention paid to the cultivation of the intellectual faculties was balanced by country hikes, calisthenics, gardening, and woodworking. Cogswell also attempted to maintain the more paternal, affectionate relationship with his students that he had observed at Hofwyl. But perhaps most significantly, the school Cogswell established at Round Hill retained Fellenberg's dichotomous sense of society and its educational needs. Although Cogswell's vision was less overtly classist, he continued to envision a hierarchical society of distinct levels with distinct educational needs.

In bringing back to America the elitist element of Hofwyl there was considerable irony. Initially, Cogswell's Federalist friends had directed him to the school in order to learn more about its methods of educating the poor. But as James McLachlan observed, while Cogswell was there, he became more "entranced with the education of the rich." Returning to America, Cogswell continued to argue that the needs of students of limited means and abilities must be addressed—one task of his school involved "patiently fitting them for the places, for which Providence and circumstances seems to have designed them." But it was the school's "higher object" to train those who were more "liberally gifted." Their education was Round Hill's "more sacred trust," for these more talented students must be in "their generation the lights of the world and the guardians of public prosperity."[47]

The elitist character of Round Hill reflected a significant fact about the lessons Cogswell learned at Hofwyl. To the extent that this young Federalist reformer was influenced by the European reformers, his was a selective imitation. Cogswell still thought within the intellectual context shaped by his Federalist past, and thus the innovations he adopted were only those compatible with the Federalist sense of the world and the place within it of people like himself. This is even more evident within those parts of the European vision he rejected. The differences between Round Hill and Hofwyl, perhaps even more than the similarities, reveal a great deal about the persistently Federalist character of the educational system Cogswell and his Federalist friends envisioned. For example, Cogswell was not willing to abandon altogether the traditional curriculum in his school at Round Hill. Although he embraced a more varied program, he retained a belief in the importance of classical subjects. Throughout his career he lamented the "new doctrine of exploding classical studies." Nothing, he believed, could substitute for this "early discipline for the mind." In particular, he was distressed by the tendency among educational reformers to abandon these studies for "some miserable manual labor affair."[48] He was genuinely committed to a broadening of the curriculum. At Round Hill his was a "two-fold object, the culture of the human powers and preparation for actual life." But within this combination, the former served the most noble purposes. Although an education which prepared a person for the active business of life was "unquestionably the first claim," the development of the mind through a more traditional curriculum, including classical studies, was education's "most exalted office."[49]

Further characteristic of Cogswell's Federalist approach to education was his criticism of the Europeans' excessive emphasis on experiential learning. Especially at Yverdun he was not persuaded of the effectiveness of a pedagogy that emphasized the senses over the intellect. This emphasis on experience and observation "would exclude memory altogether as a medium of instructing, and make use of reason alone."[50] At Round Hill, therefore, there was only selective methodological innovation. Students were not instructed as an undifferentiated mass as they were at other American schools; instead, they were individually assigned books and worked through them at their own pace. But memorization and recitation continued to be the primary form of instruction. Cogswell continued to believe that education was more about the dissemination of existing truths than the rediscovery of knowledge, and that it relied more on the teacher's knowledge than the student's experience. Cogswell may have sought to modernize the process of education and loosen up the curriculum, but he remained wedded to a vision of education and culture that was still hierarchical and a sense of knowledge that was still authoritarian.

Like the other Federalist educational reformers, Cogswell drew selectively from the ideas and examples that surrounded him. Although they drew from the ideas of Rousseau, Pestalozzi, and Fellenberg and felt pressured to meet the challenge of the other states, they developed a vision that was still grounded in Federalist tradition and ideology. Especially in their vision of the university, the educational institution to which the contributors to the *North American Review* paid the most attention, they operated with a balanced appreciation for both the old and the new, an appreciation for innovation but also a persisting sense of the importance of hierarchy, order, and the value of accumulated experience—the need for general education but also the necessity of more elite forms of education and more specialized training for the "wise and the good."

In acknowledging the need for innovation, these young Federalists began with the recognition that American, and even New England's, society and culture could no longer be addressed with the assumption of intellectual and cultural homogeneity. They recognized that pluralism was a fact of republican life. As part of their general adaptation to this new world, they looked for and found the benefits inherent in pluralism. William Tudor could thus praise the diversity within Harvard and conclude that in its religious and intellectual variety Harvard stood on "broader ground." Its intellectually eclectic faculty, "borne about by various currents and eddies of opinion . . . uncertain where they will land at last," was offered as a positive development, not a cause for alarm. But much of this confidence lay in their belief that this diversity could, and in the new order would, be contained within the tightly regulated structure of the university. If the future did indeed hold little intellectual consensus, the "various currents and eddies" at least would be contained within the structure and decorum of an orderly institution. There the diversity that threatened disorder outside would be subjected to a regulated schedule of lectures, recitation, and rigorous exams. Tudor, in this spirit, even argued the necessity of academic gowns and well-maintained grounds. They were trifles, he admitted, but such details "give effect to solid things." And if Harvard's students were to learn the "self-government and voluntary moderation" necessary for life in a free society, the university must provide a model.[51]

Edward Everett advanced much the same logic in his criticism of the

University of Virginia. Jefferson's decision not to include a chair of divinity violated not just Everett's religious sensibilities but also his understanding of the university's role within the increasingly pluralistic American society. The exclusion of religion from the university would only drive the here-to-stay forces of diversity into "various theological camps pitched throughout our country." Rather than providing a forum for reconciliation, an example of toleration and decorum, the university through this decision threatened to inflame the "sectarian spirit" and exacerbate the divisive tendencies within America's democratic society.[52]

George Henry Bode carried this logic still further in the *North American Review* in his calls for a national university. Such a university, he argued, would temper not only religious and intellectual diversity but also regional and political division. Drawing together young men from all parts of the nation, a national university would check their local prejudices and regional jealousies. Recalling Washington's unfulfilled dream of just such a national university, Bode questioned "how much fierce contention, arising from the insanity of party spirit and mercenary politics, might have been spared!"[53]

Providing an example of order and decorum amid diversity was only one part of this vision of the university. Closely connected was the understanding that from within this controlled environment some sort of consensus would emerge. To the varied and divisive problems of contemporary life, America's brightest minds would apply the calm but rigorous methods of scholarly research and produce a set of principles and policies for broader dissemination. Everett argued that the murkiness of the American legal system might be clarified in this way. The "multitude of books, the want of a digested system . . . the confusion and obscurity" of American laws and treaties, would find in the university and "the manner of learning" the clarity and system "wanting in the records of the science itself." James Luce Kingsley suggested that the confused state of the common schools might be remedied through the same approach. By transferring the superintendence of these schools from local boards and lay visitors to the university, America's common schools would receive "new vigor."[54] Levi Frisbie argued that even questions of morality would benefit from the guidance of the university.

Frisbie made this argument in discussing the common sense philosophy so central to the thought of Federalist Unitarians. There was, he reminded readers, a difference between "moral sense" and "moral science."

Although all men did indeed possess the former, thereby enabling them to sort out basic questions of morality and even religion, there was still a need for the latter. As human affairs were often "complicated and remote," questions of morality and religion often required more systematic and scientific exploration. For Frisbie, Harvard's Alford Professor of Natural Religion, Moral Philosophy, and Civil Polity, the ultimate "safety of society" lay in its continued supervision by men of intellect and learning, in the "jealous scrutiny of a sound philosophy" by men "whose habits and studies will lead them to a rigid superintendence of whatever is proposed."[55]

The vision of the university gradually taking shape in the pages of the *North American Review* acquired further coherence in the calls for more thorough and obligatory graduate professional education. The traditional methods of training for medicine and the law—study and apprenticeship under the tutelage of a practicing professional—were far from adequate. The resulting education was haphazard, incomplete, and constantly interrupted by the often more compelling affairs of an active practice. Progress had been made in recent years. There were now six graduate medical schools in the United States and two law schools. But less than half of the country's professionals had received their training at these institutions.[56]

To remedy this problem professionals launched campaigns both to improve the quality of these graduate institutions and to bring about more universal attendance. In supporting the General Hospital, Boston's doctors emphasized its "collateral advantages"—the centralization of medical knowledge and its more ready access to students of medicine at Harvard. Referring to Boston's loss of leadership to the city of Philadelphia, they argued that medicine needed to be practiced as a profession, not as a trade, and that the difference lay in more rigorous, systematic forms of education. In addition, the Boston Medical Association employed the threat of professional isolation against individuals improperly trained. Members of the association agreed to not associate or consult with physicians who did not possess either a degree from the Harvard Medical School or letters of approbation from the Censors of the Massachusetts Medical Society.[57]

To improve the character of legal training, Harvard announced the appointment of two new professorships of law between 1815 and 1817. The announcements were greeted with enthusiasm by supporters within the

Federalist press. Until now, "Juridicus" complained in the *Boston Weekly Messenger,* the law and its practitioners in America were "perhaps the most loose and imperfect, possible." The absence of formal academic training produced lawyers who sacrificed informed opinion for "flippant and ready utterance" and a legal system characterized by "irregularity of proceedings . . . looseness and laxity of practice . . . [and] frequent contradictions in judicial opinions." It was, in short, "everything but what it ought to be, a uniform rule regulating the intercourse of society, giving stability to property, protection to the weak, and confidence to all."[58]

Isaac Parker, chief justice of the Massachusetts Supreme Court and Harvard's first Royall Professor of Law, was more politic regarding the status of law and learning in America. If these had suffered in the past, it was because the more fundamental exigencies of Americans' colonial existence had required their attention and demanded that higher learning take a back seat. But he also agreed that America was at something of an intellectual and institutional crossroads, and what had been adequate in the past would no longer suffice. Parker thus suggested that a general course of legal studies be pursued by all Harvard students. For the person planning a career in the law, he proposed two years of graduate study before entering into an apprenticeship. Just as Frisbie had allowed for a certain degree of common capability in questions of morality, Parker suggested that a rudimentary understanding of the law was essential for men of "liberal education" in a republican society. But, also like Frisbie, Parker asserted that true expertise, ultimate authority on questions of law, would be reserved to a minority. The law, like morality, would remain "a science for the few to understand and practice."[59]

John Thornton Kirkland, Harvard president and *Review* contributor, summed up these sentiments in arguing that professional preparation should be an essential part of the university's mission. The current haphazard methods of training in medicine, law, and even the clergy must be replaced by "systematic education" within the confines of the university. In making this argument, he summarized the emerging vision of the university. Within its decorous and orderly ivy-covered walls, the confusion and variety of American life would find order and systemization. Through specialized graduate study, the university would prepare a corps of genuine professionals capable of taking the wisdom of the university back to society in order to impose some of its clarity upon it. In describing these products of the university, these Federalist visionaries conjured up something of the traditional vision of the Harvard man. For almost two centuries, Parker argued, Harvard professors had boasted, as Parker did now, that "within these walls, the moral strength of our country is to be formed. . . . this interesting mass of youth dispersed over our towns and villages, will occupy the pulpits, the chambers of the sick, the bar, the bench of justice, the seats of the legislature, the halls of Congress, the chair of state." But in the new vision being explored by Parker and others in the *North American Review,* the qualities and qualifications upon which this new breed of leaders would base their status were to be different. If the old Harvard man had led and inspired respect through his "moral strength," the new Harvard man would lead with the authority inherent in more specialized training. If the old law and its old practitioners had filled the need in the past, it was now imperative that these "bold and ignorant pretenders give place to the skilful and scientifick." [60]

Not everyone embraced this new vision of the university taking shape in the pages of the *North American Review.* Reflecting republican sensibilities, many of these critics attacked the class character of higher education, more specifically the link they assumed between a college education and a leisure class. While some argued that the absence of such a class in America made colleges unnecessary, others feared that colleges would create such a class. A too highly educated class, these critics argued, would be an unproductive one. In addition, they disapproved of the young Federalists' suggestion that universities be publicly funded. They pointed out that costs per pupil were much higher at the university level than at the elementary level, and that public funding would injuriously divert monies away from elementary and grammar schools. They argued that universities were traditionally the province of the wealthy, and that even a publicly funded college would attract only those students able to afford a delayed entry into the workforce. [61]

But for Federalist reformers public funding for higher education was a necessity. For starters it seemed the most expeditious way to salvage America's academic reputation. "While small states in Europe, whose positions we can hardly trace on our maps, are endowing universities," remonstrated Sparks, "we are contented tamely to submit to the reproach of doing absolutely nothing." American plans for a national university foundered for lack of support, complained Everett, and "we leave it to despots, to build universities as the toys and playthings of their slaves." Only public funding could provide the amount of money necessary, argued Everett. Private resources were inadequate to fund universities in America. The sort of "overgrown estates" and "privileged orders" upon which European institutions depended were "a relic of a state of society which never existed among us." What America did possess, Sparks added, was abundant public lands to the west. The 1785 ordinance that made a portion of these lands available to new states to support their educational efforts was a good start, he argued. But its logic ought to be extended to the older states as well. Sparks calculated that an allocation of 9.4 million western acres would enable the eastern states to meet a broad range of educational needs. Nor, argued Kingsley, would this public funding of a university represent a tax on the poor for the benefit of the rich. The rich would always find a way to educate their children, even if it meant sending them abroad. The poor, on the other hand, must depend on public universities if they were to reach those educational heights "which otherwise will fall exclusively into the hands of the rich."[62]

Less frequently, but perhaps most importantly, these Federalists argued that public funding, and ideally federal funding, was necessary in order to free the university from the intrusion and influence of local interests. In Connecticut, Kingsley had seen the best interests of education "sacrificed to local and individual interests, partial benefit, and narrow views." Jared Sparks expressed a similar concern regarding North Carolina. There he worried that high-minded proposals for the improvement of transportation and education would be defeated by local and state legislators animated by "short-sightedness, narrow policy, love of popularity and perhaps selfishness." In the past, even the salaries of university professors had fallen victim on occasion to the "whim or caprice of a party."[63]

If the university was to fill its critical role in the Republic, it must be protected from this local legislative interference. If academics were to be allowed to study and digest, find harmony amid pluralism, and produce for the public a unifying vision, they must be insulated from the very disorder they were trying to correct. Federal funding would address all these concerns. It would provide the university both the financial stability it needed to approach European standards and the autonomy it required to fulfill its social responsibilities.

Within the pages of the *North American Review*, young Federalists thus outlined a comprehensive vision of the university and its role in the Republic. Constructing a vision of academic reform that wove together curriculum, structure, and funding within a more general vision of society, these young Federalists made an intellectual contribution many historians have linked to a much later period. Laurence Veysey, for example, argued that the vision of these early reformers lacked concreteness. Only in the years between 1865 and 1890 did the theorists of academic reform generate a "coherent intellectual history."[64] But the contributions of these young Federalists suggest that these early efforts were far more coherent than Veysey acknowledged. Moreover, it is arguable that in the recently founded law school at Harvard, antebellum academic reform moved beyond theory—that, in fact, these young Federalists provided the intellectual rationale for a very concrete process of reform already begun.

With the appointment of Isaac Parker as Royall Professor in 1815 and of Asahel Stearns in 1817 to coordinate a program for resident graduate study, the Harvard Law School began its historic existence. The school's real origins, however, must be traced to an earlier date. Since the previous century criticism of the apprentice method of preparation had been voiced throughout America. In response, the College of William and Mary established the nation's first law professorship in 1779, and in Connecticut, Judge Tapping Reeve founded the Litchfield Law School. Offering a more complete course of preparation than William and Mary, the school at Litchfield drew students from throughout the country. In its fifty-year existence it trained over a thousand lawyers, including over sixty congressmen, ten governors, and two justices of the United States Supreme Court. Other than these, however, American colleges were slow to address the calls for improved legal education. Ezra Stiles proposed a course of legal studies at Yale in 1777, but nothing came of it until 1812. Although the Isaac Royall chair at Harvard was endowed in 1781, over thirty years passed before Harvard fully funded the chair and made an appointment.

Harvard's failure to implement Royall's request more quickly has been explained in several ways. Charles Warren argued that the delay was caused by the War of 1812. The surrounding political distractions and economic dislocation made organizing and funding the position difficult. Arthur Sutherland suggested that the delay was caused more by internal questions regarding the suitability of a law school within the college. "If education was to be practical, it would not be academically respectable; if it was to be respectably academic it must be professionally unprofitable." And most recently Gerard Gawalt has argued that the delay in establishing the law professorship at Harvard had more to do with resistance offered by the profession itself. Many lawyers believed that the apprentice system provided an adequate means of preparing lawyers and maintaining professional standards. In addition, it offered an effective means of controlling entry to the profession and thus regulating competition and protecting fees.[65]

None of these explanations excludes the other. No doubt more pressing political affairs distracted college officials from implementing the endowment. No doubt entrenched lawyers within county bar associations resisted any challenge to the control they exercised over the profession. But Sutherland's suggestion that implementation depended on the college rethinking itself accents the importance of these young Federalists' efforts. In helping to overcome the resistance and inertia coming from all directions, the new vision of the university they offered seems to have been critical to the newborn law school as it attempted to get on track.

Beyond this contribution, however, it is difficult to find evidence that this new vision of the university had any significant immediate impact. If historians have failed to acknowledge these early efforts, the failure of these intellectuals to inspire more widespread reform may explain their neglect. To an extent this failure was due to the widespread Republican opposition. While these Federalist reformers sought to strengthen the university, Republicans sought to strengthen the common schools. While Federalists sought to protect these institutions of higher education from the meddling and supervision of legislative bodies, Republicans sought to strengthen this branch of government. While Federalists sought to elevate the man of education and expertise, the specialist in possession of scientific and esoteric knowledge, Republicans sought to glorify the common man. But Republican opposition was to be expected. More surprisingly, and more effectively, Federalist efforts at implementation were obstructed by their own internal disagreements. Although they seem to have agreed on the importance of the university and its centrality within the social order, their attempts to reform Harvard, the very first step within this broader effort, were marked by dissension and ended in failure.

The need to reform Harvard was painfully apparent to everyone who had observed the great universities of Europe.[66] George Ticknor, Edward Everett, Joseph Cogswell, and George Bancroft had all returned with a humbled sense of America's finest academic institution, but also a missionary's commitment to its improvement. Nor were they alone. A number of alumni and Harvard supporters were disturbed by the unruliness of the student body and the college's tarnished reputation. The four young academics saw in this concern, along with President Kirkland's support, the opportunity to move Harvard toward the great universities of Europe.

But this proved far more difficult than first believed. Neither Cogswell nor Bancroft experienced much success or satisfaction in their Harvard careers. Cogswell felt unsupported by the Harvard Corporation in his attempts to improve the library. Bancroft, with his effete manner and arrogant ways, quickly became the target of student jokes and pranks.[67] Within two years both had left, eventually to start their school at Round Hill. Consequently, it was left to Ticknor and Everett to lead the reform effort. With Everett increasingly distracted by thoughts of a political career, the task fell almost exclusively to Ticknor.

The proposals he advanced were marked by their realism. Harvard was a long way from Göttingen. The first step, he thus argued, was to turn Harvard into a "well disciplined high school." The students' behavior must be improved. They drank excessively and spent far too much time in Boston. The academic standards and methods of instruction were also poor. The primary means of instruction was the recitation; students were assigned lessons and then evaluated on their ability to recite them back to the tutors. In recent years the school's faculty had grown, and the lecture program had been increased, but these remained poorly integrated within the rest of the curriculum. Student attendance was irregular, notes were rarely taken, and the material was not incorporated into their lessons or examinations.

To remedy these problems Ticknor recommended that entrance exams be more rigorous and that instructors be required to teach and not just monitor recitations. The students should be grouped according to ability, rather than alphabetically as they were currently, and annual progress and the awarding of degrees should be determined by an outside group of examiners. To improve discipline he also suggested that students be required to wear uniforms on and off campus throughout their careers. Not only would this breed élan, it would make misconduct less anonymous.[68]

Despite the reputation Ticknor enjoyed and Kirkland's professed support for reform, Ticknor's proposals were greeted with more irritation than enthusiasm. The faculty charged him with stirring up local feeling against Harvard and creating unnecessary concern. But in 1823 the "Great Rebellion" provoked the Board of Overseers to explore the cause of reform further. Student life at Harvard had always been characterized by a certain degree of unruliness, but the class scheduled to graduate in that year was an unusually rowdy bunch. Their secret gatherings, bonfires and explosions, mistreatment of tutors, and disrespect for professors had kept university officials on edge for four years. In addition, a division had emerged in the student body between the "high fellows" and the less rebellious "blacks." When one of the blacks informed on a high fellow, leading to the rowdy's expulsion, his classmates pledged to leave school until he was reinstated and the informant was removed from the commencement exercises.[69]

Faced with so overt a challenge just days before commencement, the most important event of the academic year, when so much attention was focused on the college, school officials decided to expel forty-three of the seventy seniors—including the son of John Quincy Adams. The officials hoped with this action to signal their intentions to crack down on student misbehavior, but this show of resolve was not enough for observers on the outside. The Massachusetts General Court refused to renew Harvard's annual grant, and reformers seized the opportunity to advance their case more forcefully. This group, which included James Jackson, Joseph Story, George Emerson, and John Gorham Palfrey, began to meet at Ticknor's home. Their eventual recommendations to the Board of Overseers drew largely upon Ticknor's plan, as well as his new recommendation that the college be divided into departments, and that the students be allowed to focus their studies more narrowly once they had completed the core curriculum. Noting that students needed to be more thoroughly prepared for the more complex professional careers that awaited them and expressing the emerging emphasis of his peers on specialization and professional expertise, he urged the university to increase its course offerings and encourage more concentrated advanced study. Once students had mastered a list of largely classical courses—Greek, Latin, moral and political philosophy, rhetoric, mathematics, physical science, and history—they should be allowed to pursue expertise in such elective areas as chemistry, anatomy, botany, and modern languages.

From this point onward the controversy was driven more by political than pedagogical questions. The faculty continued to oppose Ticknor's efforts, arguing for the most part that any efforts at reform should be initiated internally. Ticknor's committee, the faculty complained, was composed of more outsiders than insiders—several alumni and supporters from Boston's Federalist community and only one other faculty member, James Jackson. In addition, both Ticknor and Jackson were nonresident professors and as such somewhat removed from the rest of the faculty.[70] As a result, the current controversy took on the added dimension of turf warfare. The resident faculty united in their opposition to these externally generated reforms, and even the faculty members who had encouraged the formation of this ad hoc group, Andrews Norton and Henry Ware, along with some of Ticknor's best friends, including Edward Everett and Jared Sparks, opposed the implementation of the committee's recommendations.

The controversy grew even more complex when the resident faculty proposed that they alone should be allowed to serve as Corporation Fellows. The Corporation, which served as a board of trustees, had originally been composed of faculty members. But by 1820 it had become the custom to select businessmen and professionals to fill these roles. Arguing that merchants should no more run a school than academics should meddle in business, Norton suggested that the historical character of the Corporation should be restored.

Neither the Corporation nor the Board of Overseers, the board of local citizens—ministers, public officials, and prominent men of affairs—charged with advising the Corporation, endorsed this faculty proposal. But within this sensitized climate they also shied away from the sorts of sweeping reforms suggested by Ticknor and his group. They did approve the introduction of departmental organization of the college, regroup the students by ability, and urge the introduction of a few electives. But these were only half measures, and in the following months they were effectively undermined by a noncompliant faculty.

With significant reform all but a dead issue, the controversy entered its final phase with the resignation of President John Kirkland in 1828. Charged with administrative and fiscal incompetence by Corporation Fellow Nathaniel Bowditch, an ally of Ticknor, Kirkland resigned, leaving Everett and Ticknor as the leading candidates to succeed him. But in the end the Corporation selected the more moderate Josiah Quincy. Neither Ticknor nor Everett was all that interested in the position. Ticknor hated all the academic infighting, and Everett was set on a political career. But it seems that the Fellows were moved less by these considerations than by an interest in terminating the controversy. In Quincy they chose a capable administrator and a moderate reformer. During his ad-

ministration the number of course offerings was increased and concomitantly the opportunity for student choice. But he was far from a visionary.
The more ambitious components of the reformers' agenda were abandoned. His "Scale of Merit" restored the traditional methods of recitation
and examination. And his affirmation of Harvard's traditional structure
prevented the development of the more specialized curriculum Ticknor
and his peers prescribed.

Ticknor was able to advance some of his progressive ideas within his
Department of Modern Languages. But broader efforts at reform went
unpursued until after the Civil War.[71] Although he eventually would be
credited with breaking up the "intellectual sterility" of American academia and preparing the way for the modern American college, in the short
run his efforts brought more frustration than success. And perhaps most
painfully, this controversy shattered the messianic unity of the young
Federalists driving the reform. At the peak of the controversy, Ticknor
submitted an article to the *North American Review* advancing his position.
But shying away from the fight and fearing further internal disagreement,
the *Review* decided not to print it. Ticknor retreated in disgust; he never
again submitted an article to the journal. The conception of the university
placed at the heart of these young Federalists' institutional vision had
stalled on the pages of the *North American Review*.

Even the new law school these young Federalists promoted at Harvard
did not fare well in this decade. The choice of Isaac Parker to fill the
Royall chair proved to be a poor one. A respected chief justice of the state
supreme court, he lacked both the temperament and the time to be an
effective professor. Described by Joseph Story as "a good-natured, lazy
boy when at college . . . a good-natured, lazy lawyer . . . a good-natured,
lazy judge," he was known on the bench more for his instinctive sense of
justice than for the depth of his legal understanding or the discipline of
his mind. He "always decided right," concluded Story, "but gave miserable reasons for his opinions."[72] The lectures he offered were shallow
and fell far short of providing any systematic training in the law. Asahel
Stearns, given the task of creating a more systematic course of graduate
study, had more time and discipline than Parker. Under his direction the
law school developed a more comprehensive program of lectures, directed
readings, dissertations, and moot courts. But the law he taught was becoming quickly obsolete. Emphasizing classical land law, he neglected the
sorts of law increasingly necessary in the expanding Republic. He offered

nothing pertaining to the new forms of business organization and regulation and nothing to prepare students for the increasingly complex and important relations between federal and state governments. As a result the school failed to attract students—by 1828 there were only two—and the college demanded the resignation of both professors.[73]

Not all of the institutional objectives articulated in this journal were as unsuccessfully pursued. Although these young Federalists failed to advance their vision of the university, they did succeed both in advancing the cause of judicial reform and in defending the common law against Republican reformers.[74] In doing so they furthered a process begun by their fathers. Perfecting the machinery of the American judiciary and clarifying the character of American law were tasks made necessary by the American Revolution. The termination of the British courts required the formation of new institutions, and the rejection of English rule raised questions concerning the status of English common law in America. In Massachusetts the constitution ratified in 1780 fell far short of answering all these questions for the system adopted was inefficient and complex. Litigants were provided access to too many appeals, the attorney fee system encouraged lawyers to prolong cases rather than resolve them, and the bench suffered from an inability to attract quality jurists. Reform was widely discussed, but it was not until the election of Jefferson, and the subsequent recognition that the judiciary offered the best refuge and means of protection for Federalism, that concerted measures were taken.

The leading figure in these efforts was Theodore Sedgwick. A High Federalist, he left public life when Jefferson was elected, but the offer of a seat on the state supreme court brought him out of retirement. Apparently recognizing this as an opportunity to strengthen the court as a Federalist stronghold, he advocated a series of measures designed to strengthen the judiciary and, in particular, increase the power of judges. In order to attract better judges, he urged that salaries be raised and that judges be allowed a share of the fees collected by the court. To increase their power relative to juries, he argued that juries should never be allowed to interpret the law—a practice not uncommon during the pre-Revolutionary period. This was a responsibility better suited to the bench. And to ensure that the court spoke on questions of law in unified rather than divided language, he recommended that a single judge be allowed to preside over most trials, rather than the entire court, and that the court's decisions be published.

To the extent Sedgwick could convince Republicans that these measures were aimed at increasing efficiency he won their support. But they resisted all measures that promised to strengthen the power of the judges and the professional attorneys. They opposed his attempts to raise salaries and attach a pension to court seats. They defended the right of juries to interpret the law. They proposed that more cases be heard by justices of the peace and that some sort of local arbitration boards be established. They pressed for the right of laymen to argue their own cases and attacked lawyers as leeches preying upon the public.[75] They also suggested that judicial seats be made elective offices just like the other branches of government. Finally, Republicans argued that the system of law itself needed simplification. They suggested that the system of common law be replaced by a simpler code—a system that would be accessible to laymen and defined by legislative rather than judicial bodies.

Despite this opposition Federalist reformers managed to enact much of their program between 1803 and 1810. A new system whereby single judges were allowed to hear cases was initiated, the decisions of the state supreme court were collected for publication, and the exclusive authority of the judge to interpret the law was established. The power of juries was reduced so much that lawyers began appealing cases regularly, and successfully, on the grounds that the jury had ruled contrary to the instructions given them by the judge. But the status of the common law remained in dispute. During the 1820s Republican critics were still finding it at odds with America's historic and democratic character. Why, they asked, should the American legal system be ruled by this complex web of precedent and tradition rather than a code of clear and accessible legislative acts? The common law, they argued, served only to muddy the legal waters and left common people at the mercy of lawyers. Why, in a democracy, these Republican reformers asked, should the makers of law be unable to understand it? Why should the branch assigned the task of interpreting the law be allowed, in addition, to make it? Why, in a country which traced its existence to a formal declaration of independence, should the English common law continue to exert so much influence?

The young Federalist contributors to the *North American Review* engaged aggressively in this debate. Although they feigned a scholarly consideration of the entire question, they were almost unanimous in their defense of the common law. Edward Everett was one of the few to disagree. Praising the code of Justinian, he argued that legislative codification might save lawyers time and provide laymen easier access to the law. Henry Dwight Sedgwick, although siding clearly with the majority, admitted he, too, was troubled that the greater part of American law, albeit the "better part," was "neither traditional . . . nor statute . . . but judicial law, enacted by the sole authority of the judges."[76]

But few other Federalist commentators seem to have been so troubled. The vast majority of the contributors to the *North American Review* rallied unequivocally to the defense of the common law. It was, argued Parker, the "recorded wisdom of times which are past, drawn from every civilized country in ancient and modern times." It represented, quite simply, the "learning and experience of the ages." Joseph Porter agreed: the common law was an indication of a civilized country. This web of precedent was a barometer of a nation's sophistication; "in exact proportion . . . as those are advanced in civilization and refinement, do these become numerous, extensive, and intricate."[77]

Nor had the common law been thrown out, along with imperial rule, in 1776. It was true that the American common law was rooted in the English. But since its introduction, it had undergone a process of evolution and elaboration. By definition, the common law was "an elastic garment" made to fit a particular situation at a particular time. Although rooted in English tradition, by the time of the Revolution, the American common law was markedly independent, linked, perhaps, as "separate branches of the same tree" but singular enough to be classified as autonomous.[78]

The rejection of imperial English rule thus did not represent the rejection of common law. Nor did the Declaration of Independence reduce man to that state of nature which would have meant the obliteration of all existing law. The common law persisted and was presupposed in the writing of the Constitution. Although Federalist jurists rejected the more extreme argument that the English common law had rushed in to fill all of the gaps left by the vagueness of the Constitution and statutory law, they were adamant in their belief that an American common law was a continuous and essential component of the American legal system.[79]

Now more than ever, these jurists argued, the common law was a necessity. The "complexity and variety of human actions" required a complex legal structure, said the "pseudo-republican" Joseph Story. Caleb Cushing agreed that "the shifting multitudes of a polished commercial people, whose interests embrace the whole range of the globe," depended on an equally elaborate system of law. No statutory code, added Nathaniel Appleton Haven, which like a "coat of mail . . . admits of but few movements," could serve the needs of a dynamic and expansive people.[80] Nor could the legislative branch be expected to keep proper pace. Cumbersome and cautious, the legislature could never apply the time or the expertise necessary; it could never "investigate the complicated details of this most intricate and extensive and rapidly growing of all the sciences, take up title after title, rule after rule, principle after principle."[81] Common law—judicial law—provided a remedy for this defect within the democratic system. To those who pointed out the contradiction inherent in this vision, these clever advocates responded that it was they who were the true defenders of freedom. "It is not in lands of liberty and equal rights that the business of codifying flourishes," argued Porter.[82] Although attractive on the surface, these attempts at codification and simplification were dangerous, agreed Parker somewhat more paternally. The "complexity of the laws is the price of freedom . . . despotism alone is equal to the task of establishing a simple and invariable standard."[83]

Through the cleverest of inversions Federalist jurists were able to argue that they were the true defenders of the liberty, diversity, and dynamism of democratic society. Cushing might concede to the reformers that the multiplicity of legal journals was making the law excessively complex and suggest a more selective process of compilation and publication. But Porter would not concede even this. These reports, even in their duplication and excess, were "precisely the way by which all the sciences improve." Yes, they made the law more complex; yes, they made it all the more inaccessible to the common man. But the man of "real science," the man upon whom the legal system must depend, did "not very often complain of the multiplication of books upon his favorite theme."[84]

The defenders of the common law carried the day, and in a final piece of intellectual arrogance, they speculated on these questions within the context of America's historic role. The quality of English jurisprudence was slipping. Theron Metcalf, one of America's most distinguished legal scholars, argued that English law was muddied by vestiges of its feudal past, and its current practitioners were far from Blackstone and Coke. The quality of American legal science, on the other hand, was making dramatic strides. "Under circumstances of national tranquility," noted Nathaniel Haven, "the science advances with surer, because soberer steps."[85] The United States Supreme Court in its "greater patience of research . . .

higher reach of intellect, [and] profound ratiocination," added Metcalf, was far superior to any British court. American jurisprudence, added Haven, displayed greater creativity and inclusivity than its stagnant British counterpart.[86] Cushing saw a propitious sign in the first edition of the *United States Law Journal and Civilian Magazine.*

Was this to be the mark that America would make on the world of law and government? While Republicans continued to wax eloquent on the future of American democracy and proclaimed the advance of its egalitarian philosophies around the world, Caleb Cushing's ability to see in the American perfection of the common law the fulfillment of the American experiment provides a measurement of how far these young Federalists had reconciled themselves to democratic society, yet how far apart from Republican conceptions of that society they still remained. While Jackson announced the advent of the common man, Cushing celebrated the advancement of a far more narrow group, "writers of inquisitive minds, sterling sense, deep science, and patriotic sentiment." This vanguard of specialized and carefully trained men of science would elucidate America's "grand, but yet unfinished system of civil polity . . . as a model for the imitation and guidance of other nations."[87]

By the election of Jackson, these young Federalist innovators had thus gone a long way toward reimagining the institutional framework of the young Republic. Confronted with a political system that was less secure and accessible than in the past, they invested in extragovernmental organizations that aimed at the same goals of social cohesion. As this vision unfolded, these organizations grew into more permanent institutions that defined and were maintained by a professional, specialized elite. Holding this institutional framework together was a web of law that required scientific and professional execution. At the center of it all lay the university, incorporating the eclecticism of the democratic society within its decorous walls but disseminating back to that society a more unified and authoritative set of moral, religious, and legal truths.

For many of these young Federalists it was indeed a promising vision. But for those who looked more closely at its terms and implementation, it was not an entirely reassuring one. It relied on an understanding of the university that bore little resemblance to American realities. Even the most moderate of reform measures, those which would have provided only a half step toward the fulfillment of its academic institutional goals, met resistance or outright failure. And even where these Federalists' efforts were more successful, there was a troubling discordance with the broader directions of American society. The vision of the specialist contrasted sharply with the celebration of the common man. In addition, the defense of the common law contained an understanding of America's political mission which meshed poorly with more popular conceptions. Thus although the theoreticians of the *North American Review* may have drawn some hope from this vision, it was far too early to proclaim their attempts at institutional adaptation a success.

Even at the time theirs seemed an ambiguous achievement—and as the century progressed the nature of their achievement, the extent which their efforts could be labeled successful, grew even more unclear. In 1837 Edward Everett appointed Horace Mann to a seat on the newly created State Board of Education. Mann was a logical choice, having guided the founding bill through the state legislature. Everett no doubt also appreciated the similarities between Mann's educational vision and that earlier articulated in the *North American Review.* Centrally administered, publicly funded, and staffed by university-trained teachers, the state educational system envisioned by Mann was structurally compatible with that laid out by young Federalist reformers. Moreover, Mann's pedagogical theories were rooted in the Unitarian theology and faculty psychology so central to the young Federalists' view of man. Much like Joseph Cogswell, Mann argued that schools should address the physical and emotional development of their students, as well as their intellectual and moral growth. Teachers should cultivate relationships with their students based more on affection than fear and strive to build an appreciation for knowledge, rather than its mere accumulation. Through a carefully structured and age-sensitive system of learning, schools should aim ultimately to nurture in their students those higher faculties which would make them not only self-governing individuals but also productive citizens.[88]

But if the creation of this state system and Mann's appointment represented something of a victory for Everett and his *North American* friends, it was a tenuous one at best. Their vision may have been realized, but any hope that this would stabilize their social status or strengthen the positions of men of their caste in the emerging institutional order was disappointed, for the normal school established in 1838 as part of this vision for the training and certification of teachers admitted only women. By this time the cause advanced in the *Review* had been appropriated not only by Mann but also a new group of reformers led by Robert

Rantoul Jr. For these men priority should be given to the preparation of female teachers—largely "because there is more unappropriated female talent . . . because females can be educated cheaper . . . and will teach cheaper after they are qualified."[89]

There had always been a certain blind spot, a curious limitation regarding the role of women within the educational vision of these Federalist reformers. For all their foresight in discussing the university, despite all their support for a broadening of educational opportunities, they failed to anticipate, or perhaps refused to acknowledge, the feminization of teaching already under way as they wrote.[90] Granted, the more rapid process of feminization was still a generation away. Between 1840 and 1865 the percentage of male teachers in Massachusetts public schools would drop from 61 percent to 14 percent.[91] Still, by the 1820s women were playing an ever larger role, especially in primary education.

The closest thing to an endorsement of this trend by these young Federalists was offered by George Ticknor in his 1824 description of Boston's free schools. This system, which he recommended as a model for imitation, contained a lowest tier—primary schools teaching reading and spelling to 2,600 children, ages four to seven—staffed by female teachers. But a perhaps more significant proposal was offered in his discussion of the Lancastrian school method written in the same year. As communities attempted to address their growing educational needs, he argued, rising costs would require some innovation. His recommendation was that the Lancastrian system be explored. As most effectively modeled at a high school in Edinburgh, this system used older students to instruct the younger. The system of "mutual instruction" promised greater student involvement, expanded student attention, and most importantly, reduced instructional costs.[92]

What makes Ticknor's suggestion so important is that it was offered at a time when New England's schools were turning increasingly to women teachers, primarily as a means of curbing costs. Although educators initially argued that women were suited only to teach the younger students, the fact that women earned significantly less than male teachers encouraged administrators to hire women at all levels of education with increasing frequency.[93] Ticknor's recommendation of the Lancastrian system in this context thus represents not just a cost-cutting proposal but an alternative to, if not rejection of, the feminization of teaching already under way.

At least Ticknor acknowledged the participation of women in the field. Somewhat curiously, the other contributors to the journal failed even to comment on their efforts. Given the fact that contributors regularly affirmed the nurturing sensibilities of women and women's unique contributions to children's literature, their failure to outline more explicitly a place for women in their educational vision is all the more surprising.

Perhaps the explanation lies in their more pressing commitment to the cause of professionalization. Although they did not discuss the role of women, they repeatedly discussed the importance of improved teacher training and more thorough graduate school preparation. Orville Dewey complained that "there are schools for the education of the clergy, of lawyers, and physicians. Why should there not be schools for teachers of youth? There are special qualifications for this profession, qualifications as peculiar and specific, as for any other of the learned professions." George Henry Bode added that not only did a teacher need "as serious and thorough a preparation for his practice, as a divine, or lawyer, or physician," but the advancement of the other professions rested on the promotion of teacher education—"the standard" of the others "will be raised, in proportion to the general improvements in education." Both contributors to the *North American Review* encouraged state legislatures to establish and fund institutions for teacher education. Jared Sparks argued even further that this should be the states' highest educational priority. "Legislative aid in favor of education," he suggested, "is wanted in nothing so much at present, as in providing some means for creating a better supply of teachers in the common schools."[94] But to the extent that the professionalization of education was critical to their vision of the new institutional order, it was equally critical that they not allow the inclusion of women in this vision. For given antebellum concepts of work and power and the period's notions of gender and aptitude, to include a place for women would undercut much of what these young men hoped to accomplish by advancing the cause of teacher professionalization. By including a place for women in their vision of professionalization, they would undercut its credibility and thus its promise as a guarantor of status and power.

The tightrope these Federalists walked in promoting the professionalization of teaching without endorsing its feminization was reflected in Samuel Sewall's review of Catherine Beecher's pamphlet on education. Beecher, as principal of the Hartford Female Seminary, complained that teacher preparation did not rise to the level of the other professions. Parents demand more expertise from their shoemaker, she argued, than their children's teachers. She coupled this with the suggestion that motherhood required similar preparation. "What is the profession of a woman? Is it not to form immortal minds, and to watch, to nurse, and to rear the bodily system?" In responding to this problematic take on professionalization, Sewall seconded her concerns about teacher preparation but ignored her comments on motherhood. In addition, in discussing her argument he employed gender-exclusive language. The teacher should ensure that "the boy" understands, not just regurgitates, and the teacher—"he should endeavor to interest his pupils."[95]

Perhaps what made Beecher's argument ultimately acceptable to the editors of the *North American Review* was that she went no further than to call for female teachers in female institutions. Moreover, in doing so she implicitly suggested that they were ill suited for boys' schools. Teaching depends, she said, on a degree of familiarity between teacher and student, an "intimate knowledge of feelings, affections, and weaknesses." While this made women uniquely suited to the teaching of girls— "female institutions ought to be conducted exclusively by females"— they were, by the same logic, poorly suited to positions in the more numerous and influential boys' schools.[96]

But if women were thereby sacrificed to the greater cause of professionalization, the young Federalists were doubly disappointed. If the opening of the normal school at Lexington dashed their hopes of preserving the male hegemony of the teaching profession, the future course of professionalization represented an even broader challenge to their ambitions. Contrary to any hope that these efforts would serve to strengthen their own privileged positions in America's changing society, they appear ultimately to have loosened their own lock on these positions of status. Far from providing a new means of securing their own status and reestablishing their own public importance, their efforts to professionalize certain occupations and institutionalize and objectify the paths of entry seem instead to have laid the groundwork for these young Federalists' eventual displacement by members of the middle class.

Burton Bledstein has argued that the culture of professionalism emerged during the mid-Victorian era as a means of reconciling the twin urges of the aspiring middle class—the one toward innovation, enterprise, and mobility and the other toward control, self-regulation, and discipline. Within the concept of professionalism, with its regulated paths to social and occupational advancement, they found a tool by which these potentially conflicting elements of middle-class culture could be reconciled—a set of "universal and predictable rules to provide a formal context for the competitive spirit of individual egos."[97]

Bledstein's conclusions regarding the importance of professionalism for the middle class are difficult to challenge. But the cultivation of a similar ethic of professionalism by young Federalists in the years following the War of 1812 renders Bledstein's conclusions regarding its class and period of origins questionable. Bledstein was quick to point out that class was more a cultural than a socioeconomic designation, a set of attitudes about one's place and potential in society rather than a fixed station in the social hierarchy. Nevertheless, his argument that professionalism provided a means of "emulating the status of those above one on the social ladder" implies that even this cultural class had a certain socioeconomic basis.[98]

Yet clearly the upper-class contributors to the *North American Review* and their friends James Jackson and John Warren at the Massachusetts General Hospital and Josiah Quincy at City Hall had much earlier articulated this same ethic of professionalism. Like the ambitious middle class Bledstein described, they recognized that "educated knowledge was the beginning of power," and they would have found confirmation of their efforts in his conclusion that by the second half of the century, "legitimate authority now resided in special places, like the courtroom, the classroom, and the hospital; and it resided in special words shared only by experts."[99]

It would seem that the culture of professionalism was less a creation than an appropriation of the middle class, that the ethic being articulated by members of Boston's upper-class Federalist community was by midcentury appropriated by the middle classes as a means of regulating their own ambitions and attaining occupational parity with the upper class. In this there is more than a little irony. Although Boston Federalists articulated this vision as a means of enhancing the occupational and social stability of democratic society, they also saw in it a means of preserving their own elite status. Within the concept of specialization and expertise, they envisioned a means of compensating for their loss of status in other arenas. But in their objectifying and institutionalizing the paths of entry, in making graduate education and state licensing rather than an apprenticeship within the office of a practicing professional the means of acquiring professional status, they opened the door to middle-class advancement. Consequently, the more thoroughly their ethic of professionalism was established, the more difficult it became to retain control of the professions as status preserves for the upper class. As with their literary agenda, the more successfully they advanced their ideas, the more quickly they hastened their own displacement.

This can be seen most clearly in the results of their efforts to professionalize the law through the advancement of graduate education. Underlying their efforts to improve the Harvard law program was the premise that the "scientification" of the law would protect their status. Through the systemization of legal education, they would redefine the law as a profession for a uniformly and rigorously educated elite. The impact of their efforts has been described—although these efforts were perhaps critical in providing intellectual support for the new school, poor leadership and a dated curriculum hindered the school in its first years. But although the law school struggled throughout the 1820s, it enjoyed great success in the 1830s. Many scholars have attributed this success to the appointment to the law school faculty in 1829 of Joseph Story, whose prestige attracted far more students to the college.[100] But Gerard Gawalt has argued that the real source of Harvard's increased enrollment was the passing of a new set of state licensing statutes in 1835. These enabled a student to enter the practice of the law after taking an eighteen-month course of study and passing an exam. Because an apprenticeship still lasted three years, prospective lawyers could more quickly enter practice through a graduate education, which cut their preparation time in half.[101]

The windfall for Harvard, argued Gawalt, was dramatic. It is after this point that enrollments increased significantly. But although marking the success of young Federalist efforts to standardize legal education, locate training within the university, and redefine law as a science and a profession, these new statutes also had the ironic effect of opening up access to the bar and eliminating the hegemony that New England's upper class exercised over the profession. Gawalt has demonstrated that the apprenticeship system ensured limited access to the profession. With county bar associations restricting the number of clerks allowed in an office and demanding that local study precede local practice, established attorneys could control entry to the profession and consequently maintain both the financial and the status rewards of exclusivity. While the rest of America was moving toward an increasingly open and democratic set of conditions, he argued, "the legal class in Massachusetts, at least, was becoming an increasingly closed profession." But these new statutes eliminated this hegemony. As young Federalists saw their efforts to professionalize the law realized, entrance into the legal profession became, contrary to their intentions, "at least superficially, more attainable for people without family wealth or connections."[102]

A similar argument could be made in regard to perhaps their greatest institutional achievement—their defense of the common law. On the surface this appears to have been the culmination of a long process through which the power inherent in the courts shifted from juries to judges and highly trained and specialized attorneys. It appears to be the epitome of what these Federalists sought to do—to create a system whereby the disorder threatened by an expanding and increasingly pluralistic community was contained by a legal system which rested power in a small group of highly educated men. William Nelson has illustrated that within the eighteenth-century legal system, the jury held the balance of power. Allowed to rule on questions of law and fact, the juries acted as effective checks on both judge and lawyers. This was partially the result of the courts' structure. As most trials were presided over by a panel of judges who often presented conflicting instructions to the jury, juries were left with the ultimate power to rule on the points of law involved. The power of lawyers was equally limited because their essential responsibilities dealt with procedural rather than substantive questions—their primary task was not to argue a point of law before the jury but rather to maneuver the court through a series of procedural devices to that point of law upon which the jury should rule. But the power of juries was also rooted in the moral and cultural unanimity from which they spoke. Judges, as agents of the state, could not rule counter to the wall of cultural and moral consensus represented in the jury. Consequently, control over the content of the law lay with the people as represented by juries. "The legal system could not serve as an instrument for the enforcement of coherent social policies formulated by practical authorities, either legislative or executive . . . when those policies were unacceptable to the men who happened to be serving on a particular jury."[103]

But in the half century following the Revolution, all this changed. The cultural unanimity that had given the public its coherence and strength slowly gave way. The forces of libertarianism let loose by the Revolution opened the door to competing religious groups and ethical codes. The resulting ethical confusion both demanded some response from the courts and enabled judges and lawyers to strengthen their own positions. With juries no longer able to draw upon consensus, it was left to judges to impose direction and uniformity and to highly specialized lawyers to weave the common law into a coherent legal framework.

From this angle it appears that the defense and preservation of the common law completed the process of transferring power from the people as represented by juries to the legal establishment. Within the new system, as Nelson described it, the jury "ceased to be an adjunct of local communities which articulated into positive law the ethical standards of those communities" and became instead only "the adjunct of the court," controlled by judges and lawyers highly trained and drawn from the upper class.[104] But there was also a corresponding shift in the character of the law that must have been less satisfying for these Federalists. Although the advance of pluralism left their status within the judicial system enhanced, it also worked to replace the traditional law, which valued stability and the preservation of the status quo, with a system that encouraged change and competition and accepted the legitimacy of instability. The new law posited a conception of the contract that retained nothing of the traditional understanding of "fair exchange," elaborated an understanding of property which encouraged its more easy transfer, and redefined debt and bankruptcy in such a way that excessive risk was no longer seen as a sinful attempt to advance beyond one's station but instead became the positive and necessary concomitant of an expanding capitalist economy. As Nelson and others, including J. Willard Hurst, have pointed out, while the pre-Revolutionary understanding of law pursued objectives that were more moral than economic and articulated conceptions of property, contracts, and the community that ensured stability, the new system of law valued "dynamic rather than static property, property at motion or at risk rather than property secure and at rest."[105] While pre-Revolutionary law acted to preserve the privileged status of the economic elite, the new system, according to Lawrence Friedman, sought to "further the interests of the middle class mass, to foster growth, to release and harness the energy latent in the commonwealth."[106]

As a result, although these Federalists may have convinced themselves that they had succeeded in placing themselves at the top of the legal system and preserving a system of common law that required maintenance and interpretation by experts, the character of the law over which they would preside was inherently unstable. If successful in the short run in preserving their status, they helped foster a legal system which in the long run would facilitate their displacement.

For the young Federalists of the *North American Review,* their efforts were indeed double-edged. Much like their efforts to establish a national literature, it appears that the more they succeeded in advancing their agenda, the further they undercut their own positions. Success bred failure; success in advancing their vision only opened the door to their displacement. As they advanced the cause of professional education, they only accelerated the rate at which aspiring members of the middle class were able to challenge their hegemony in the professions. As they succeeded in defending the common law against codification, they failed to ensure that the law itself would not prove hostile to the stability they pursued. As they elaborated a vision of the highly specialized expert, they articulated a vision that hinted at detachment as much as integration, that threatened to isolate them in their expertise rather than bring them status and recognition. Within the pages of the *North American Review,* these young Federalists thus laid out a promising vision, but where realized, it did not serve them as they had hoped.

CHAPTER 7

HISTORY

➤➤ In the years between 1815 and 1828, the contributors to the *North American Review* elaborated a vision that promised both their continued influence and the preservation of social order. In implementing the vision, they met considerable resistance. And within the vision itself there were troubling undercurrents and a continuing disagreement with the more general directions of American thought and society that, in retrospect, should not have been ignored. Yet overall, this vision represented an impressive rethinking of their fathers' conservative ideology. Moreover, despite its flaws, it seems to have effectively reconciled these young Federalists to the changing social and political landscape. Whereas their fathers had reviled the republican town hall filled with the "breath of fat and greasy citizens," William Tudor spoke prosaically of the annual public school ceremonies.[1] Here education was honored, merit was rewarded, and young boys were introduced "into the public forum, where they are hereafter to discharge their duty as citizen." Far from unsettling, Tudor found it "the most pleasing, and certainly the most republican festival, I ever witnessed."[2] Whereas the last generation had identified Jefferson as a hapless dreamer, the dupe of the French and the subverter of the Constitution, members of the younger generation labeled him a true patriot, overrated perhaps as a thinker but a vital member of the founding generation nonetheless.[3] And whereas the Louisiana Purchase and the resulting expansion westward had portended for their elders the decline of New England's influence and the subversion of the American polity and culture, Edward Everett was able to see in the movement west the advance of both civilization and culture. America's frontier population was not crude, its advance was remarkably rapid, and despite the shifting of population and political power, New England "continued to advance in population, wealth, and arts with no perceptible diminution in the ratio of progress."[4]

For these young Federalists the articulation of a viable conservative vision for life in democratic society left them reassured amid the political and social changes that surrounded them. In addition, it brought them more confidently to terms with what they perceived as the overall course of history. No single feature of their thought stands out more sharply in contrast to the ideology of their parents than their confidence in the general progressive path of history. No feature of their thought reveals more fully their coming to terms with democracy than their willingness to share in the age's historical optimism and faith.

A certain historical optimism can be discerned in the earliest periods of New England culture. Framed within the terms of Christian millennialism and encouraged by the Puritans' sense of their errand of reform and regeneration, New Englanders' confidence in the direction of history and their place within it was voiced from the start. Although on occasion members of the clergy bewailed the state of immorality or spiritual declension using the language of the Apocalypse, the stridency of their rhetoric suggests their pessimism was more the exception than the rule. The regressive view of temporal history that defined premillennialism was never very well suited to New England's sense of itself, and thus by the time of the Great Awakening postmillennialism and a belief in America's central place within history's progressive course were central features within New England's religious and cultural identity.

For most of the eighteenth century, certainly through the Revolutionary period, this millennial-based view of historical progress was a critical component of American ideology. Not only did it reenforce the American sense of self, but it offered an interpretive framework for analyzing historical events. During the imperial crisis it helped Americans identify the forces at play, and during the war itself it provided what Ruth Bloch has called the "visionary dimension of American Revolutionary ideology."[5] But in the years following the Revolution, as political and social conditions changed, premillennialism and its inherent historical pessimism rose to the surface of orthodox New England Congregationalism and New England Federalist thought. Well suited to the siege mentality of religious and political orthodoxy, premillennialism helped to explain the infidelity that threatened America from abroad, the materialism and decay of civic virtue that plagued the body politic in New England, and the usurpation of Federalist power from Boston to Washington, D.C. For Federalists like Fisher Ames, the theological and historical pessimism of premillennialism offered both explanation and consolation for their political and social displacement.

But the Federalists of the next generation rejected this historical pessimism. They rejected the premillennial gloom of their fathers and joined their democratic co-patriots in their visions of almost inevitable progress—their visions of a steady and mechanical course of history that would lead toward social and political perfection. In so doing, they embraced a sense of history that served Americans in a variety of ways. It provided a call for reform and social improvement; by placing perfection in the foreseeable future, it imposed a demand for increased social responsibility. But it also provided a rationale for expansion and the most chauvinistic forms of nationalism. Given Federalism's tradition of social paternalism, it is not surprising that these young Federalists would embrace a vision of history that encouraged increased social responsibility. But given the older fears of regional displacement and Federalists' self-conscious cultivation of moderation and gentility, it is surprising to see the extent to which they also embraced that element of this historical vision that justified reckless expansionism and the displacement of an entire race.

Among the more ardent defenders of expansion and the consequent removal of the native populations was Lewis Cass.[6] A frontier soldier and statesman, an eventual Democratic presidential hopeful, he expressed views that were perhaps the predictable product of his experience and his politics. But having been born in New England of Federalist parents and educated at Exeter, he retained ties to the seaboard and an audience in the *North American Review.* A repeat contributor to the journal, he offered his "realistic" appraisal of the Indian character and its implications for national policy. Cruel and savage, knowing only hunting and war, in Cass's view the "noble savage" of James Fenimore Cooper and John Heckewilder was not of the "book of nature."[7] There was, he granted, something intriguing in the Indians' form of government and system of justice, but not so intriguing as to earn for them an unlimited right to possession of the land.[8] Cass had no patience for the "system of legal metaphysics, that would give to a few naked and wandering savages, a perpetual title to an immense continent."[9] It was folly, he said, to argue that these savages could fix the boundaries of civilization's advance. Although it was perhaps regrettable that this placed a body of "wretched, forlorn" people on the country's frontiers, the fault was their own.[10] It was their unassimilable character, their failure to imitate the example of whites, and their persisting improvidence and lack of industry that brought them to their fate, not any mistreatment on the part of the white settlers.

Cass was not entirely unsympathetic. He suggested that efforts be taken to protect the Indians from white traders, that the sale of alcohol be restricted, and that a sum of money be appropriated annually for the purpose of civilizing the Indians. But these, he acknowledged, were measures of limited value and at best would only postpone the inevitable. Eventually the Indian must "disappear with the forest . . . whose existence seems essential to his own."[11]

It is perhaps unsurprising that Cass, a frontiersman, would develop a cavalier attitude toward the impending extinction of a race. It was perhaps to be expected that as a Democrat he would justify these affairs in the name of expansionism and manifest destiny. Less understandable was the extent to which his unrelocated, politically unconverted New England brethren echoed his views. Edward Everett, in particular, stands out for the extent to which he shared Cass's ideas. Everett would draw attention in 1830 as a friend of the Native American for his opposition to the Removal Act. His biographers have succeeded in establishing his reputation as "the chivalrous champion for the just and honorable treatment of the Indians."[12] In doing so, however, they have had to look past the position he initially maintained. Although Everett may have eventually opposed Jacksonian attacks on Native American rights, it is clear that in the 1820s he held no greater respect for their culture or territorial claims.

Everett argued, much like Cass, that "barbarous tribes have but a partial and imperfect right in the soil." The right of a more civilized people to occupy and improve surrounding territories was undeniable. Once these settlers were established, he argued, further principles of natural growth and improvement made encroachment upon Indian lands unavoidable. In this emphasis Everett's argument was somewhat different than Cass's. While natural law provided the initial right to settle an unimproved coast, natural laws of development made white usurpation of Indian lands less an issue of right than historical inevitability. The settlers possessing the "arts of civilized life" grew in numbers and power far more rapidly. Forests were turned into cornfields, hunting grounds into farms. As the white population grew, liquor and guns were introduced, vices that the natives could neither resist nor control, and their dissolution was guaranteed that much more quickly.[13]

Everett, like Cass, consequently believed that the extinction of the Indians was inevitable, a cost of the unalterable course of historical progress. But even more than Cass he seems to have been indifferent to their fate and less tolerant of those who urged that a remnant of their culture be preserved. What was worth preserving, he asked, their religion, their form of government, their mode of life? America's purpose, he argued, should be the promotion of knowledge and piety, not Indian knowledge and Indian piety. Nor was Everett willing even to concede that there was an element of tragedy in these events. What made the passing of the Indians into extinction a "melancholy fate? In proportion as the Indian generations passed off, civilized generations have come on. . . . Had not the Europeans come, the Indians would have died in the course of nature as before, and been succeeded by other generations of Indians, to lead a barbarous and wretched life, and die like their fathers. The Europeans came; and—by causes as simple and natural, as they are innocent—the barbarous population, as it has passed off, has been replaced by one much better, much happier."[14]

Everett was not the only member of his circle to anticipate the ultimate extinction of the Indians. Jared Sparks believed it "a few years only . . . before the remaining Indians will become finally extinct."[15] Nor was Everett the only one to place their fate within the inevitable and largely blameless context of progress. It was unfortunate, wrote Nathan Hale, that civilized society pressed the Indian to his fate with "indecent haste." But beyond this there was little cause for criticism. Their fate was but "the natural course of human events . . . the certain consequence of industry, enterprise and skill, to prevail over indolence and ignorance." It was yet another expression of the entire American experience in which the present "is always overwhelming the past, and throwing it into insignificance and obscurity."[16] Still, it is Everett's attitude that stands out most sharply. An urbane scholar, he would not seem the sort amenable to such a reckless view of expansion. Nor as a classicist, trained to find perfection in the past, was he the sort one would expect to see in history's inevitable progressive flow justification for its casualties.

This view of history and, in particular, the racial attitudes within it, shared by so many members of Everett's caste, have troubled historians for years. The incongruous juxtaposition of genteel culture and reckless expansionism, of social reform and racist indifference, of adamant abolitionism alongside racial theories premising white superiority, has long challenged the students of New England culture and the biographers of its most prominent intellectuals. Reginald Horsman has offered among the more convincing explanations. He argued that through the Revolution both the historical and anthropological confidence of the Enlightenment held its ground. New England intellectual elites accepted the fundamental unity of all mankind, traced racial differences to environmental factors, and argued that the condition of all could be raised to equal heights through the course of educational and historical progress. But in the early nineteenth century this confidence was subtly undermined. The need to defend slavery amid the Revolutionary rhetoric of freedom and to justify westward expansion and its increasing brutality placed this confidence under considerable stress. As these pressures increased, the set of "practical racial attitudes" that had existed for some time alongside the Enlightenment confidence, attitudes which posited the fundamental and unameliorable inferiority of nonwhites, gained a wider audience. In the decades after 1815, these practical racial attitudes went looking for more credible intellectual support, and they found it in the new scientific studies of race. The disciplines of philology, phrenology, and physiology combined to generate a set of racial theories that would pervade American intellectual circles and justify both African slavery and Indian removal and even extinction.[17]

Horsman's argument is compelling, and it seems to a certain extent affirmed by the interests of the young Federalists contributing to the *North American Review.* Ticknor and Everett studied under Johann Friedrich Blumenbach, a transitional thinker in the development of these theories, and Ticknor formed a close personal relationship with the German anthropologist. Ticknor and Everett were exposed to his argument that while there was a single origin to the human species, five distinct types or races had been environmentally generated over time. Although none was inherently inferior, according to Blumenbach, the nonwhite races did result from a degeneration of the original human stock. In Göttingen they visited Blumenbach's skull collection, and Ticknor had to admit that the physiological evidence of distinct races pointed out by the scholar—"the fair forehead and Grecian nose of that Circassian . . . the wide interval between the eyes of that Calmuck and the projecting chin of that Hottentot . . . the low sensuality expressed in the sharp projection of the upper jaw of that Jew"—was "certainly all there."[18] But they offered no further discussion of these ideas, and Everett never framed his position toward Indian policy in the 1820s in these terms.

Similarly, although several contributors to the *North American Review* did express an interest in the major currents of scientific thought, in particular the blossoming study of languages, the discussion was tentative at best. The works of the German philologist Johann Adelung were reviewed, and the entire question of linguistic and human origins was discussed. But their commentary is noteworthy for its reluctance to fully embrace these theories regarding the Asiatic origins of a gifted race and its westward migration. James Luce Kingsley thought the question of language communities interesting but found little historical proof. Jules de Wallenstein was also intrigued by the question of language migration but, drawing upon the American philologist Peter Stephen Du Ponceau, argued that the evidence did not yet support any dramatic claims. Lewis Cass was willing to believe that the multitude of Indian languages could be traced to a single stock, but he noted that to date there was no etymological proof. John Pickering would not go even this far. His study concluded that the old myth of Hebraic origins was utterly unfounded, and he had difficulty finding evidence of commonality even among the three main Indian languages.[19]

Occasional remarks did echo those of scientific racialists. Edward Everett's belief that intermarriage might quicken the inevitable absorption of the Indians paralleled the recommendations of polygenesists who argued that only in this way could Indians overcome their inherent limitations.[20] But the only explicit commentary on the new racial theories was made by Gamaliel Bradford in a review of William Lawrence's *Lectures on Physiology, Zoology, and the Natural History of Man*. Bradford was openly contemptuous of these lectures. Lawrence's theory that the white races were "superior to the dark races in mental improvement and the arts of civilization" and the phrenological theories of Gall and Spurzheim that underlay Lawrence's work were refuted, argued Bradford, by "the most common observation."[21] He maintained the Enlightenment position regarding the importance of environment in determining the relative status of the races and offered as proof the barbaric state of certain Scottish clans. In the process he mocked the shallow scientism of Lawrence's skull comparisons and offered in support of his views the works of an African poet.

Similarly, Caleb Cushing explored the political events in Haiti as a means of "judging of the intellectual dignity" of the African race. He found their condition somewhat primitive, their language corrupt, and their morals low. But these Cushing traced not to any inherent limitation but rather to the barbaric form of slavery imposed by the French. "Never was a servitude more complete, never was abasement more hopeless, never was ignorance more deplorable." These, he argued most importantly, would be mitigated over time. Reviewing the state and progress of Haitian political development, he concluded by explicitly refuting the scientific racialists who argued that Haiti's black population lacked the "wisdom, the knowledge, the force of mind required to perpetuate their national being."[22]

Thus while these questions may have become important components in the defense of Indian policy in the 1830s and 1840s, at this point they were not. The suggestion that men like Everett revised their Enlightenment universalism in the wake of scientific racialism seems unlikely. Of far greater significance in the formation of their views on Indian policy would seem to be the cultural warfare amid which these policies were being pursued. Although contributors to the *North American Review* were clearly aware of the work of Adelung in linguistics and Lawrence in physiology and the phrenological studies of Gall and Spurzheim, they were far more sensitive to the flood of anti-American rhetoric spewing out of Europe. It seems more plausible, therefore, that their views on Indian removal, and the sense of history in which these views were contained, were formed less in response to the new scientific theories than in reaction to the attacks on America from the British and European press.

Lewis Cass explicitly framed his defense of American Indian policy in rebuttal to attacks in the English press. Responding to charges in London's *Quarterly Review* that America was systematically driving the Indian to extinction, he insisted that American treatment of the Indian was just and clearly more honorable than that of the British.[23] Although Everett never made explicit reference to these particular criticisms of American behavior or policy, his reaction to foreign criticism in general makes it more than plausible that his defense of expansion and Indian displacement was influenced by these attacks as well. Everett was, after all, perhaps the most markedly offended by these attacks on American culture. Educated in Europe and still conscious of the ties of language and culture between Britain and America, he nonetheless grew "exhausted with finding the most absurd misrepresentations of his country credited, and the ignorance which prevails with regard to us."[24] Unable to ignore them, he wrote response after response defending American culture and way of life. In fact, these attacks, and the cultural nationalism they generated, seem to have become one of the determinative elements in Everett's thought. They informed his interpretation of America's past. Revisiting the American Revolution in the wake of these attacks, he described it as rooted in the "oriental spirit" that guided British policies in the past and inspired the "indiscriminate and virulent abuse" in the present. The attacks on American culture were just the most recent expression of the "fixed policy of the paternal councils of England, to keep the continent of America, as far as possible, in the savage state, in which they found it."[25]

These attacks also influenced Everett's assessment of contemporary American society. His defense of the western populace was at least partially informed by the "truly atrocious" remarks of the British press on this topic. Whereas earlier he too had voiced concern over the crudeness of life on the frontier, against these foreign critics he suggested that what was truly remarkable was that a society so young should "exhibit all the essential features of a high stage of civilization."[26] An attack by German critics led him even further to a defense of the pragmatic and utilitarian bent of American culture. Against their charges that Americans' obsession with "material life" had bred a preference for cattle shows and swine breeding over a Venus de' Medici or a Laocoön, Everett suggested that a "noble bullock . . . whose iron neck and compact frame are clothed with an almost silky fur, whose beautiful shape seems the very compound of symmetry and strength . . . [was] as worthy an object of curiosity." This professor of classics, who in earlier works had lamented America's neglect of the fine arts, now argued that "more has been done for human happiness, by the introduction of this small-boned and kindly fattening breed of swine, than by the publication of Winckelmann's history of the ancient arts."[27]

Everett's defense of Indian removal thus seems only one part of a far more dramatic intellectual shift triggered by these attacks in the foreign press. His apologia for their extinction, and celebration of the progressive course of history of which it was a part, was only one piece within a more comprehensive shifting of intellectual orientation—a transferal of cultural loyalties from Europe to America and a reorientation of his historical focus from antiquity to the present. It is telling that among the few statements by an English critic with which he agreed was one which noted the progressive outlook of Americans. "Other nations boast of what they are or have been—but a true citizen of the United States exalts his head to the skies, in the contemplation of the FUTURE grandeur of his country. . . . Others appeal to history; an American to prophecy." Everett agreed, yet phrased it in tellingly more Anglophobic terms. "An American's heart dilates at the prospect of the glorious career before him, which he and his children are to travel; an Englishman looks up to the summits from which he has descended, and tells you how high they be." [28]

The effect of European criticism on Everett was thus to reorient him culturally and historically—to see in the Western Hemisphere what he had initially sought in Europe and to project into the future what he had earlier idealized in the past. This reorientation was reflected most clearly in his call for support of the revolutionaries in Greece. To a certain extent one can detect the residues of a more regressive view of history in Everett's call to arms. The classicist's attachment to the seat of learning and democracy and the Christian's medieval revulsion at the presence of a "Mahometan power" in a Christian nation speak clearly in his characterization of this conflict as "a war of the crescent against the cross." [29] But even more vehemently, he denounced the European balance of power politics that left Greece in Turkish hands. Both Russia and Great Britain could help, but as neither was willing to see Greece fall into the hands of the other, they sacrificed the duties of religion and culture to one of geopolitics. [30]

Confronted by such cowardice and cynicism, Everett framed the new Greek crusade in the language of America's progressive mission. These events, he argued, "must bring home to the mind of the least reflecting American, the great and glorious part, which this country is to act, in the political regeneration of the world." Criticizing those European nations which for centuries had assumed leadership in world affairs but now "stand aghast at the spectacle," he urged America to recognize Greek independence and private citizens to support the cause with money and supplies. [31] The Greek crusade was thus not a step toward the reestablishment of a golden age but a step in the transferal of the seat of its principles to the west and a projection of its perfection into the future. Greece had stood for centuries as the seat of learning and the symbol of liberty, Everett argued, and that "liberty is the lesson, which we are now appointed to teach." Adding a note of inevitability to his historical vision, he promised, "It may be written in sand and effaced, but it will be written again and again, till hands now fettered in slavery shall boldly and fairly trace it, and lips, that now stammer at the noble word, shall sound it out in the ears of their despots, with an emphasis to waken the dead."[32]

Everett was perhaps the member of this circle most obviously moved by foreign criticism to a new set of cultural and historical sensibilities. But he does not seem to have been alone. William Tudor's resentment of foreign criticism no doubt contributed to his sense of European decadence and his belief that the forces of progress had permanently moved west. Reviewing Europe's recent history, he saw some evidence of improvement. In France the monastic system had been eliminated, the lower class had been slightly raised, and a new middle class had been created by the redivision of property. But overall he was pessimistic. "Incurably diseased. Loaded with impositions, crippled with debts . . . devoured with enormous standing armies, polluted with the desires and habits of war," Europe, he concluded, offered "no solid hope that the miseries of its inhabitants can have any termination."[33]

Jared Sparks's indignation over repeated foreign taunts no doubt fed his perception of the degraded condition of European affairs. In the confederation of European states achieved at Vienna he saw "a conspiracy" against liberty, "a combination to perpetuate ignorance, delusion, and slavery."[34] Whereas this sense of European decadence had led Everett to embrace the cause of the Greek patriots, for Sparks it led to support for the emerging republics of South America. There is an unmistakable sense of hemispheric pride in Sparks's celebration of South American independence. "The atmosphere of America is not one, which can ever be breathed freely by kings and emperors," he offered both as warning and in self-congratulation.[35] In contrast to the "confederated despotisms" of Europe he offered the Congress of Panama. Sparks called this confederation of republics, which established a forum for the resolution of national differences, the exploration of international law, and the interpretation of treaties, "among the most remarkable events of political history."[36]

Sparks's specific focus may have differed from that of Everett, but it represented the same sort of geographical and historical reorientation.

For both, the center of liberty now lay in the Western Hemisphere; for both, its perfection lay at the end of an inevitable and progressive course of events. Everett, too, saw in South American affairs matters of trans-historical importance. Initially he was more cautious than Sparks, sympathetic toward their cause but urging neutrality in the conflict between Chile and Spain. But, illustrating yet again the determinative role in Everett's thought played by European criticism, he turned to full support for the cause of the republics when it became linked in his mind to European attacks on America. He labeled an 1826 attack on American culture by the Austrian Johan Georg Hülsemann "the most narcotic lampoon" he ever read. Arguing that it originated in the Austrian cabinet, he suggested it held a more "practical importance"; it was part of a conspiracy to undermine republican institutions, an element in the efforts of Spain, Austria, and France to restore monarchical institutions in the Americas. Having made this connection, he now encouraged "the zeal and vigilance, with which we ought to cherish that sympathy between ourselves and our sister republics."[37]

But if the pressure of foreign criticism encouraged these men to reorient themselves culturally and historically, it was a shift not without its tensions. The sort of expansion they endorsed, the version of progress they affirmed, was filled with challenges to their conservative sensibilities and vision of social order. In Greece the cause of independence, although ennobled by its place within the historical process and its classical heritage, was led by a somewhat primitive batch of patriots. In South America the cause of progress, albeit clear, was traveling on the backs of peasant revolutionaries often more savage than noble.

Some members of this Federalist circle consequently were far less willing to embrace these causes and the vision of history behind them. Nathan Hale, for example, conceded the inevitability of events in South America but was more cautious in declaring his support. True, the independence of Mexico and South America would further the course of progress by giving "a spring and animation to commerce," similar to that which accompanied the original discovery of the region. But the participants in this movement were too unpredictable. Iturbide was clearly no Washington, and the people of South America were "not fitted by their education and character . . . either to govern themselves, or to be governed without the assumption of extensive powers in the chief magistrate." Francis Gray agreed. Although he wished the revolutionaries success, he saw in these events neither the unalterable sweep of history nor the flow-ering of America's spirit of liberty. Instead, they were precipitated by events in Spain and carried to South America prematurely. He supported those who argued that the southern republics lacked the "maturity of in-tellectual and physical resources sufficient to secure the object with ease," and he concluded that the whole crusade would best be delayed "two or three centuries."[38]

Even among those most taken by this sense of history there appeared signs of tension and ambivalence. Jared Sparks, for example, was con-vinced that history was playing out its noble course in the Western Hemi-sphere. Progress was inevitable—the spirit of liberty would proceed, and civilization would advance. But he was troubled by the casualties en route. While Everett was able to reconcile the advance of civilization and the annihilation of a race by arguing that progress meant the spread of civi-lized societies rather than the conversion or improvement of primitive peoples, Sparks seems to have clung to the Enlightenment belief in the improvability of all men. By 1826 he had concluded that the extinction of the Indians was inevitable; however, he traced this not to any inherent defects on their part but rather to a history of mistreatment at the hands of the whites. It was too late to remedy, but the villain was white brutality, not the impersonal sweep of history.[39]

In a similar way Sparks voiced ambivalence concerning the advance of civilization in the Pacific. As with his comments on western expansion, he sided ultimately with the forces of progress; he praised the efforts of Christian missionaries and prayed for their ultimate success in bringing the natives of the South Pacific into history's flow. But he voiced more than a hint of doubt concerning their efforts. He was struck by the resis-tance of the natives to the influence of civilization. Even those who trav-eled to Europe and America for education quickly regressed to their na-tive ways upon return. Somewhat tentatively, he even noted that to a certain extent civilization brought more harm than good. In New Zea-land the arrival of firearms had turned their relatively small-scaled con-flicts into far more bloody contests. It was true that their thirst for war preceded the arrival of guns, but "the rage for killing has burnt with the more fury, in proportion as the means of doing it with the greater facility have increased."[40] In contrast to the questionable advance of civilization, he noted the gentle "voice of nature" that contained its own logic and kept all things in balance.[41] Despite the Pacific natives' barbarism and passion for war, he was struck by the genuine affection that existed among family and friends. Despite their social primitivism, he was intrigued by the genius of nature that fitted out a form of government so well suited to their condition. He even described superstitions like the taboo as logical and effective tools for social order.[42]

For the young Federalists of the *North American Review,* the adoption of the democratic and historical confidence of the age was thus not without its ambiguities. Few were as able as Everett to embrace this vision of history and all its concomitant beliefs without tension. Most were more sensitive to its casualties and less confident in the inevitability or benevolence of its sweep. Despite their acceptance of history's progressive course, they remained anxious to preserve a vision of society that was essentially conservative. Somewhat ironically, they pursued a vision of history that was both progressive and conservative, a vision that acknowledged change, turmoil, and expansion but looked ultimately to harmony and order.

The thought of William Tudor is most illustrative of this inclination. Tudor, like the others, embraced the democratic vision of progress and expansion. He accepted the changes his elders deplored and found in the diversity and motion of republican society much to celebrate. But although welcoming the diversity and calmly confronting the centrifugal forces at play, he seems to have taken ultimate comfort in certain centripetal forces which would reharmonize society and ensure that progress remained essentially conservative. This sense of history was revealed in his discussion of political parties. Calling political parties "inevitable and indispensable," he seems fully reconciled to the organizations his ancestors considered the greatest threat to republican government. But his acceptance of them was linked to a sense of their mechanistic rise and development. Parties formed around the ambitions of men excluded from power. While denied power they adopted crowd-pleasing and often extreme views. But once in power they retreated from their former views and adopted the more centrist policies of their old adversaries. This had been demonstrated by the Republicans. Decentralizing and populist while on the outside, they adopted, once in power, the nation-building measures of the Federalists. Suggesting that ultimately the development of parties might be predicted as accurately as "the return of comets," he described a process in which parties not only rise and develop but also gravitate toward a set of conservative and Federalist policies.[43]

Tudor did not make it clear what force would pull the parties to the center. He was similarly vague in discussing his sense of the nation's religious future. Here again he spoke confidently and supportively of the country's commitment to religious toleration. It was, he suggested, the greatest lesson America offered to the world. But in discussing individual denominations, he struck a less ecumenical chord. The Methodists, in particular, with their "nasal whinings . . . and itinerant preachers . . . strange assemblies in the fields, and . . . violent, enthusiastic excitement in their worship," were singled out for ridicule. Nor did his relegation of this church to regions where "religion comes periodically, like the fever and the ague," provide a convincing endorsement of regional diversity. In fact, in discussing his own Episcopal Church, he hinted at a future in which one denomination would incorporate all. His actual forecast was framed more cautiously. The church, he said, should in the future hold "a much larger relative proportion to other denominations than it now does." But in his praise of its ancient and timeless forms and poetic and solemn prayers and in his conclusion that "all rational minds may find shelter within its pale," there is the suggestion that Tudor's sense of history included a gravitational pull toward ecclesiastical reunification not unlike the pull toward centrist politics.[44]

What exactly would pull the religious and political extremes back toward the center was never very clear. But if somewhat vague in explaining the historical process in these instances, he was far more specific when talking about commerce. For Tudor, commerce was to be understood in the broadest of terms. It referred not just to the activity of merchants but included the marketing of surpluses produced by farmers, craftsmen, and intellectuals. Everyone sought to create these surpluses, and no one was content with mere subsistence; everyone wanted to produce "beyond his own immediate wants, to secure a greater power of ulterior gratification." Thus everyone was some type of merchant, every exchange of products, information, or techniques was at bottom a commercial venture. With commerce so broadly defined, its significance was great. The movement of commerce "is to the nation what the circulation of the blood is to the body." It produced not only economic advance but also "liberty, enterprise, science, and morality." It had "made known the rights, enlarged the capacity, multiplied the comforts, and ameliorated the condition of mankind."[45] More powerful than both the sword and the cloth, the advance of civilization, culture, and even religion had less to do with the high-minded efforts of disinterested men than the working out of man's acquisitive spirit.

This was indeed a significant conclusion. Federalists of the past had viewed such egoism with far more alarm. John Thornton Kirkland, writing in 1801, for example, expressed the more organic and high-minded sense of the individual's role in the community in condemning "the avaricious digging for riches, the ambitious climbing for power, the emulous panting for fame." [46] Egoistic interests were the demon to be suppressed, not the force to be ridden to public improvement. But in Tudor's thought this egoism would actually unite individuals and nations within a web of common purpose and common direction.

Nor was Tudor alone in identifying egoism as a necessary and ultimately positive force within the historical process. Other Federalist writings similarly described history as a certain unfolding of the commercial spirit, a mechanistic process that was driven by egoistic interests, or that at least required passage through a stage of exploitation and egoism. Henry Tudor, in describing his "pedestrian tour" through the northeastern states, reprimanded Boston provincials who assumed barbarism and discomfort lay just outside the coastal cities. Quite the contrary, he found "good roads, tolerable inns, a well cultivated country, growing orchards, an intelligent people, and all the good things of life." True, he encountered some impertinent and vulgar commoners, and in upstate New York he witnessed Yankeeism at its worst—crude entrepreneurs for whom no natural marvel was beyond exploitation, no vista too sacred to be despoiled by "sawmills and slabs . . . red and yellow paint, and 'English Goods, and W.I. and N.E. Rum.'" But twenty years hence, he projected, this valley would be "covered with villas and villages." These Yankee entrepreneurs, this "active, overreaching, bustling race, whiskey-makers and drinkers, store-keepers, millers and traders," would prove "the ignoble founders of future elegance." [47]

This reconciliation of progress and conservatism, of individual ambition and social harmony, was attempted with somewhat less success in the area of politics by William Powell Mason. He too broke ranks with traditional Federalist philosophy, which required that political efforts be guided by disinterested pursuit of the general good rather than self-interest. Instead, he expressed a similar willingness to accommodate the spirit of the age in noting the inevitable presence of ambition and lust for power in republican governments. The "peculiar conformation of our political system not only presents stronger incentives to a wide and more general spread of this ambition . . . but it also furnishes infinitely more abundant means of gratifying it." The reality of political equality and the accessibility of public office made political ambition the inheritance of every republican child. Nor was he certain that this ambition, being the "spring and origin of so much good as well as so much evil," either could or should be removed.[48]

In the end Mason retreated from the conclusion toward which he was heading. Unlike Tudor, Mason was unable to completely embrace the march of self-interest and ambition. He thus rejected the notion that this "political energy" was a force too pervasive to be controlled for the perhaps deluding but "happier view of the human character and of its capacity for improvement." Unable to ignore this energy's existence yet unwilling to give it free rein, he found comfort in the vision of "future Franklins" who would rise up and prove to the world that "political energy and national and individual virtue are not incompatible."[49]

But in placing ultimate confidence in the peculiar character and genius of men like Franklin, Mason revived the question that plagued this generation. Despite the sense of influence and status they achieved through the *North American Review*, despite their claims to persisting power through the maintenance of the nation's legal and educational institutions, many seem to have held lingering ambitions of still greater power, lingering fantasies of the sort of political power and widespread influence exercised by their forefathers. Beyond the comparatively pedestrian influence they exercised as literary critics, scholars, and judges, they seem to have been still intrigued by the possibilities of even greater influence, the sort exercised by the truly great men of the past.

This would seem to be the unspoken question underlying the multiple biographies that the young Federalists of this era produced. Everett, Ticknor, Sparks, Tudor, Cushing—they all undertook the study of great men and in doing so attempted to answer for their own generation the most dramatic question of purpose. Having reconciled themselves to a historical process that in many ways was foreign to their upbringing and sensibilities—a process that included and even depended upon the entire range of human qualities and vices, a process that seemed driven by great impersonal forces—they now attempted to discover what special role they, or individual men in general, could play.[50]

To a certain extent they found room for hope; they found that there was still a place for the great man. Despite the mechanistic and ignoble forces at play, there was still a part to be played by the man who could rise above these forces and influence the events and people that surrounded him. George Ticknor's look at Lafayette was representative. Surrounded by events larger than any individual and forces perhaps ultimately beyond control, Lafayette was able to identify that critical moment when the individual could gently direct events. These moments did not come often. History for the most part must follow the "progress of general intelligence and political wisdom" rather than the exertions of a single player.[51] But on occasion an opportunity arose when a speech, or even a simple gesture, could have profound effects.

For Ticknor the illustrative moment was when the French mob marched on Versailles to capture the queen. Lafayette reluctantly followed, in hopes more of tempering the mob's actions than of assisting in them. When the critical moment arrived, "a moment of great responsibility and great delicacy," he demonstrated the qualities of greatness.

> The agitation, the tumult, the cries of the crowd, rendered it impossible that his voice should be heard. It was necessary, therefore, to address himself to the eye, and turning towards the queen, with that admirable presence of mind, which never yet forsook him, and with that mingled grace and dignity, which were the peculiar inheritance of the ancient court of France, he simply kissed her hand before the vast multitude. An instant of silent astonishment followed, but the whole was immediately interpreted, and the air was rent with cries of "Long live the queen! Long live the general!" from the same fickle and cruel populace, that only two hours before had embrued their hands in the blood of the guards, who defended the life of this same queen.[52]

Caleb Cushing's study of Christopher Columbus provided a similar lesson about greatness. Described as a man of singular habits, genuine piety, and great courage, Columbus struck Cushing as historical proof of the potential of the great man to shape history—one of those men "whose acts stand forth in high relief on the page of history, and who seem . . . singled out by destiny to impart a new direction, and communicate an extraordinary impulse to the age in which they arise upon earth."[53]

But if in this passage Cushing seems to have acknowledged, even more

than Ticknor, the potential of the great man to shape history, in others
he placed an even greater emphasis on the context in which greatness
could surface and the limitations on its persistence. Columbus may have
been a man of singular character, but an entire web of circumstances and
individuals assisted him in his pursuits. Well-placed relatives, a fortuitous
marriage, an influential cleric, and a supportive queen all played essential
roles in his success. And although with their aid he did manage to rise
above superstition and intrigue, he was only able to do so for a short
while. Another batch of individuals and events, most prominently the
death of Isabella and the enmity of Ferdinand and his agent Bobadilla,
combined to bring him down.[54] Columbus's character may have brought
him temporary greatness, but in the end "the elements seemed to con-
spire with the injustice of man" to restore his mortality.[55]

Alexander Everett's brief account of the life of Marie Antoinette also
emphasizes the limitations impeding those who would be great. His general view of history as driven by larger-than-life forces was similar to
Cushing's and Ticknor's. Like them, he also suggested that the individual
could exert some influence on occasion. A skillful Austrian official managed to reconstruct the traditional alliance system; a scheming peasant
girl managed to unsettle the royal family and bring the queen into public
disfavor. In particular, he suggested that a stronger king could have redi-
rected events in France to some extent. Everett conceded that there were
"general and remote causes" for the revolution that were beyond control;
a revolution could not have been prevented altogether. But "occasions
repeatedly offered themselves, when a slight exertion of vigor on his part,
would have given an entirely different turn to subsequent events."[56]

Everett, clearly fascinated with the figure of Marie Antoinette, suggested that she, in fact, possessed more qualities of greatness, more
strength and resourcefulness, than the king. But in her inability to alter
events despite these attributes of individual power, there was a sobering
lesson on the limitations of the individual. Marie may have been a strong
figure, but she also was entangled within a web of court intrigue, national
ambition, and individual jealousy. Because she had been promised from
birth to the king of France in order to seal an agreement between Austria
and France, every detail of her life, from her education to her dressing
habits, was dictated by this web of circumstance. In the end her words
reveal the range of forces and conditions that restrict the individual in-
clined to greatness. "For myself, I could act with vigor; I could shew my-

self, if necessary, on horseback; but to what effect? There would be at once a general cry of Austrian influence, and female management."[57]

Ticknor, Cushing, and Alexander Everett thus concluded that although there were still opportunities for the exertion of greatness, chances for the successful exertion of individual power and influence were sharply circumscribed in terms of frequency and effect. Opportunities arose, but only rarely; events could be shaped, but only temporarily; history could be altered, but only at the fringes.

William Tudor's study of James Otis reached a somewhat different but equally sobering conclusion. Perhaps the most thorough attempt to answer this question concerning roles and influence, his conclusions were no more encouraging. Written in 1823, the work offers a closely researched and argued review of the Anglo-American debate between 1763 and 1776. Tudor's meticulous concern for detail and moments of scholarly objectivity suggest that he answered this question about roles and purpose with a personal commitment to scholarship. Yet his treatment and even choice of Otis suggest that Tudor was looking for an answer to these questions that went beyond a life of scholarly observation.

In Tudor's history, Whig and orderly, Otis's role is critical. He is given credit not just for mobilizing certain intellectual forces—the first to clarify the Americans' feelings about taxation and representation—but also for fathering the popular cause. Tudor makes much of John Adams's observation that Otis's speech before the Boston town meeting sowed "the seeds of patriots and heroes." Drawing upon "a promptitude of classical allusions, a depth of research, a rapid summary of historical events and dates, a profusion of legal authorities, a prophetic glance of his eyes into futurity, and a rapid torrent of impetuous eloquence, he hurried away all before him. American Independence was then and there born."[58] For Tudor, Otis clearly represented a man of not just scholarship and wisdom but passion and influence. He offered an example of the potential of the man of letters to shape and direct popular causes.

Yet this was a vision and a model laced with ambiguity. If Tudor emphasized Otis's determinative role in some places, in others he emphasized the truly popular nature of the rebellion, not dependent on any one man but rooted in "the virtue, intelligence and courage every where diffused among the citizens." If at times he credited Otis with fathering the Revolution, at others he fell back upon a more deterministic sense of history. Liberty was a product of the irresistible "spirit of the age,"

spreading wherever "commerce, intelligence, and enterprize can pene-
trate." From within this historical perspective, the role of a man like
Thomas Cushing seemed more suitable. Bland and conciliatory, he
proved a "useful agent" to both the patriot cause and the greater historical
process.[59]

Yet despite this sense of history, Tudor was drawn to the lives of a
different class of men, men who proved as passionate as they were erudite, men who seemed to shape history rather than merely serve it. Despite his scholarly caution, he was fascinated by men like Jonathan Mayhew, whose apocalyptic language and "solemn enthusiasm" clashed with
Tudor's genteel tastes but were nonetheless "suited to the times," and
Charles Chauncey, whose fervent commitment to the American cause
and belief that "if human efforts should fail, a host of angels would be
sent to support it" probably offended his Unitarian rationalism but nevertheless expressed an attractive streak of patriotic zeal.[60]

If Tudor did indeed finally see in the lives of Mayhew, Chauncey, and
Otis a more exciting example for the contemporary man of letters, it was
a conclusion filled with inconsistency and edged with a warning. Otis was
brilliant and influential, but also manic and unbalanced. The passion and
intensity of his thought may have given birth to a revolution, but "his
disposition was so ardent, and his mind so excitable, that its natural tendency, under aggravating circumstances, was to insanity." In the mode of
his death in 1783, when he was struck down by lightning, "demolished at
once by a bright bolt from Heaven," Tudor found a certain apocalyptic
seemliness.[61]

This conclusion may or may not have been the one Tudor set out to
find. But it was one with which many Federalists of this generation were
comfortable. It meshed well with their sense of history and the sort of
social order they imagined—a history of general forces regulated by a
web of educational, juridical, and literary institutions, a history not dominated by powerful individuals or excited groups but one in which organizations of professionals and experts established the parameters within
which these individuals and groups were contained. Nathan Hale was one
of these. He was embarrassed, for example, by the overreaching citizen,
the "public spirited gentlemen, who think it their duty to favor congress
with their speculations on all subjects." He was embarrassed by the "ha-
rangues" from those who stepped beyond the bounds of their expertise
and offered opinions on everything. Matters of great national interest

required careful, informed deliberation, to which Hale would offer only that which he was qualified to provide, "a few statistical and economical statements."[62]

A few statistics, a few facts, the proceeds of their specialization and expertise. Wasn't this after all what this more complex age required? Wasn't this the source of their status and the essence of their new roles? Joseph Cogswell felt a bit sheepish critiquing the work of the western explorer Henry Schoolcraft from his Massachusetts desk, but the sort of loose, unscientific observations Schoolcraft offered were no longer adequate. Why didn't they carry "the instruments necessary to make the requisite observations"? Where were the facts about mountain heights and river currents, water temperatures, and latitude and longitude? The world no longer had much use for "loose and indefinite" observations of nature; it needed precise, scientifically obtained information.[63]

Josiah Quincy seems to have agreed. In fact, this former congressman and future mayor of Boston went so far as to suggest that the world was in greater need of scientists than of statesmen. In earlier stages of society, the exertions of individual leaders were important, but as society advanced and grew more complex, it became shaped "less by the activity of particular individuals, than by the mass of intellectual, moral, and physical powers." In such a society there was less need for speeches and heroics than that "facts relative to the civil condition of the people . . . be collected and generalized." In the most dramatic statement regarding the evolution of society's needs and the shifting roles of the wise and the good, Quincy suggested that the forging of a nation begun by the Revolution and advanced by the architects of the Constitution would eventually be completed by the compilers of statistics. The work of nation building today required fewer Madisons and more Timothy Pitkins, social scientists who could gather statistics concerning the economic and commercial status of the nation, researchers who could gather "the facts belonging to the condition of our society" and thereby place public policy in the hands of science, rather than in the crucible of individual or party ambition.[64]

If for some this sense of history was satisfying, if it meshed well with their sense of society and their roles within it, for others it seems to have been somewhat depressing. It was not very exciting, and it was far from inspiring. And wasn't that one of the roles that history should play? Shouldn't the country's history provide a chronicle of past glories, a record of the great men and events that made the country what it was, a collection of the sacred memories and national myths that defined Americanism? How could the mechanistic sense of history described by Tudor and Sparks and Alexander Everett and the sober sense of men's roles within it described by Hale and Quincy provide a sense of national identity strong enough to unite all America? Without a more inspiring record of the nation's great men, those Daniel Webster called "the real treasures of the country . . . the regalia of the republic," how would Americans respond to those foreign critics who said the nation lacked a soul?[65] Without a more inspiring vision of history and America's place in it, how would we respond to those who, perhaps accurately, described America as a restless nation of wanderers, with "no fixed and settled feeling of affection for the spot, on which you were born and bred"?[66]

There was an understandable disagreement between Hale the engineer and Webster the orator on these questions. But it is an error to see their positions as extremes within the young Federalist community. More accurately, they should be viewed as competing elements within the Federalist vision—like the tensions within their understanding of literature and its obligations—a tension not just between individuals but within individuals who wrestled to maintain and reconcile these conflicting ideas within one vision of history and their place in it.

Edward Everett, for example, at times could sound like Hale. History was a somewhat mechanistic process of progress within which men of his class played the part of technicians fine-tuning the institutions that shepherded its travelers. England's current problems were connected to the failure of its statesmen-technicians to recognize the obsolescence of its traditional institutions. Industrial innovations had shifted the structures of power in England, vastly increasing that possessed by the owners of technology. Their machinery represented an addition to their influence equivalent to hundreds of millions of men. And "a people, moving with the energy of three hundred millions of working arms, cannot be kept organised in the old way."[67]

The statesman-technician could accomplish much through his continual retooling of the social and political institutions, even successfully combat the problems of overpopulation and hunger. Everett and his brother Alexander made this argument in a series of articles on Malthus. Although they challenged his conclusions, they did not reject his mechanistic view of history. Where Malthus erred, in fact, was in not recognizing the full range of mechanical forces at work in the historical process. Just as population grew by certain natural laws, so also did the means by which this growth could be sustained. Population growth was followed "immediately by a division of labor; which produces in its turn the invention of new machines, an improvement of methods in all departments of industry, and a rapid progress in the various branches of art and science."[68] The Everetts concluded that by a careful maintenance of the social and political institutions, the problems of poverty and hunger, which were primarily ones of distribution, could be largely eliminated.

But if Everett thus at times could voice a set of ideas that foreshadowed notions of technocracy, at others he articulated an entirely different vision of society and history, their character and purposes, and the role of men within them—a sense of society held together less by institutions than by bonds of sentiment and memory, a sense of history driven less by impersonal forces than great men, and a vision of both in which men like himself were not just scientists and technicians but philosophers and statesmen. In reviewing Richard Henry Lee's memoirs, for example, Everett argued that what was lacking in America was a sense of historical memory—the "historic recollections" that bound a people together as a nation, providing a common sense of origins and identity. These identifying myths existed in the states individually, but at present the Union was only a "metaphysical and theoretical thing." He thus encouraged the production of histories like these so that the nation could grow in "that veneration which time alone confers."[69]

Everett seems to have agreed with his brother that societies were more than just contracted associations, groups of free-willed individuals who band together out of fear or weakness. In an article on Cicero, Alexander Everett rejected Hobbes's argument that the natural relation between men was one of hostility, and also the premise of Rousseau that in nature man was "wholly isolated, and disconnected from all the rest." Instead, he argued, societies were expressions of man's "social instinct . . . one of the principles of our nature," and consequently not the artificial result of agreement but an organic expression of human nature.[70] This understanding of society's origins affirmed the fundamental conservatism of both Everetts, and it led Edward toward the more organic vision of society and history. If society was more than just covenant, but instead an organic elaboration of human nature, the bonds of memory and identification must be nurtured. This could be accomplished best by the cultivation of Americans' historical memory through biographies, historical narratives, and even the theater.

The culmination of this more romantic and organic sense of society and history was Edward Everett's biographical sketches of Napoleon and Ali Pacha. Even the choice of subjects spoke to this increasingly prominent romantic bent in his character. But the conclusions regarding great men did so even more. Whereas his brother Alexander and Caleb Cushing had concluded that great men struggled long and generally unsuccessfully to raise themselves above the events and conditions that surrounded them, Everett's subjects succeeded mightily. While the others concluded that moments of influence and transcendence were short-lived, Everett celebrated the greatness of Ali Pacha, who managed to achieve and maintain power for over sixty years "by the sole energy of character and fertility of personal resources."[71]

But if Everett was pulled toward this vision of history, Francis Calley Gray was drawn in the other direction. He, like Everett, seems to have tried balancing both visions of history and man's role. On occasion he echoed the views of Webster and Everett that the study of history should be directed to the formation of the national character. Historians were, he argued, "the guardians of the publick instruction. . . . the founders of their country's fame, they only can render her illustrious by celebrating the achievements of her heroes." Moreover, they should seek to inspire public service by throwing out the bait of fame and recognition. Why else do men strive as they do? "The momentary plaudits of the crowd? No; they toil for immortality, and the hand of learning only can give them their reward."[72]

Gray also echoed Everett's romantic orientation in urging historians to avoid the dry recitation of fact and instead "appeal to the feelings as boldly, though not in the same manner, as the poet or the orator." Like his more celebrated colleague William Hickling Prescott, Gray seems to have drawn from Scott a lesson in the potential of history to fuse the objective and the romantic. The historian should not abandon impartiality, but he should not confuse this for apathy. His work should consequently strive to "catch with the eye and describe with the pen of the poet those general features and striking peculiarities . . . and recalling them, as it were, into existence, place them living and moving before us."[73]

On other occasions, and sometimes in almost the same breath, Gray would shy away from this romanticism and the subjection of the discipline to these purposes. The romantic notions of history he voiced in the abstract were replaced with a more disciplined, scholarly objectivity when confronted with a particular example. Thus despite calling men to public service with the promise of immortality, he refused to join Tudor in celebrating the importance of James Otis. Arguing that American independence represented the convergence of several broad, popular forces, he concluded that "the declaration of Independence would not have been made a day later, though James Otis and Patrick Henry had died in the cradle."[74] He similarly refused to share in the romantic notion of South American independence and urged a similar caution in exploring America's own Revolution. American independence was indeed a significant achievement. But it should be understood for the set of particular events that it was. Those who tried to read into it some transcendent historical force or into the motivation of the colonists some romantic instinct for liberty would be looking in vain. Too often, Gray complained, speculating men tended to find too much design and coherence in historical events. The historian had an obligation to cast more sober, disciplined eyes on the past.[75]

It is perhaps understandable that Everett the scholar turned statesman and Gray the historian would ultimately lean in opposite directions on this question. That one would eventually conclude that society was an organic web of memory and myth, that history was a grand movement toward progressive ends, and that great men could carve out niches of glory within its flow, while the other would tend to be more circumspect about history's direction, its uses, and the role that men play within it, is perhaps the logical extension of their differing sensibilities and careers. But beyond this it says something about just how much these two had come to terms with the sort of options facing men of their caste in the new order. Gray, the scholar, seems to have been entirely at ease with the detachment that his role demanded. The aloofness, the removal to the edges of society and history where he could gain the best vantage on the past, was a position with which he seemed quite comfortable.

But Everett was not. He seems to have worried about the dangers of marginalization inherent in the scholar's life. Harvard, he wrote early in his career, was far too limited an arena for a man of his talents and temperament. "I die daily of a cramped spirit, fluttering and beating from side to side of a cage," he wrote in 1821.[76] As his career advanced, he grew even more concerned about the prospects of marginalization. The printing press, he argued, had done much to improve the condition of mankind. But once it separated the artist and scholar from their audience, substituted the written page for the public performance, the man of letters had lost "the social principle."[77] He had lost the immediate interaction with his audience that ensured a sort of organic bond between them. Much the same change was responsible for the deterioration of public oratory in Congress. The distance between orator and constituent had destroyed the mutual interaction that had made public discourse the crucible in which the statesman and the public created policy. The hollow forms of discourse that remained lacked not only eloquence but also authenticity as a vital process within a living body politic.[78]

For Everett, this marginalization threatened the organic nature of society upon which his vision of public service depended. But more importantly, it invoked specters of personal impotence. In this fear there is more than a little irony. The one who had more than all the rest publicly embraced the popular sense of history and America's role in it was the one left most fearful of the place it left men of his class and breeding. The man who, driven by foreign criticism, had developed the most complete apologia for American culture and society was the one left most haunted by the specter of displacement. The man who had most emphatically embraced America's historical optimism, its messianic sense of expansion and conquest, and most enthusiastically embraced the transferal of cultural leadership from the European to the American continent was left now the most haunted by a vision of where all this left men like himself. Perhaps within the role of scholar and scientist, experts in possession of esoteric knowledge, the keys to America's educational and judicial machinery, the Federalist of the 1820s could find some prestige and influence. But there also loomed the possibility that these roles would relegate the Federalist to the fringes of society, where rather than find status, he would find isolation, and rather than earn respect as a vital member of society, he would invite curiosity as the scholar set apart, the man out of touch, the "man in advance of his age."[79]

CHAPTER 8

LEGACY

→→As Andrew Jackson rode triumphantly into the city of Washington for his inauguration, the old guard of the Federalist Party looked on in disbelief and despair. The revolution in American politics initiated by Thomas Jefferson seemed completed in the election of this Tennessee Democrat. At least Jefferson had been restrained by his "constitutional timidity," William Sullivan would note in later years.[1] Never had the "intelligent people" of America, added Massachusetts congressman Samuel Clesson Allen, seen in such an exalted position a man of such "bad character—a man covered with crimes."[2]

But for the younger generation of Federalists, Jackson's election held little of the same apocalyptic significance. True, he may not have been their favorite candidate. But having long ago shed their parents' vicious partisanship and antirepublican paranoia and resolved to adapt to the new realities of democratic America, these heirs of the Federalist tradition watched Jackson's election with more curiosity than alarm. The complacency with which they greeted Jackson's election speaks convincingly of the success they perceived in their efforts to adapt and be reconciled to the new political and social realities. And clearly the young Federalists of the *North American Review* could look back at the first dozen years of the journal's existence and the ideological and institutional adaptations they developed in its pages with a considerable degree of satisfaction.

By the time of Jackson's election they had launched a crusade for the development of a national literature that they believed would answer America's critics, improve public morality, and strengthen the cords of national sentiment. In the process they also carved out for themselves a position as vital members of this new order. As literary critics they not only would promote the nation's literary achievements, they also would exercise an influence on both the artists and the public, providing the necessary parameters for the former while shaping the tastes of the latter. Within this role they believed they would more than equal the political influence of their fathers; they would surpass it by cultivating the sensibilities and values antecedent to political behavior.

Within the institutional framework they developed in the *North American Review,* they outlined a social order which allowed for diversity while at the same time promoting unity and harmony, an order that accepted equality and tolerance while also preserving hierarchy. Within this institutional framework they also carved out a niche for themselves—men of unusual education and training, specialists in possession of the technical and esoteric knowledge needed for the maintenance of America's complex legal, commercial, and social order, men whose training and detachment enabled them to identify within America's eclectic culture the canon of literary, legal, religious, and moral truths to be disseminated through the educational, religious, and juridical institutions.

And finally, in the understanding of history articulated in the journal they outlined a vision of progress that brought them into agreement with the popular confidence of the age without sacrificing their conservative appreciation for social unity and hierarchy. They described a course of history—inevitable and progressive—that promised the advancement of America's messianic democratic agenda while simultaneously preserving order and social harmony. Here again they identified purposes for men of their class either as the technicians responsible for the institutional adaptation to the historical process or as the statesmen and leaders capable of steering people and nation through the ultimately inevitable but not unnavigable currents of history.

There was indeed much within the vision articulated by these men during these years that suggests they had successfully adapted their fathers' conservative ideology to democratic America—much to suggest that they had come to terms with the egalitarianism and antielitism of democracy while yet retaining a vision of their own responsibilities and actual capabilities as "the wise and the good"—much to suggest that they had grown comfortable with the individualism and diversity of contemporary society by identifying the means by which these forces might be reintegrated within a unified order driven by a vision of the general welfare. And the recurring expressions of this ideology throughout the nineteenth and twentieth centuries suggest that this ideological adaptation was of more than temporary importance. Within their organic view of society and their belief that the interests of the whole were more compelling than class or group interest, they articulated an ideology that has found repeated voice throughout American political history. Within their insistence upon a certain level of decorum in all aspects of public life, their demand that traditional standards of morality and behavior be cultivated and reenforced through conscious efforts of social, cultural, and institutional elites, they helped perpetuate a conception of the social order that is still broadly tapped. In the elaboration of an ideology that combined a conservative temperament with an openness to reform, a bias toward stability and an appreciation for historical continuities, but also an awareness that history is movement, and that progress depends upon change, these young intellectuals helped construct a peculiarly American form of conservatism.

But there was also much within this vision and the attempts to see it realized that must have troubled these young intellectuals. The *North American Review* spoke throughout this period to a very limited audience. With a peak circulation during these years of roughly 3,000, any hope that the journal might shape the public's literary tastes and establish the parameters of the nation's literature had to be qualified at best.[3] In addition, the efforts of these young Federalists to implement the institutional reforms they prescribed were greeted with considerable resistance. The establishment of the common law was a significant and enduring achievement, the steps they took to institutionalize their fathers' philanthropic efforts paved the way for further reforms, and the progress they made toward the professionalizing of the fields of law and medicine would ultimately prove important. But the educational reforms they placed at the center of all this were slower to take root. The number of graduate schools increased only slowly, and their vision of the modern university, comparable to German models, would not be realized for another half century. Even their attempts to reform Harvard, the institution closest to their own interests and most susceptible to their influence, had little effect during these years.

In addition, there lurked within the vision itself disturbing undercurrents that threatened to undermine both the viability of the ideology they prescribed and the status it offered to its architects. Although their literary theories seemed to offer influence and status, their recurring celebration of genius and its privileges threatened to undercut both. Running alongside their calls for a literature that was accessible and moral were contrary conceptions of art that defied regulation, of the artist who stood above social obligation and critical censure, and of the discriminating reader who earned by his tastes the right to indulge and escape. In a similar fashion, although their institutional vision contained a prestigious place for the man of specialized training, there lingered in this picture the prospect of marginalization—a reduction of the specialist's significance in proportion to the reduced breadth of his vision, a transformation of the man of learning from a respected savant to a myopic pedant. And finally, although their historical vision promised progress and ultimate order, it also challenged the primacy and even the necessity of their own contributions. Although it suggested that diversity would ultimately find unity, it conceded that, more often than not, individuals were only minor agents—inconsequential players traveling impotently within the broader and impersonal forces of history.

Indeed, as the century progressed, it appears that many of these undercurrents rose to the surface, and many of the more discordant elements of their vision compromised the effectiveness of their adaptation. Even more ironically, it appears that unintended consequences haunted their successes—even at those points where they succeeded in realizing their vision, the concomitant of their success was failure; the reward for their contributions was censure and displacement. For example, although they succeeded in carving out a new literary synthesis, one which enabled the flowering of a distinct American literary culture, they did so at great cost—for the literature to which they opened the door proved ultimately hostile to their own contributions. As the romantic national literature they helped foster shed itself of neoclassical vestiges, it grew beyond the conventions and limitations these young Federalists hoped to preserve, in fact, beyond the dictates of critics altogether in its celebration of individual genius and unfettered self-expression. Similarly, although they paved the way for academic reform, in particular the advancement of professional education, their success only opened the door to their usurpation. As they succeeded in regularizing graduate education for the law and medicine, they found their own hegemony over these prestigious occupations challenged by the rising middle class. Finally, although they succeeded in reconciling themselves to the historical confidence of the age, they did so by surrendering their positions as objective critics of society and politics. In the process of defending American behavior and answering American critics, in successfully assuming the role of apologists for American policy, culture, and behavior, they not only sacrificed their own regional interests and violated their personal sensibilities, but most importantly they denied the nation the voice of introspection and self-criticism it needed.

Any ultimate assessment of their contributions and their success must deal with this mixed record, with this conservative blueprint for elite influence alongside a recipe for intellectual isolation, with the construction of an ideology which has persisted into the present alongside the empowerment of cultural and social forces that proved hostile to their own more finely nuanced goals. Any assessment must ask whether these young Federalists successfully adapted their fathers' ideology to the new realities of democratic America or just paved the way for their own displacement, whether they successfully carved out a place for the intellectual in American society or provided the philosophical and institutional framework for his marginalization.

Many of these men would have argued that they were successful, and many of their careers do suggest a successful reconciliation of elitism with democracy and of intellectual pursuits with public influence. William Tudor moved from the *North American Review* to diplomatic posts in Lima and Rio de Janeiro. Edward Everett went from the journal and a career in academia to the governorship of Massachusetts and a seat in the United States Senate. Caleb Cushing's public career included a seat on the Massachusetts Supreme Court, four terms in Congress, and ambassadorial positions in China and Spain. Nathan Hale and Francis Calley Gray served several years in the Massachusetts state senate. But a closer look at the lives of individuals suggests that this reconciliation was never quite complete—that there lingered tensions between their visions of public influence and the sort of careers through which they hoped to achieve this.[4]

William Prescott established himself as perhaps the most eminent literary critic in America during the 1820s, and his work remains among the most highly regarded of the period. His historical studies earned him even greater recognition. His *History of Ferdinand and Isabella*, published in 1836, was praised at home and in Europe as among the most significant historical works of the decade. His subsequent *Conquest of Mexico,* published in 1843, was equally well received. Traveling to Europe in 1850, he was awarded an honorary degree at Oxford and lionized throughout the Continent. Suggesting that literary endeavors could earn recognition and influence comparable to political life, George Ticknor described Prescott's tour as "the most brilliant visit ever made to England by an American citizen not clothed with the prestige of official station."[5]

But beneath these testimonies to the successful reconciliation of literary life and public recognition lay lingering doubts concerning career and importance. By 1837 Prescott had concluded that literary criticism was an essentially worthless form of literary activity, unfair to the author and of little value to the reader. Moreover, he lamented that the *North American Review* had become, or perhaps he sensed always had been, "weak and waterish." American criticism, he complained, lacked "the business-like air, or the air of the man of the world, which gives manliness and significance to criticism." He continued to chide his friends in politics about their choice of careers and their abandonment of scholarship. But over and over again, in sometimes subtle and sometimes very overt ways, he expressed dissatisfaction with the nature of the literary and academic life. He railed impatiently, for example, against the critics of his work and the "pedantic spirit which under the despotic name of taste, would reduce them to all one dull uniform level." In a striking convergence of romantic sensibilities and inherited social arrogance, he chafed against the yapping of smaller minds and lesser men. "Originality—compensates for a thousand minor blemishes," he argued. "The widest latitude should be allowed to taste and to the power of unfolding the thoughts of the writer in all their vividness and originality."[6]

The life of a scholar, after all, always had been something of an uncomfortable fit for Prescott. A person of dashing good looks and stately carriage, he struck a figure well suited to the opportunities and social station of his father's generation. But the narrowing of political opportunities was rather poetically complemented by a college accident that left him partially blind. Restless as a student, equally bored practicing law, he adopted his literary and historical work in something of a desperate attempt to find a career which satisfied the demands of his Federalist heritage. "It is of little moment whether I succeed in this or that thing," he once confessed, "but it is of great moment that I am habituously industrious."[7]

The elaborate methods by which he pursued his studies offer testimony to the persistence of his Federalist sense of social responsibility. Never really liking to work, always driven more by his "duties towards his fellow men," he employed a regimented schedule and countless tricks to drive himself forward. Carrying an envelope filled with little slips of paper on which he had written down his faults, he regularly evaluated his behavior and disciplined himself for the life of study for which he was poorly suited. His secretary, Edmund Otis, later admitted that this drive to be useful yielded an unhealthy "uniformity, regularity, and order in his mode and habit of living. . . . I sometimes thought that he had reduced life to such a system, and regulated his every action so much by rule, that there was a danger of merging volition in a mechanical, clock-work existence, and losing liberty in the race for knowledge and fame."[8]

If he ultimately succeeded, if he managed to achieve recognition and a sense of usefulness through the vehicles laid out by his young Federalists peers, it was not without its ambiguities. Despite the distinction he drew between literary and civil history—the former of narrow scholarly interest, the latter more broadly directed and of interest to every man with civil or religious rights to defend—there seems to have persisted a degree of doubt that the writing of any history was all that useful a contribution to public affairs. There remains more than the suggestion of relative impotence in the image of Prescott laboring half-blind in his study, beneath the fabled "crossed swords," a legacy of his own grandfather and his wife's who had faced one another in the Revolutionary War, composing a review of Byron or writing a letter to Ticknor debating the existence of Petrarch's Laura.

If Prescott represented the Federalist-scholar frustrated by the narrowness of his public service, dissatisfied with the passivity inherent in his adaptation of Federalism to democratic society, Everett represented something of the opposite. Unlike Prescott, he abandoned a career in academia to pursue one in politics. Unlike Prescott, he very early recognized the limitations of an academic life and pursued influence through more traditional channels. But like Prescott, he found his career unsatisfying. Although achieving considerable political success, he emerged no more satisfied with his adaptation of Federalism than was Prescott. Like

Prescott, he found his attempts to reconcile literary sensibilities with the traditional Federalist call to public service ultimately unsuccessful.

On the surface Everett's career appears one of tremendous success. In a political and literary career spanning four decades, he seems to have reconciled the Federalist vision of elite governance with democratic society. A United States congressman at age thirty, he served five terms in Washington (1825–35) and then four terms as governor of Massachusetts (1836–40). From the State House he moved to the Court of St. James's as the United States minister, and from there to the presidency of Harvard College in 1846. In 1852 he was appointed secretary of state after the death of Daniel Webster, and then to the United States Senate in 1853. A successful public life was culminated with the vice-presidential nomination of the Constitutional Union Party in 1860.

Everett's career was significant both for its success and for its apparent reconciliation of literary and political ambition. Not only did he succeed in both areas, but reminiscent of the old school Federalist, he managed to move back and forth between them, in fact using one arena as a vehicle to the other. His political career was launched and then facilitated by Webster, who was first drawn to Everett by an article the young scholar wrote for the *North American Review* in 1823. His nomination as a candidate for Congress was largely inspired by a Phi Beta Kappa address he delivered in 1824. Speaking on the literary prospects of the young Republic, he wove together erudition and patriotism and subsequently emerged in the public eye and ran for Congress as the scholar-statesman-patriot.

In addition, there is a certain symmetry to his literary and political careers, a certain consistency in theme and emphasis. The most vehement defender of American culture against foreign attack while writing for the *North American Review,* he made one of his more significant contributions to American diplomacy in 1850 with a rather strongly worded response to the Austrian charge d'affaires Hülsemann who had criticized American intervention in Austrian affairs. While denying any interference, Everett offered no apologies and minced no words in contrasting American power and influence with those of the Hapsburgs, whose country was no more than a "patch on the earth's surface." The nationalism he first exhibited, perhaps first cultivated, in the pages of the *North American Review* was further reflected in his response to the Tripartite Convention proposed for the United States, Great Britain, and France in 1852. As secretary of state Everett rejected this agreement, which would have guaranteed Spanish control over Cuba. Claiming no territorial ambitions, Everett nonetheless argued that Cuba's fate was a question for American, not European, resolution. Using language that could as readily have described Everett's response to foreign criticism of American literature and culture, N. L. Frothingham described his response to Britain and France as "a truly American document . . . the greatest Manifesto that has ever been made to the European nations from these shores."[9]

But if in many ways Everett's life does suggest success—his reconciliation of literary and political careers, integration of the intellectual in politics, and adaptation of Federalism to changing political conditions— there were tensions and anxieties throughout that left this success far from unqualified. To a certain extent these tensions were rooted in flaws more personal than cultural or generational. Extraordinarily sensitive to criticism or attack, he met political disappointment with bitterness, suspicion, and a sense of betrayal that bordered on paranoia. But the sources of Everett's dissatisfaction went beyond these personal failings. They seem to lie also within the very balance he tried to strike, the adaptation and transition he tried to effect.

His reputation as an eloquent and erudite speaker and the confidence he possessed as a person capable of shaping people and events were both gained at Harvard as a scholar and professor. These skills and this sense of himself helped launch his political career. But they also led to a series of political indiscretions. Accustomed to the relative anonymity of academia, he seems to have been unprepared for the sort of scrutiny attached to political life. Used to discussing topics of narrow academic interest before lecture halls of admiring or, at worst, indifferent schoolboys, he seems to have been insensitive to public feelings on issues of more vital interest, or perhaps overconfident in his ability to shape public opinion. In one of his first speeches in Congress, he wandered into an indiscreet defense of slavery that struck his constituents as offensive and more seasoned politicians as politically naive.

He also carried with him from his celebrated but comparatively cloistered life at Harvard too much of the old Federalist understanding of power and its uses. In his 1836 governor's inaugural address, he suggested that state power might be necessary to curb immoderate abolitionist talk. In arguing that antislavery rhetoric might incite slave insurrection or provoke sectional discord, he voiced a not uncommon concern among northern moderates. But in threatening the use of governmental power to suppress these forms of speech, he completely misread public feeling and provoked considerable anger. In a similarly dated demonstration of power, he demanded as Harvard's president that the faculty attend all chapel services in order to improve campus discipline. When the faculty resisted, he pursued legislation that would have forced compliance at the expense of all future administration-faculty relations.

In both instances the arrogance Everett acquired as a celebrated scholar and speaker and the understanding of power he inherited and exercised unmodified from his Federalist ancestors led him to impolitic actions and failure. At Harvard, in particular, his arrogant approach to his office and misunderstanding of the political realities of the college led to a series of failures and disappointments. His achievements should not be ignored. He did secure the funding from Abbott Lawrence for the construction of a new school of science, and he did lure Louis Agassiz to the university. But by the end of his term, after childishly frequent threats of resignation, he had abandoned most serious attempts at reform to concentrate instead on a campaign to restore the old Harvard seal. Complaining that the current seal, with the word *Veritas,* was anti-Christian, he resolved to see the original motto *Christo et Ecclesiae* restored. Pursuing the issue, as his biographer gently phrased it, with "a meticulous persistency in the mat- ter . . . somewhat difficult to understand," he reduced his tenure as presi- dent to this one objective. Telling himself that "should I do nothing else during my Presidency but restore the venerable seal of the University, I shall feel that I have deserved well at its hands," he left Harvard satisfying himself on perhaps this one issue alone.[10]

If the balance Everett thus attempted to strike was impossible—if the man of literary sensibilities could no longer function in politics, if the Federalist could no longer adapt to the realities of power and public scru- tiny, Everett was among the last to admit it. At times he seems to have edged toward this realization. Political defeat, public criticism, or even personal tragedy usually would prompt him to imagine a refuge in schol- arship. Amid fears of Senate nonconfirmation in 1852, he consoled him- self with the literary opportunities political defeat would create, "more congenial perhaps to my character and more favorable to happiness."[11] When his daughter died in 1843, he went so far as to outline the scholarly project in which he would seek solace.

Intellectuals outside of politics were quick to point out the impossi- bility of the balance he was attempting to strike. Most pointedly, Emerson described the "political brothers" who attended Everett's presidential inaugural ceremonies at Harvard. Far from acknowledging any vital link between academia and politics, they came, said Emerson, "to grace with a sort of bitter courtesy his taking of the cowl." Criticizing less their disrespect than their prostitution of Everett's talents, he directed most of his venom at Webster whose "evil genius . . . warped him from his true bias all these twenty years, and sent him cloud-hunting at Washington and London, to the ruin of all good scholarship, and fatal diversion from the pursuit of his right prizes." Most bitingly, Emerson mocked the emptiness of Everett's political contributions. He concluded that Everett had never been more than "a mere dangler and ornamental person."[12] Truer than Everett would ever admit, Emerson's assessment did not shake Everett from his attempt to be both intellectual and statesman. As a result he concluded both careers largely dissatisfied. His great literary works were never pursued, and although he was elected or appointed to the highest offices, he was plagued by suspicions, insecurity, and a sense of unappreciated talent that left him imagining Machiavellian plots and fatal illness.

It was understandable that the public role to which Everett eventually committed himself—the role through which at the end of his life he believed he could successfully function as both an intellectual and a statesman—was as an orator. From 1856 to his death in 1865, he traveled around the country speaking primarily about the glories of George Washington. As the Civil War approached, he responded with neither the power of political office nor the analytical detachment of the scholar, but instead with a memorial to Washington as the unifying vision capable of overcoming sectional discord. Expressing perhaps the most important but also the most uncertain premises of the Federalist vision—its extreme confidence in language and its exalted sense of the ability of great minds to influence events—Everett concluded his public career eloquently reminding America of its former greatness.

Within the lives of both Everett and Prescott, one senses not only a failure to fully reconcile the competing elements of their vision but a failure to fully escape the demands of their fathers' generation. Despite their early criticism of their fathers' shortcomings, despite the reworking of Federalism they believed necessary, one senses that their fathers' generation continued to hang over them, calling them to fuller participation in public affairs and a more vital influence on contemporary events. Everett could not escape the shadow of Washington. In the end it was only this icon from his Federalist past that could see the country through its current trials. In the end Prescott could not escape the memory of his Revolutionary era grandfather, in whose shadow he literally worked. Even more poignantly, in the end he could not transcend the expectations of his father. At his father's death Prescott recalled his duty "to guide myself through the rest of my pilgrimage by the memory of his precepts and the light of his example." Recommitting himself to the literary labors that his Federalist past demanded but which he found so difficult, he held up as inspiration a perhaps double-edged specter: "He still lives, and it must be my care so to live on earth as to be united with him again and forever."[13]

Within the lives of both men thus lies the suggestion that young Federalists did not wholly succeed in adapting their fathers' ideology to the new conditions of America. The roles they worked out fully satisfied neither their search for intellectual integrity nor their hope for public influence. Whether defining new roles as scholars and critics or pursuing old roles as statesmen, they remained somewhat unsatisfied with the hybrids they achieved. Alongside this generation must be placed successive generations of New England neo-Federalists and intellectuals whose lives and complaints testify to an even more negative assessment of their efforts. Henry Adams's complaint that nineteenth-century America was ill suited to men of his breeding and education has become a textbook account of the century's rejection of the Federalist tradition and the resulting displacement of its heirs. Henry James's lament that modern America held no room for literary men like himself further suggests that all attempts to create a place for the intellectual within the bustle and volatility of American society failed miserably.[14]

Many students of New England and American culture have affirmed these men's sense of displacement. Noting the integration of this Brahmin cultural elite in the first part of the century, they also have described its gradual marginalization in the second. They have described a process of evolution through which the political displacement experienced in the first part of the century was matched by a cultural displacement in the second. Just as the Federalist politician was removed from the center of the political stage, the neo-Federalist intellectual was moved from the center to the fringes of American society or forced to take refuge in pockets of "high culture" by the end of the century. Within this evolution the only limited success of this generation seems affirmed. One senses that if these young Federalists did succeed, they did so only for a while; if they did indeed reconcile the man of letters to the new democratic realities, their formula was a problematic one, and it held up for only a part of the nineteenth century.

Martin Green has argued, for example, that Boston culture must be broken into two periods. During the first half of the century, it was distinguished by its effective integration of all the different kinds of power—financial, political, intellectual, and administrative—within one web of assumed responsibility. Most importantly, he argued, within this web the "other kinds of power" acknowledged and respected the intellectual and consequently awarded "a high place to the life of the mind." As a result, the intellectual was able to exercise authentic power, and in return he was encouraged to recognize his obligations to society. Pedantry and artistic isolation were held in contempt—the antithesis of the man of learning's obligation to pursue a "fusion of the private and the public." Within this "really healthy culture," the man of letters could balance his sense of intellectual superiority with his democratic confidence and achieve a sense of authentic integration, feel himself "fully a citizen—both as democrat and as aristocrat." [15]

This is a description of Boston culture with which the contributors to the *North American Review* would have agreed and from which they would have drawn hope. Its portrait of integration and influence for men of their education and class offers evidence of their successful adaptation. But Green also noted that during the second half of the nineteenth century, much of this changed. The fusion of public and private, this reconciliation of literature and politics, of culture and society, came undone as the man of letters was replaced by a new type of civic leader—businessmen and machine politicians. These new office seekers cast a more suspicious eye on culture while, on their end, the activities of intellectuals grew less confident and even confused. Some intellectuals made concessions to the new conditions by promoting literary forms that did not stretch or challenge the social consensus—they offered up the "easy, safe, tame art with which the philistines felt comfortable." Others retained a commitment to high culture but did so from within an understanding of its exclusive and esoteric nature. These pursued "serious" literary careers, not as citizens but as "aesthetes." Maintaining an uncomfortable position in the middle were those who embraced these more esoteric forms of art but insisted on placing them before the entire community—they embraced forms of art that were "more obscure, learned, expensive . . . out of ordinary reach, and out of relation to moral or social reality," but despite these qualities they continued to believe in their general powers of edification.[16]

Although the old synthesis fell apart, a few examples of the old model persisted. Green offered Ticknor's nephew, Charles Eliot Norton, as evidence of the "continued vitality" of the earlier fusion of the private and the public, an intellectual who retained a commitment to both high cultural standards and broad social obligations, a literary man who continued to believe that literature should go beyond the safe and the tame and that this ambition was a necessity for, not a threat to, the general society. But he did so without the broader cultural or institutional support earlier generations enjoyed. Whereas his uncle consequently "was what he believed in," moving "among people and institutions which to some degree realized his ideals," Norton only "stood for what he believed in; the people and institutions around him were visibly losing vigour and needing protection."[17]

Within Norton's peculiarity lies the conclusion that the young Federalists of the North American Review ultimately failed. Within the isolation and irresponsibility of the aesthete one recognizes the ultimately irrepressible undercurrents of the North American Review. Within Boston aesthete Bernard Berenson's argument that "the world consists of one's personal friends, one's thoughts and one's dreams" lies the suggestion that the literary ethic of indulgence and escape completely displaced the more socially responsible components of the Federalist literary vision. In Green's conclusion that culture became "an alternative to, a refuge from reality," there is evidence that the romantic components of Boston's literary vision ultimately triumphed over the neoclassical. In his description of aestheticism as an "approach to the world as a place of line, colour, and form, rather than of right and wrong," there is the suggestion that these young Federalists ultimately failed to balance the demands of aesthetics and morality.[18]

Nor is Green the only scholar to note this transformation within the culture of Boston and in so doing to point to the ultimate failure of these Federalist intellectuals. Frederic Cople Jaher argued similarly that what distinguished antebellum Boston society was the combining of commercial and cultural values. Mutually supporting one another and reenforced by marriage, this alliance of businessmen and intellectuals made the Boston Brahmins the exceptional cultural and social class that they were. Jaher did not agree with Green on the relative strengths of each group within this relationship. His argument that the business elements dominated the cultural stands in marked contrast to Green's description of a "really healthy culture." But his point that prior to the Civil War the two were fused together, only to become unraveled after the war, suggests a similar process of social atomization. Although disagreeing on the prewar balance, he was in agreement that in the second half of the century Boston Brahmins became increasingly exclusive and aristocratic. They held less confidence in their ability to reconcile social and cultural values and increasingly took refuge in a more aristocratic and purely aesthetic view of culture. Contrary to the earlier fusion of cultural pursuits with an active engagement in the world was James Russell Lowell's conclusion that culture could only be preserved by a genteel class sheltered from the world by hereditary wealth. Contrary to the earlier confidence in the abilities of the intellectual or the artist to weave together aesthetics and social activism was the belief that culture was threatened by the "violation of the abstract by the concrete, of contemplation by action, and of culture by power."[19]

Scholars looking more broadly at American culture in the nineteenth century have reached similar conclusions. Lawrence Levine, for example, has traced a similar process of cultural fragmentation. Whereas at the beginning of the century all members of society participated in the same culture, watching Shakespeare together and singing the same operatic arias, by the second half of the century there had emerged two distinct cultures. The artistic forms previously shared were seized by the custodians of "high culture" and elevated to the status of cultural icons beyond innovation or criticism. No longer part of a shared and interactive cultural experience, they were "sacralized" as monuments to perfection. Although some continued to believe that even in this form culture served a public function—examples of beauty and decorum to be modeled for the lower classes needing polish and restraint—others denied any broader social function of art and defined the role of the upper class as one of benefactors and protectors. It was their responsibility not to disseminate art but rather to preserve it, not employ it toward didactic ends but rather to enshrine it, pristine and uncompromised, regardless of its unpopularity or commercial unprofitability.[20]

Levine's application of this argument to Boston supports the conclusions of Green and Jaher. Their identification of the aesthete is echoed
by Levine's description of Henry Lee Higginson who argued that the
Boston Symphony should maintain the highest artistic standards regardless of the resulting inability to attract an audience and of John Sullivan
Dwight who demanded cultural forms that made concessions to neither
the audience nor the performer. For these men the monuments of classical culture should be presented without interpretation or variation in the
transcendent and permanent forms in which they were created.[21]

There is considerable consistency within all these portraits of Boston
and American culture. They all portray a unified culture giving way to a
more fragmented one. They contrast the intellectual and cultural leaders
of the first half of the century, integrated within the broader society and
playing important roles, with the aesthetes of the second half of the century, shut off from avenues of greater public influence. They contrast the
confidence of the earlier cultural leaders in the ability of culture to influence society with the late-century custodians of high culture who substituted preservation for dissemination as their goal. This portrait of
withdrawal and fragmentation has been reenforced by the work of other
historians who have suggested that this cultural retreat was complemented by a residential and social withdrawal. Both Oscar Handlin and
Barbara Solomon noted that during the second half of the century, Boston's upper class withdrew to its own suburbs, isolated its children in private schools, and took sanctuary within the Anglophilic decorum of the
Episcopal Church. Robert Dalzell more recently has described the economic and social dimensions of this retreat. Although in the first half of
the century Boston's commercial elite explored new manufacturing possibilities and energetically engaged in wide-ranging social endeavors, during the second half of the century both their business and social efforts
were more narrow and nonexpansive. Their agenda, he argued, had always been essentially conservative—to stabilize their economic status, to
find more secure avenues than commerce for themselves and their children, and to develop business activities that left them more time and energy for public service. Whereas in the first half of the century this led
them to broad efforts—the construction of new industries and institutions and participation in a variety of charitable organizations—by the
second half of the century their efforts tended to inhibit, rather than expand, New England's economic base, and the organizations in which they

participated and the charities that they funded served more exclusive purposes and clientele. The broad-based subscription drives intended to forge community cohesion while serving community needs were replaced by more elite forms of fund-raising for institutions like the Maclean Asylum that served an increasingly elite class of patients.[22]

The portrait of Boston society that finally emerges is a remarkably consistent one, pointing to the failure of these Federalist intellectuals to define a role for themselves of full participation in social and cultural affairs. The only disagreement among these historians lies in their explanations as to how and why this all occurred. For Green the decade of the 1840s was pivotal. In these years Irish immigration swelled to the point that the homogeneous culture which made the integration of culture and society possible broke down. Unassimilable and openly resistant to integration, these immigrants forced an institutional and political response that left the upper-class intellectuals marginalized and impotent. For Jaher the divisive impact of immigration was combined with the eclipse of Boston's commercial power by New York. Displaced politically by machine politics and commercially by New York merchants, Boston Brahmins turned more exclusively to careers in religion, education, and letters. For Levine the retreat of the upper class to the refuge of "high culture" was prompted by the challenge of the middle class in the cultural arena similar to its challenge to elite hegemony in politics, business, and society. "High culture," in Levine's argument, was the defensive response of upper-class members to the usurpation of their roles in all facets of American life.

There is considerable logic in all of these explanations. But what stands out after analyzing the young Federalists of the *North American Review* is the extent to which they themselves contributed to their own displacement, the extent to which their cultural and social isolation represented not a forced retrenchment but rather a logical unfolding and consequence of their own ideas. If by the end of the nineteenth century New England Brahmins and intellectuals found themselves cut off from the more central avenues of power, isolated within narrow communities, and engaging in rather narrow cultural pursuits, it was largely the logic of their own thought that was to blame. If by the end of the century Boston Brahminism had become characterized by asocial aestheticism and cultural elitism, it was the logical elaboration of the young Federalists' ideas about the uniqueness and privileges of genius, the legitimate social indifference of art, and the permissible escapism of the elite audience. If by the end of the century Brahmins had been displaced within the institutional order by the middle class, if they no longer singularly enjoyed the status and influence that accrued to medicine and the law, it was largely the result of their own success at professionalizing these fields and objectifying the means through which they were accessed. In short, if by the end of the century these heirs of the Federalist tradition were isolated within a divided culture, their isolation and this dichotomy represented less a cultural or social defeat at the hands of external forces than the consequence, albeit unintended, of their own efforts—less the result of Irish immigrants or rival commercial interests than of the failure of these young Federalists to fully reconcile and retain control over the competing elements within their literary, institutional, and historical visions.

Moreover, if the separation of culture and society and the deintegration of the intellectual did indeed grow out of the troubling undercurrents of elitism and aestheticism voiced in the *North American Review,* it is also true that an ethic of social engagement and responsibility persisted stubbornly in the background of late nineteenth-century Brahmin culture. If the heirs of this Federalist class found themselves displaced in the institutional order as a result of their own efforts, it is also true that a few refused to accept a position on the fringes and forced themselves back to the center of public affairs. Green recognized the persistence of this more complete social and cultural ethic in Charles Eliot Norton, and Levine acknowledged it in men like John Philip Sousa who continued to argue that culture had didactic responsibilities. George Fredrickson has argued more thoroughly that this residual call to public service provided a continuous challenge to intellectuals tempted to retreat. Although some did withdraw into transcendentalism and its ethic of self-cultivation, others like Francis Lieber and Horace Bushnell urged intellectuals to reconstruct the private and public institutions essential to the preservation of "institutional liberty."[23]

These intellectuals urged others to resist the romantic temptation to withdraw and called them to assume their traditional responsibilities as leaders. During the Civil War they embraced the war effort as a means of purifying the nation and cleansing it of its democratic excess. They celebrated Brahmin heroes like Robert Gould Shaw as examples of the sort of unique leadership they could provide. And they modeled in the Sanitary Commission the possibilities within highly organized professional action to solve social ills. Although in the years following the war these intellectuals were largely disappointed—their leadership remained rejected, their institutional model not widely imitated—they persisted in their commitment to social action. Sobered in their expectations, they continued in their resolve to serve "on whatever terms American society offered."[24]

Fredrickson reminds us that the social ethic of nineteenth-century intellectuals should not be oversimplified. His work is complemented by Christopher Lasch's study of twentieth-century intellectuals who refused to accept the disempowered positions in which American society placed them. For Lasch the persisting call to social action was reflected in the exaggerated, sometimes contradictory attempts of intellectuals to be men of action worthy of public roles.[25]

Thus, while pointing out the fact of retreat and consolidation, the tendencies within Brahmin culture and the institutions that supported it toward exclusivity and aestheticism, we should stop well short of identifying the young Federalists as failures. If we conclude that in the end it was their affirmations of aestheticism and artistic isolation that held most sway by 1900, we cannot ignore the vestiges of the more complete Federalist vision that remained visible into the twentieth century. Even more, we cannot ignore the importance of their intellectual blueprint for the development of American culture and society. Even if they did fail to permanently reconcile the competing elements in their vision, the innovations they prescribed, in some instances the transitional positions they articulated, proved crucial to the cultural and institutional developments of the nineteenth century.

It is perhaps the ambiguous character of their achievements that helps us most in understanding the place of intellectuals in America; it is perhaps the very ironies that lace their efforts that are their real legacy to American intellectuals. Much like the more general history of intellectual life in America, their difficulties cannot be explained simply by the advance of hostile forces such as anti-intellectualism, democracy, pluralism, revivalist evangelicals, or populist politicians. Their troubled place in American affairs was rooted in the ambiguities within their own efforts, in the particularities of their own response, their own form of adaptation. If these New England intellectuals left themselves and future generations of American intellectuals in an ambiguous position, it was not through their unwillingness to adapt, nor was it the fault of forces beyond their control. It was their success which bred failure, their achievements which

led to their own censure, their reforms which caused their own displacement. They were challenged and ultimately replaced within the new institutional order by the middle classes not because they clung defensively
to the old order, but because they led a reform movement which opened
the door to these rising social forces. They brought censure upon themselves not for being inflexible but for being just flexible enough to prepare
the ground for an even more progressive generation of intellectuals. They
compromised their ability to serve the nation as critics and analysts not
because they were indifferent to its policies or direction, but because they
were perhaps too anxious to preserve a voice in national affairs.

If American intellectuals are best understood as victims of their own
contradictions and marginalized by their own logic, the intellectuals
of the *North American Review* provide us an explanation as to why. If
American intellectuals more generally found themselves embracing philosophical and artistic positions that contained anti-intellectual implications or that ultimately reduced their influence, if they found themselves
anxious to serve society in more complete ways but restrained by their
unwillingness to make the political or ideological concessions necessary
to do so, if they felt themselves unappreciated at the same time that they
were being emulated, if their success in realizing their ambitions or gaining a broader acceptance of their thought only left them more insecure
and even replaced by those imitating or usurping their thought, then the
intellectuals of the *North American Review* do indeed illuminate the enduring complexities of American intellectual life.

There is more than a suggestion that these same New England intellectuals might illuminate similar questions pertaining to British intellectuals—that if they did not actually influence British intellectuals, they at
least anticipated by a generation or so corresponding developments in
British literary culture and intellectual life. The possibility is suggested
through a comparison with a group of intellectuals in Britian who in
many ways were similar to the young Federalists of the *North American
Review,* a group which could be considered, in fact, their British counterpart, the young Scottish intellectuals writing for the *Edinburgh Review.*

In many ways their story and that of their journal are very similar to
that of the American group. Founded in 1802, the *Edinburgh Review* provided a mouthpiece for a group of intellectuals whose political and professional prospects had been similarly circumscribed by events. Like the
young Federalists of the *North American Review,* they found their political

ambitions checked by shifting social and political realities. The French Revolution cast a pall over Scottish intellectual life in the early nineteenth century—in its wake Tory rule grew increasingly oppressive, debating societies were virtually silenced, and Whig leaders were isolated. Political dissent and free thought drew charges of Jacobinism, and consequently many of Scotland's young intellectuals took refuge in London.[26] There these intellectuals found greater intellectual and political freedom. But they also found themselves essentially removed from the center of political life. As a result, their work initially took on a more detached and analytical perspective. As Biancamaria Fontana has explained, left "unconstrained by the limited horizons of the day-to-day strategy of the opposition," their work adopted a range that was more broadly historical and a tone more philosophical.[27]

But if like the intellectuals of the *North American Review* in their depoliticization, if similar to them in being forced from the center of political affairs, the Scots were much different in the direction toward which their views evolved. Whereas most of the American group concluded that this nonpartisan intellectual activity was essential to their continued influence, the Scots eventually recommitted themselves to political activism. Ironically, the philosophical premises that they inherited suggested just the opposite tack. The thinkers of the Scottish Enlightenment had argued that the key to social and economic progress was the development of a commercial economy. More general prosperity, improved standards of living, the growth of the middling classes, were all dependent on the unfettered advancement of the commercial economy. Political forms were, in fact, largely irrelevant. Progress and reform could be achieved under a monarchy as easily as a republic. Within both the benign effects of commercial economy advanced inevitably, within both the voice of the political economist could hold sway.

But the French Revolution, which had initially served to remove these intellectuals to the fringes of political affairs, also served eventually to convince them of the importance of political action. The misery and frustration, the failure of Physiocratic reform, the advance of the revolution beyond the understandable and acceptable reforms of the National Assembly, all shattered the complacency of their vision. As a result, these young intellectuals were forced to rethink their views regarding the relative unimportance of political structures and political agency. Quite simply, they concluded that these did matter. The form of government under which progress hoped to advance did make a difference, and persistent, skilled political activity was necessary for its advance. Theorists could not simply place hope in the inevitable force of their ideas but must engage in the more practical work of political organization.

Unlike the *North American Review,* the *Edinburgh Review* became an overtly partisan journal. The founding intellectuals of each recognized the power of the people and its force in politics, both groups believed it was their job to help shape and direct public opinion, but the *Edinburgh Review* went further to an advocacy of direct political action. Some of its most important contributors—Henry Brougham and Francis Horner— entered politics, while others were satisfied to adopt a stance decidedly more political than that adopted by the *North American Review.* In both forms, the intellectuals of the Scottish circle expressed their belief in the importance of politics, their belief that political activism was one of their responsibilities as intellectuals.

The intellectuals of the *North American Review* group stand out in their refusal to regrasp political activism as a necessary part of their roles as intellectuals. Perhaps the political climate was more hostile, perhaps Jacksonian America was less receptive, perhaps they were personally less well suited. Or perhaps they were more committed to the purity of intellectualism, the necessary removal and distance required for true scholarship—perhaps they continued to heed Buckminster's suggestion that the intellectual should remain removed from the inevitably compromising realm of politics. The intellectuals of the *Edinburgh Review* did indeed compromise, or recast their efforts to serve their political ends. They allowed the political implications of the literary works submitted determine their acceptability; founder and editor Francis Jeffrey's religious skepticism was carefully silenced in order to prevent the political fallout. In this light, the refusal of the intellectuals of the *North American Review* to similarly reembrace political activism seems a testimony to their intellectual integrity—less a reflection of any political timidity or preference for a position on the fringes than an expression of their intellectual strength. If in comparison to the intellectuals of the *Edinburgh Review* they remained more isolated and even frustrated in their inability to shape events more directly, their frustration seems the work of their own logic.

Moreover, although the two groups and their journals diverged during these years, by midcentury English literary culture was moving closer to the position staked out by the *North American Review*. By the 1850s the polemical character of the *Edinburgh Review* and *London Quarterly* had lost favor. More preferred, according to Stefan Collini, was a new type of journal which spoke from a different stance and aimed at a different audience. Not so narrowly partisan as their predecessors or so narrowly academic as the journals that would emerge at the end of the century, these new journals spoke not to the party faithful or the academic specialist but rather to the well-educated but broadly interested "clever university man." These new journals, such as the *Saturday Review* (1855) and *Macmillan's* (1859), were serious and informed without being pedantic or overly specialized. Much like the *North American Review* they spoke to a range of interests, commenting on literature, reform, institutional development, and contemporary affairs. And like the *North American Review* they remained consciously nonpartisan politically, while at the same time far from indifferent culturally and socially. Like the *North American Review,* although they refused to serve as an extension of a party, they did represent the philosophy and ideology of a particular culture. Neither narrowly academic nor coldly analytical, these new journals depended upon "a fairly intimate acquaintance with the larger cultural conversation" within which they participated. Like the *North American Review* these new journals were concerned less with upholding an explicit political agenda than with contributing to the elaboration of the "imagined community" of which they were a member.[28]

If the *North American Review* anticipated by a generation the sorts of literary journals that would emerge in England in the 1850s, the *Review's* cultural nationalism anticipated a similar tendency in British literary culture during the second half of the nineteenth century. In the first half of the century, British writers and critics were not indifferent to the character and importance of their national literature, but there was nothing of the *North American Review's* messianic enthusiasm in their interests. Relatively stable politically and prosperous commercially, undivided internally, and unprovoked by foreign press—or at least confident enough culturally to be indifferent to any foreign criticism—British literary culture was not inspired to explore, until the mid to late century, the nationalistic questions that much earlier had preoccupied the *North American Review.* There was an interest in grammar and lexicography, but not until the second half of the century did English critics turn their attention to the character and importance of their literature, not until then did they

become more concerned with anthologies than dictionaries, with defining the canon of British literature than the rules of English grammar.[29]

Even the position of intellectuals in British society seems to have been
anticipated by New England intellectuals. Their emergence as a class in
Britain at the end of the century no doubt owes more to institutional
developments than the example set in America. The reform of the university, the advance of science, the fragmentation of the liberal arts into
distinct disciplines, had more to do with the emergence of an intellectual
class as an "isolated cultural elite" than the examples set in Boston.[30] But
in the late-century British conflict between the "gentlemen don" and the
"research-ideal," between the older vision of the intellectual as aristocratic
savant and the newer conception of the intellectual as a detached scholar,
one sees, removed by several generations, the tension laid out much earlier in the *North American Review*. When the students of Macaulay and
Froude, the historians of the grand narrative, were challenged by the
new "fact-grubbing," research-oriented, archive-based historians, they
gave voice to the debate earlier held between Daniel Webster and Nathan
Hale, between Edward Everett and Francis Gray.[31]

To argue a causal relationship or even one of influence would be im-
prudent. No doubt the peculiarities of British social and cultural life had
far more to do with the elaboration of British literary culture and intellectual life than these young New England intellectuals. But the similarities are considerable and the differences in timing curious. If there is
little to suggest that antebellum American intellectuals directly influenced British intellectual life, it seems safe to argue that the cultural and
intellectual developments in America were largely prompted by the cultural and intellectual pressures exerted by England—that the character
of American literary culture and the role of American intellectuals were
largely reconsidered and redefined as a result of the criticism from the
British press. In this realization there is perhaps the ultimate irony—
as American intellectuals struggled to defend American culture against
British criticism, they carved out a niche for themselves that anticipated
similar developments in Britain by at least a generation. As they fended
off the ridicule of British travelers and press by promoting American culture and outlining a series of institutional reforms, they anticipated similar developments in British cultural and social life. As these embattled
New England intellectuals reconceived the literary journal, reimagined

the university, and reconceptualized their place in society, they modeled the future direction of British intellectual life.

If in the end these American intellectuals foretold the direction of not only American intellectual life but also English, if they anticipated the character of both American and British literary culture, the entire question of success and failure becomes terribly confused. Ultimately it is decided by what one chooses to emphasize—the stimulus these men offered American cultural independence or the position in which they left the intellectual, the personal success of these men in preserving the status of their class or the vehicle they offered for middle-class mobility, the effectiveness of their response to foreign criticism and the resulting effects on American identity or the intellectual support they provided for American expansion. Even if the conclusion is that on their own terms they were ultimately unsuccessful, that is, they failed to situate the man of letters unambiguously within a culture that valued hierarchy as well as equality, the general good as well as individual interests, and social obligation as well as self-cultivation, one should not forget the variety of ways they contributed to the formation of American society and culture.

If even on more personal terms we conclude that this generation was generally unsuccessful in achieving its aims—if most did ultimately fail, like Prescott and Everett, to fully reconcile the conflicting demands of their Federalist upbringing with the realities of republican America, some consideration must be given to those like George Ticknor who seem to have denied the generalization and concluded their lives more fully at terms with surrounding events.

In 1835 George Ticknor returned to Europe. Still shaken by the death of a son the previous year, he resigned his position at Harvard and embarked on a three-year tour emphasizing concerns for his wife's health. But his departure was also moved by a profound sense of failure. His tenure at Harvard had not lived up to the expectations he brought to the appointment in 1819, and in leaving he cited not only his family concerns but also his long-standing disagreement with college officials over "what the college can be, and what it ought to be." [32]

In many ways the Europe to which he returned offered a series of striking contrasts to the disappointments he had experienced at Cambridge. The failure of his academic reforms, the resistance in America to intellectual rejuvenation, and his own personal disappointment surrounding the failure to win the respect and prestige he believed his scholarly achievements warranted contrasted sharply with the honor and recognition awarded intellectuals in Europe. In Dublin he was moved by the knighting of William Rowan Hamilton, an unprecedented distinction for a man of scientific or literary achievement. In Florence he made repeat visits to the gallery—"a sort of holy place in the arts"—where great minds from the past were memorialized in stone. In Dresden he was moved by the tribute to Böttiger, a professor of archaeology, paid him by his students upon his death. Parading in absolute silence, they gathered at his home to sing hymns on the night before his burial. The "multitude, illuminated by the torches which the young men tossed wildly about as they advanced in absolute silence," stood in ironic contrast to the pyrotechnic mischief directed against Harvard faculty.[33]

He was moved further by the historical and cultural richness of Europe that America could not rival. At a music festival in York celebrating the anniversary of the king's coronation, Ticknor passed through a range of unrepublican emotions. When "the vast audience rose . . . [and] the shout of 'God save the King,' broke from the choir of four hundred voices sustained by the full power of two hundred and fifty instruments and the tremendous organ," the effect, admitted Ticknor, "was electrical." Visiting the Trinity College library, he was awed by the archival treasures— Newton's and Milton's papers, the "venerable remains of two of the greatest men . . . the world has ever seen."[34]

But if tempted to the edge of cultural infidelity by Europe's respect for intellectualism and its cultural richness, he pulled back. By the end of his trip, his American sensibilities and cultural loyalties seem to have been not only secure but also strengthened. Although he suggested that America could use more antiquarians like the one he met in Berlin, his praise for this church historian was filled with ambiguity—"buried in books, so near-sighted that he can see little more than an inch beyond his nose, and so ignorant of the world that the circle of his practical knowledge is not much wider than that of his vision; dirty in his person, and in the midst of confusion." When he visited Goethe's home, he was struck less by the public veneration that had turned it into a public monument than the "vanity of a man who . . . came at last to think whatever related to himself to be of great consequence to the world." Far from applauding this tribute to intellectual greatness, Ticknor denounced the exaggerated sense of self-importance demonstrated by Goethe's orders for the posthumous publishing of all his papers, "much of which is mere waste-paper," and the enshrining of his personal quarters, "a very ordinary study and sleeping-room to be shown to strangers, as matters of moment and interest."[35]

Of still greater significance in this restoration of Ticknor's loyalties was a series of discussions he had with Metternich in Vienna. Although Ticknor was somewhat miffed that Metternich attached little significance to their meetings—"he ceased, I dare say, in five minutes, to think or remember anything more about me, as Sancho says, than 'about the shapes of the last year's clouds'"—he was granted three audiences during which they discussed democracy and its future in America. For Metternich, neither was promising. Democracy was "a dissolving, decomposing principle; it tends to separate men, it loosens society." True, it might make men "more curious . . . more distinct, more interesting." But there was nothing to "unite them into compact and effective masses; to render them capable, by their combined efforts, of the highest degrees of culture and civilization." Moreover, it was inherently unstable and short-lived. "With you in America," he argued, "it seems to be *un tour de force perpetuel*. You are, therefore, often in dangerous positions, and your system is one that wears out fast."[36] Ticknor's nationalism was prodded, perhaps in much the same way that he and his peers had been provoked by foreign criticism two decades earlier, and he defended America and its republican institutions. Even though Metternich's praise for monarchy's unifying powers may have struck a chord, Ticknor defended republicanism, where "individuals are of much more consequence . . . men are more truly men, have wider views and a more active intelligence.[37]

As his tour continued, this argument became a recurring theme in his journals and correspondence. He soon began to frame it within a more complete assessment of Europe, America, and their respective futures. The romantic fascination with Europe was now replaced with a more pessimistic sense of its future. "The old principles that gave life and power to society are worn out; you feel on all sides a principle of decay at work." Its middle class offered some hope, but it was surrounded by a lower class that was discontented and jealous and an upper class characterized by "weakness, inefficient presumption, and great moral degradation." In contrast, he praised the ever more apparent virtues of America where "the less favored portions of society . . . have so much more intellect, will, and knowledge." Echoing the argument he first made to Metternich, he concluded, "A man is much more truly a man with us . . . and, notwithstanding the faults that freedom brings out in him, it is much more gratifying and satisfying to the mind, the affections, the soul, to live in our state of society."[38]

This restored commitment to America was sharpened further by the pessimism Ticknor encountered among European liberals. Austrian liberalism had been crushed, and the forces of tyranny seemed strengthened. French liberals had all but lost hope in the free institutions that they had formerly championed in their own country, while American mobs and the curse of slavery convinced them that even the future of American democracy was imperiled. The result for Ticknor was not only a restored commitment to American institutions but a restored sense of American exceptionalism—a renewed sense of the uniqueness of the American experiment and a renewed awareness that its failure would have international repercussions.[39]

It was thus with a rejuvenated sense of purpose as an American, and even an intellectual, that Ticknor returned from Europe. He resolved to improve Europeans' understanding of America, in particular regarding its intellectual character. His correspondence back to Europe was filled with descriptions of the "education, intelligence, and domestic happiness" that pervaded American society. To Maria Edgeworth he described America's common schools and boasted that not only did there exist "a great deal of intellectual activity and cultivation, there is no visible poverty, little gross ignorance, and little crime." To Prince John, duke of Saxony, he claimed that "progress in wealth, in education, in civilization—is the very law of our condition, and its impulse is irresistible," and he offered Prescott's *Ferdinand and Isabella* as a "specimen of the progress of letters in this country." In response to Edgeworth's question regarding the state of metaphysics in America, he offered no apologies for Americans' practical disposition. Although America had produced no great metaphysical work since Jonathan Edwards's *Freedom of the Will,* a more "practical metaphysics" was expressed in institutions such as the Asylum for the Blind. Traditional philosophers might pay homage to the "more spiritualized and imaginative Germans," but the "wiser sort of intellectual philosophers . . . those who care to make people happy, and not to make them crazy or quarrelsome," would soon concede American thinkers their due.[40]

To complement these efforts to improve the reputation of America abroad, Ticknor led the crusade in these years to establish a free public library in Boston. Long advocated but also long delayed by Brahmin intellectuals less anxious to make the resources of the Athenæum available to the general public, the library met resistance to the day it opened. Even among those with whom Ticknor worked most closely, his demands that popular literature be made available and that all materials be circulated freely stand out in their confidence and magnanimity. Expressing a persisting sense of responsibility as a man of letters and means and a persisting confidence in the power of literature to shape the public character, Ticknor offered a variation of the argument earlier advanced in the *North American Review.* By making all sorts of literature available and "by a little judicious help, rather than any direct control or restraint," he believed popular tastes would "be carried much higher than previously thought possible."[41]

Perhaps because his own sense of purpose was restored, he voiced increased confidence in the wisdom of the people—to determine right and to direct the nation through even its most difficult challenges. When Massachusetts's fiscal problems were exacerbated by a lack of political leadership and the absence of legislative solutions, he offered confidence that "when the people do come to the rescue, they come with a flooding force." In 1846 when the nation engaged itself in "a very disgraceful war with Mexico," he offered as "one of the good signs" the fact that the war "grows less and less popular every day."[42]

During these same years he offered platitudes, primarily to his European friends, regarding the salutary operation of America's republican institutions. Presidential elections were extolled as a source of "life and energy" for the national character. "The simple fact that the eyes of the whole population are directed to two men, and their thoughts seriously fastened on the great principles by which their government shall be administered . . . give a concentration and authority to public opinion." Even more inspiring was the smooth transition that followed elections or death in office. In contrast to the twin threats of insurrection and despotic reaction that hovered over European affairs, Ticknor offered the restraint and calm that followed the death of Zachary Taylor, "without the least show or bustle, not a soldier being visible on the occasion, nor any form observed or any word spoken but the accustomed simple and awful oath of fidelity to the Constitution."[43]

Confident in the popular wisdom, republican institutions, and the course of national affairs, Ticknor in these years was a man genuinely reconciled with the new America. Not so troubled as Prescott or Everett, he seems in these years to have found a role for himself consistent with both the broader course of American affairs and his own sensibilities as an intellectual and an heir of the Federalist tradition. It was perhaps because of this that he met the approaching Civil War with confidence. Although dreading the bloodbath and condemning those, particularly in Europe, who sought to provoke the crisis to serve their own needs, he expressed repeated confidence in the people's ability to provide the necessary direction and resolve to public policy. Although he feared that neither Lincoln nor his advisers were "equal to the emergency" facing the nation, he was confident that "the people . . . are." Combining his faith in the people and his satisfaction with his own contributions as an intellectual and custodian of the public mind, he praised the unprecedented "earnestness" of the popular Union movement. Coming to terms fully with his role in the Republic and, perhaps more poignantly, with the legacy of previous Federalist generations, he described with a sense of ownership and pride the public mood, more focused than it was in 1812 and more informed than it was 1775. Perhaps the feelings "were as deep and stern in 1775," he admitted, but "it was by no means so intelligent or unanimous."[44]

It is this final comparative statement that stands out most significantly here. His confident assessment of the public mind and his proud description of its unprecedented intelligence and unanimity reflect just how fully Ticknor had come to terms with not only democracy but also the legacy of his Federalist fathers. The generation that preceded this one continued to impose a great deal of pressure on these men, exerting ultimately, perhaps, an overwhelming influence on men like Everett and Prescott. Their struggles, alongside Ticknor's content, suggest that coming to terms with democracy meant not just rethinking the place of Federalism in America but escaping from the shadows of its celebrated past—successfully adapting to the new America meant not just reapplying the culture and ideology of Federalism but also freeing themselves from the burden of its historic legacy.

Dealing with this burden lent this challenge a set of pressures perhaps as much psychological as intellectual. To the task of transcribing a set of beliefs was added the trauma of filial separation—a reworking of one's sense of self independent of, in some cases in opposition to, the prescriptions of their fathers. As if that were not enough, within the context of antebellum America, this reworking of their fathers' legacy, this reworking of their conceptions of self, meant also the reworking of their sense of manhood.

To speak in this sort of terms about any group is somewhat uncomfortable. To move from an analysis of their scholarly works, and even beyond an examination of their publicly expressed beliefs, to a discussion of the interior—an analysis of their sense of themselves as men—carries the risk of not only error but trivialization. For these men most particularly any attempt to dissect their inner feelings is intimidating. Most of these men were very private. Inasmuch as they were sympathetic to the self-probing tendencies of the emerging romantic artists and conceded to genius certain privileges of intellectual indulgence and introspection, they were themselves, almost to the man, very reserved. But these equivocations aside, there is something not only intriguing but also necessary in pursuing these sorts of questions, for if tinted on the edges with more personal questions about self and manhood, their search for a place in society takes on additional texture. These more interior issues may go far to help explain choices they made and rejected; they may help to explain the nuances within the positions these men outlined for themselves and others.

The study of manhood or masculinity owes much to the recovery of women's history in the 1960s. The questions raised regarding the place of women in society, their roles and sensibilities, the behaviors prescribed, the spheres delineated, the opportunities denied but also seized, have led logically to the exploration of sometimes similar and often interrelated questions regarding men in American society. Now, often overlapping one another in theme and methodology, men's and women's studies—or more appropriately gender studies—are pursued with a greater sensitivity to the "relational" character of male and female roles, a greater sensitivity to the ways in which gender roles and prescriptions are worked out dialectically, rather than in isolation.[45] In addition, the maturation of gender studies has coincided with the construction of a more variegated portrait of gender in America—the realization that male and female roles, as well as prescriptions for manhood and womanhood, have varied not only over time but across space, class, race, and ethnic group.

These evolutions within the discipline have paid particular dividends in the study of antebellum culture. It was within antebellum America that early students of women's history identified the emergence of "separate spheres" and the "cult of domesticity," while students of masculinity or manhood observed the transition from one model of manhood to another, from a model which valued public service and the "useful citizen" toward one which valued autonomy and individualism.[46] But benefiting from more recent research, these initial conclusions have been refined, and the result is a far richer and more complex portrait of gender in antebellum America. Women's historians have more recently explored whether these separate spheres were sources of confinement or empowerment; whether it is more helpful to approach the values of domesticity as something imposed upon women or generated by women. They have asked if all of this was more prescriptive or real, and if it had any meaning at all for women who were nonwhite and outside the northern middle class. Women's historians have also demanded more sharply drawn analytical tools; they have sorted out distinctions between "woman's rights" and "woman's emancipation," between "women's spheres" and "women's culture," and they have more critically explored the relationship between antebellum women's issues and postbellum feminism.[47] Students of masculinity have similarly challenged the polar simplicity of the separate spheres and have questioned whether nineteenth-century notions of manhood can be approached using a twentieth-century sense of heterosexuality.[48] More importantly, they have pointed out that manhood not only underwent some recasting during these years, it assumed a variety of forms throughout America. The rough-and-tumble style of southwestern frontier masculinity was much different from the self-control and sobriety that characterized northern middle- and working-class models of manhood. The linking of manhood to fraternal love, common to both upper-class abolitionists in the North and secessionists in the South, contrasted sharply with notions of manhood embraced by other northern upper-class males who valued adventurous camaraderie more than sentimentality. The emphases placed on personal restraint and sober chastity by the Men's Moral Reform Society contrasted sharply with the free-wheeling libertinism of "sporting-male culture."[49]

These more recent studies have illustrated the complexity of gender during the antebellum years. Irreducible to a period of clear and distinct spheres or unequivocal roles in antebellum America, the entire range of gender issues was extraordinarily unsettled—the evolving roles of men and women and the tensions between them, the shifting relation between family and the market, the intensity of the prescriptive literature, the troubled fascination with urban culture, the anxieties about the feminization of certain activities and fields, conflicting models of femininity and masculinity, all speak to the tumultuous state of gender. Manhood, perhaps even more than womanhood during these years, seems to have been particularly unfixed—its contested and unsettled state reflected not only in its variety of expression across class and region but also, according to some historians, in its recurring appearance as a subtext in presidential politics, professional formation, fraternal rituals, and many of the era's most sensational legal dramas.[50]

It was within this context, within this state of gender instability and reconceptualization, that young Federalist intellectuals set about to resecure a place for themselves in American society. Nor were they, by virtue of their privileged or conservative backgrounds, shielded from any of this. In fact, if anything, the sort of careers they envisioned, the arenas they identified as most appropriate to their efforts, the values they articulated as central to their new roles, placed them right at the center of this disorder. As intellectuals they linked themselves to a set of values far removed from the burgeoning creed of action and entrepreneurship. As men of scholarship and letters, they expressed a version of manhood far different from the nascent standard lauding physical attributes and achievements. As teachers they laid claim to a profession that was in the earliest stages of feminization. As advocates for a native literature, they presided over a cultural arena in which women were playing larger and larger roles. In short, as these young men carved out a space for themselves within American culture as intellectuals, they had to contend with a certain challenge from women on one side and a certain sense of manhood on the other; they had to confront women within the institutions and activities that they hoped to control, while simultaneously contending with increasingly strident understandings of manhood within the broader culture.

The significance of all this for these young men should not be misrepresented. Certainly neither Ticknor, Everett, Prescott, nor the others explicitly framed their concerns regarding influence and status in the sorts of gender-conscious or gender-anxious terms voiced by their cultural counterparts of the next generation. Emerson's complaints about the "excessive virility" of nonliterary men, Hawthorne's outburst against "a d——d mob of scribbling women," Thoreau's preoccupation with male rivalry and the competitive character of antebellum society in which he and his father both failed, and Melville's complaints about a culture defined by "sturdy backwoodsmen" reflect a more advanced set of gender anxieties than those ever exhibited by the intellectuals of the *North American Review*.[51] These intellectuals would not even express the sort of professional doubt that would trouble evangelical clergy who struggled to both engage and yet distance themselves from the women who supported their work but also undercut their positions within male culture.[52] Instead, these young Federalists, at least through the 1820s, seem to have been more confident that they could carve out roles for themselves that would satisfy their needs as intellectuals, as persons of influence, and as men.

But if confident that they could define their place in American life and reconcile it to more traditional notions of manhood, ones which emphasized the community over the individual and acknowledged the necessity and legitimacy of literary activities, they were still aware that the shifting place of women in American culture represented something of a challenge—if confident that the arrival of women into those fields and activities through which they hoped to wield power and influence could be dealt with, it still needed to be dealt with; the respective spheres of action still needed to be carefully delineated. Thus they applauded the efforts of certain female writers but reminded them that their sensibilities allowed them to contribute in very limited ways. They acknowledged a certain limited role for women in education but did not include them in their more complete vision, interlaced as it was with their blueprint for a professionalized, university-centered institutional order. They entered the ranks of antebellum reform, but only after establishing their own philanthropic organizations separated from the numerous evangelical reform associations—partially because of their interest in more permanent and professional institutions, partially because they were repelled by the enthusiasm of evangelicalism, but also because they wanted to separate themselves and their work from these female-inclusive efforts.

Perhaps even more subtly, their awareness of the problematic advances of women may account for certain peculiarities in individuals' conduct and thought. It may help explain why Henry Dwight Sedgwick and Theodore Sedgwick Jr. could become such powerful advocates for their sister's work but never gain more attention for her, much less a contributing role in the *Review*, a journal that was edited by their friends and to which they contributed. It may also help explain why Prescott framed his ultimate frustration with literary criticism in gender-laden terms—why he lamented his earliest scholarly efforts, and more generally those of the *North American Review,* as "weak and waterish," devoid of the "business-like air, or the air of the man of the world, which gives manliness and significance to criticism."[53]

The need to respond somewhat carefully to the shifting presence of women in American society may be reflected best in Caleb Cushing's contributions to the *Review* on the subject of women's social and legal status. In 1828 he took special aim at the absence of property rights for married women, a condition he called a "continual embarrassment." Rooted in ancient law and canonized by Blackstone, the reduction of married women to *feme covert*—legally dead, wholly absorbed by marriage into the legal person of the husband—could be reconciled with neither "justice, nor public policy, nor the exigencies of social life." But in calling for reform, he was quick to emphasize that he was not interested in securing some "extravagant standard of legal privilege." More specifically, he saw no connection between property rights and political rights. "The constitution of nature . . . written over the face of the universe . . . has, we conceive, settled the question, whether the female sex should exercise political franchises equally with man." Property rights needed to be extended, but broader political rights would be unwise. Nature had "clearly indicated the orbit, in which either sex should revolve; and were they to cross each other's paths, confusion and disorder would inevitably ensue to punish their rash eccentricity."[54]

For Cushing, acknowledging the need for reform and also maintaining the sanctity of the male-exclusive political realm were reconciled by conservative notions of domesticity. Property rights were a question not of equality, or even justice, but rather protection for the domestic sphere. Providing a married woman with some enduring control over her property would protect her and her children against a profligate husband. Current law, which made personal property an absolute gift to the husband upon marriage and entitled him to any profits or income from any real property the wife brought to the marriage, left women defenseless against financially inept or irresponsible husbands. The corresponding restrictions on women's behavior—a married woman could neither use nor alienate her property, nor even enter into a contract, sell goods, or lose money at cards without her husband's authorization—struck Cushing as equally absurd. These legal principles, he argued, were contrary to the respective characters and sensibilities of men and women. Whereas a man's nature led him to "his counting-room, or his office, upon the exchange, or in the forum, or wherever else the calls of interest, ambition, or duty may demand his presence," a woman's natural attachment was to the home. "Her functions are domestic; her education is domestic; her temper is domestic; the constitutions of Providence have made her domestic; her happiness, her pride, her glory, all that exalts her in estimation above the other sex, lies in the round of endearing charities, which enliven, bless, and purify the domestic circle." [55]

Cushing's framing of progressive legal principles within more conservative ideological terms suggests that ensuring the public positions of men of his caste required a careful framing of the public position and rights of women. The careful response of these men to the advances of women more broadly—in literature, education, and philanthropy—suggests that their coming to terms with America's emerging democratic society required a very careful clarification of the terms upon which women would participate in this democracy as well. And on these terms, it would seem that here again this group of young intellectuals failed. They were unable to prevent the entrance of women into teaching, and they were unable to maintain the distinction between the "male" and "female" literary spheres. As with so many of their ideological and institutional adaptations, one is struck by the ironies that accompanied even their successes. The establishment in 1838 of the Normal School at Lexington, Massachusetts, represented the realization of their vision of a publicly funded institution of professional teacher training. But its admission of only women denied these men the sort of professional hegemony and concomitant status they pursued.

Similarly the sort of distinction Cushing hoped to maintain in advocating legal reform for women along ideologically conservative lines would be lost once the issue left the hands of legal theorists and entered the political arena. Norma Basch has demonstrated that Cushing's position was not all that uncommon. In fact, the greatest headway during the 1840s in the movement to expand women's property rights was engineered by moderates like Cushing who dissociated legal from political rights and rooted their arguments in concerns about irresponsible husbands and financially victimized women and children. But once these issues made their way into the political arena, these moderate reformers

lost control of the terms upon which the debate was conducted and the
lengths to which the debate should be carried. Once introduced into state
legislatures and constitutional conventions, the debate "radiated in un-
anticipated directions," and a broader range of legal and political issues
was broached.[56] Even more dramatically, Carole Shammas has suggested
the ways in which these laws may have destabilized the family. Challenging the long line of historians beginning with Mary Beard who concluded
that they had little effect, Shammas argued that probate records reveal
a dramatic shifting of property and wealth by the closing decades of the
nineteenth century. As women gained greater control over their property
and earnings, the capital formation function of marriage was altered, and
divorce became a more practical option for both men and women.[57]

There is considerable evidence that these Federalist intellectuals failed
here again to accomplish their goals—failed to retain control over certain
professions and activities and to contribute to reform without destabiliz-
ing the broader traditional social order. Not only did they fail on their
own terms, not only did they fail to harness those forces around them in
such a way that their own positions could be enhanced, but their response
to the issues surrounding women during these years suggests that they
failed in even more profound ways as intellectuals. In the end, their need
to position themselves as men within a culture that was in many quarters increasingly contemptuous of their conceptions of manhood seems
to have prevented their responding more progressively to the forces of
change that surrounded them. In the end, their need to be men may have
compromised their ability to serve as intellectuals, to serve as social critics
and disinterested analysts or, perhaps better still, as voices for authentic
reform.

If here again they failed, perhaps the most generous, most sympathetic
assessment might emphasize the human nature of the issues with which
they struggled. Entangled in all this was not just their place in society
as intellectuals but also their place in the emerging American culture as
men—resting on all this was not just their sense of themselves as heirs
to the Federalist tradition but also their sense of themselves as their fathers' sons. For these sons of judges and legislators, for these grandsons
of Revolutionary statesmen and heroes, the call to measure up, in every
sense, may have been too insistent.

Perhaps even more fundamentally, any assessment must acknowledge
not only the complexity inherent in these questions about place and

status, not only the human drama surrounding this search for influence, but also the drama and the enchantment of the times themselves. Coming of age during the early years of the nineteenth century, these young Federalists sensed themselves surrounded by great events and great ideas. The spirits of liberty and egalitarianism, of passion and romance, and perhaps most powerfully of self-realization and individual autonomy were making themselves felt in all parts of the world. Although they recognized the danger in all this to men of their sensibilities and status, they did not hang on defensively to the past. Although they noted the effects on the traditional community, they nonetheless were attracted by the stimulus given to art, literature, and the life of the mind. And if they were troubled by the effects on the organic web of values, forms of communication, and modes of behavior that defined traditional society, they nonetheless were intrigued by the effects on this new race of men.

If they ultimately were unable to fully reconcile these historical forces, it was because they were drawn to these forces themselves. Rather than clinging defensively to the past, they responded honestly and selectively and attempted to form a genuine synthesis of what they deemed preservable from their past and attractive in the present. In the end, therefore, it is perhaps more appropriate that they be judged less by questions of success and failure than by ones regarding significance. On these terms an answer is clear. In the years following the War of 1812, these young men attempted to adapt the ideology of their parents to the new realities of democratic America. In so doing, they rejected part of their past and seized a portion of the present. Through the intellectual and institutional window they opened, a good deal of America's future came into view.

Notes

CHAPTER I. *1815*

1. The literature on Federalism is extensive. See Banner, *Hartford Convention;* Livermore, *Twilight of Federalism;* Fischer, *Revolution of American Conservatism;* Charles, *Origins of the American Party System;* Dauer, *Adams Federalists;* and Buel, *Securing the Revolution.* Banner and Fischer offer the most useful introduction to the ideology of Federalism, along with Kerber, *Federalists in Dissent.* Ben-Atar and Oberg, *Federalists Reconsidered,* is a useful and recent collection of essays.

2. Banner, *Hartford Convention,* 4, 72; Howe, *Political Culture of the American Whigs,* 2.

3. Hamilton, *Federalist Papers,* no. 10.

4. J. Adams, "A Defence of the Constitutions."

5. Banner, *Hartford Convention,* 3–10, 84–89. The theme of exceptionalism can be traced much further in New England's past than the era of the Federalist Party. For its earlier manifestations, see Miller, *New England Mind,* 432–93, and Heimert, *Religion and the American Mind.*

6. Fischer, *Revolution of American Conservatism,* 152.

7. Banner, *Hartford Convention,* 147–67.

8. Kerber, *Federalists in Dissent,* xi-xii, 4.

9. Gilman, *Journals of Emerson* 13:115.

10. Ralph Waldo Emerson, "Historic Notes of Life and Letters in New England," in E. Emerson, *Works of Emerson* 10:260.

11. Quoted in Mott, *American Magazines* 2:241.

12. Ibid.; Poe quoted in Spiller et al., *Literary History* 1:287.

13. Spiller et al., *Literary History* 1:287; Parrington, *Main Currents* 2:271–95. Some literary historians ignore this period and the *North American Review* al-

together. Russell Blankenship, in arguing that "for fifty years after the outbreak of the Revolution the intellectual sterility of New England was disheartening," leaps from the Connecticut Wits, "the last cry of a disappearing order," to the writers of the New England Renaissance. Only Unitarianism is offered as representative of any intellectual vitality in the years in between (Blankenship, *American Literature,* 272, 185).

14. Hall, *Organization of American Culture,* 179.

15. See Simpson, *Federalist Literary Mind,* 3–9; Buell, "Early National Period"; Spencer, *Quest for Nationality,* 63; Howe, *Unitarian Conscience,* 177.

16. Appleby, *Inheriting the Revolution,* 136; Field, "Birth of Secular High Culture."

17. For an introduction to this debate and some useful summaries of the historiography, see Shalhope, "Republicanism and Early American Historiography"; Rodgers, "Republicanism: The Career of a Concept"; Banning, "Jeffersonian Ideology Revisited"; Appleby, "Republicanism in Old and New Contexts" and "What Is Still American?" Appleby's essays are also contained in *Liberalism and Republicanism.*

18. Burns, *Roosevelt,* 236–37.

19. Sandel, *Democracy's Discontent,* 3–6.

20. Hofstadter, *Anti-Intellectualism in American Life,* 21; Niebuhr, "Unhappy Intellectuals," 790–94.

21. See Lears, *No Place of Grace.*

22. Oliver Wendell Holmes Jr., "The Soldier's Faith" (1895), in Holmes, *Speeches,* 59.

23. Lipset, *Political Man,* 323–26.

24. See Lazarsfeld and Thielens, *The Academic Mind.*

25. National Endowment for the Humanities Website, Dec. 1999.

26. Ibid., April 1999.

CHAPTER 2. *Fathers*

1. Quoted in Morison, *Life and Letters of Otis* 1:26.

2. Ibid., 85, 57.

3. For example, see Fisher Ames, "Equality," in Ames, *Works* 2:207–28; see also Kerber, *Federalists in Dissent,* 67–79.

4. Quincy, *Why Are You a Federalist?* 15, 18.

5. Goodman, *Democratic-Republicans,* 128–32.

6. For various positions on this spectrum, see Appleby, *Inheriting the Revolution;* Prince, "Passing of the Aristocracy"; Cunningham, *Process of Government;* Ellis, *Jeffersonian Crisis.*

7. Goodman, *Democratic-Republicans,* 97–127, 145–54.

8. See Kerber, *Federalists in Dissent,* 23–66; Banner, *Hartford Convention,* 99–103.

9. East, "Economic Development"; Goodman, *Democratic-Republicans,* 182–97.

10. For a contemporary's description of Boston during these years, see Hillard, *Life of Ticknor* 1:20–21.

11. Lowell, *New England Patriot,* 20, 19, 93, 105.

12. Bailyn, *Ideological Origins;* Heimert, *Religion and the American Mind.*

13. Quincy, *Washington Benevolent Society,* 6.

14. Josiah Quincy to Otis, Nov. 26, 1811, in Morison, *Life and Letters of Otis* 2:34.

15. May, *Enlightenment in America.* On the persistence of conspiracy theories in American politics, see Hofstadter, "Paranoid Style in American Politics."

16. Fisher Ames, "Lucius Junius Brutus," in Ames, *Works* 2:92.

17. Fisher Ames, "Equality. No. III," ibid., 213.

18. Fisher Ames, "Camillus. No. I," ibid., 100.

19. Fisher Ames, "Equality. No. VI," ibid., 223.

20. Fisher Ames, "The Dangers of American Liberty," ibid., 348.

21. Fisher Ames, "The Republican. No. I," ibid., 251.

22. Ibid., 252.

23. Ames, "The Dangers of American Liberty," ibid., 357, 360.

24. Wills, *Inventing America,* 111–31.

25. Ames, "The Dangers of American Liberty," in Ames, *Works* 2:345–46, 354.

26. See, for example, Tudor, *Oration Pronounced July 4;* see also Warren, *Jacobin and Junto,* 221–25.

27. See Ames, "The Dangers of American Liberty."

28. Wells, "Silva, No. 32," 543.

29. Resolution passed at the Boston Town Meeting, Aug. 6, 1812, in Morison, *Life and Letters of Otis* 2:50.

30. Fischer, *Revolution of American Conservatism.*

31. Banner, *Hartford Convention,* 256–67.

32. Ibid., 266n.

33. Quoted in Fischer, *Revolution of American Conservatism,* 65, 248, 66.

34. Morison, *Life and Letters of Otis* 1:261.

35. Otis to Harrison Gray, April 30, 1811, and Jan. 1812, ibid., 2:36–38.

36. Committee Report, Massachusetts House of Representatives, June 1813, ibid., 69.

37. East, "Economic Development."

38. Howe, *Unitarian Conscience,* 215. On the emergence of Unitarianism, see also Wright, *Beginnings of Unitarianism,* in particular 252–80.

39. Banner, *Hartford Convention,* 152–56; May, *Enlightenment in America,* 258–77.

40. Quincy, *Washington Benevolent Society,* 14; Lowell, *New England Patriot,* 135, 140; Dana, *Washington Benevolent Society,* 15; Sullivan, *Washington Benevolent Society,* 15.

41. For a representative Federalist critique of the war, see Lowell, *Road to Peace.*

42. Circular Letter from Old Hampshire Federalists at Northampton, Jan. 19, 1814, in Morison, *Life and Letters of Otis* 2:87.

43. Banner, *Hartford Convention,* 306–33; Morison, *Life and Letters of Otis* 2:III.

44. *Independent Chronicle,* Nov. 10, 1814.

45. Ibid., Dec. 22, 26, 28, Dec. 29, 1814.

46. Lowell, *New England Patriot,* 148, and *Road to Peace,* 11; Quincy, *Washington Benevolent Society,* 18; Committee Report, Massachusetts House of Representatives, June 1813, in Morison, *Life and Letters of Otis* 2:69.

47. *Independent Chronicle,* Nov. 17, 1814.

48. *Boston Spectator,* Jan. 7, 1815.

49. Ibid., Dec. 31, 1814.

50. Lyman to John Treadwell, Dec. 14, 1814, Hare to Otis, Oct. 15, 1814, in Morison, *Life and Letters of Otis* 2:184–88, 178–80.

51. Hare to Otis, Feb. 10, 1814, ibid., 174–75; Speech of Artemas Ward in the U.S. Congress, Dec. 1814, *Boston Spectator,* Jan. 21, 1815.

52. *Boston Spectator,* Jan. 21, 1815.

53. Hare to Otis, Oct. 1, 1814, in Morison, *Life and Letters of Otis* 2:176–78.

54. *Boston Spectator,* Jan. 28, Feb. 11, 18, 1815.

55. *Independent Chronicle,* Jan. 23, 30, Feb. 2, 9, 13, 1815.

56. *Boston Spectator,* Feb. 11, 1815.

57. *Independent Chronicle,* Nov. 10, 28, 1814, Jan. 12, 23, 1815.

58. *Boston Weekly Messenger,* July 17, 1817. For further description of this visit, see the *Boston Weekly Messenger,* July 3, 10, 1817; see also Morison, *Life and Letters of Otis* 2:206–9.

59. Livermore, *Twilight of Federalism,* 44–46, 51.

60. Morison, *Life and Letters of Otis* 2:204, 205, 212, 216.

61. Mills to his wife, Jan. 13, 1816, Jan. or Feb. 1819, Feb. 12, 1817, in Lodge, "Letters of Mills," 18, 31, 21.

62. Mills to his wife, Jan. 15, 1822, Feb. 16, 1827, ibid., 33, 51.

63. Mills to his wife, Jan. 22, 1824, 1823(?), Feb. 16, 1825, ibid., 37–46. On the

confused and contradictory efforts of Federalists in 1824 and the surprising response of Federalists to Jackson in both 1824 and 1828, see Livermore, *Twilight of Federalism,* 132−71, 216−22.

64. Mills to his wife, Dec. 23, 1825, Feb. 8, 1826, Feb. 16, 1827, in Lodge, "Letters of Mills," 47−52.

65. See Livermore, *Twilight of Federalism,* 3−46; *Boston Weekly Messenger,* Nov. 14, 1816.

66. Morison, *Life and Letters of Otis* 2:238−40; see also Formisano, "Boston, 1800−1840."

67. Lowell to Otis, Feb. 26, 1823, in Morison, *Life and Letter of Otis* 2:253−54.

68. Ibid., 1:49.

69. *Columbian Centinel,* Feb. 19, 1823.

70. Ibid., June 7, 1823.

71. Ibid., June 11, 1823.

72. Otis, *Letters in Defence of the Hartford Convention.*

73. Ibid., 50, 92, 94, 89, 27.

74. See Formisano, *Transformation of Political Culture,* in particular 269−301.

75. See Howe, *Political Culture of the American Whigs;* Buel, *Securing the Revolution.*

76. Otis, *Letters in Defence of the Hartford Convention,* 92.

CHAPTER 3. *Sons*

1. On Buckminster's life, see Lee, *Memoirs of Buckminster;* Simpson, "Era of Joseph Stevens Buckminster." For further discussion of the literary circles involving Buckminster, see Tyack, *George Ticknor,* and Hillard, *Life of Ticknor.*

2. Prescott's father, William Prescott, sat between 1789 and 1819 on the General Court, the governor's council, and Boston's court of common pleas. He was also a delegate to the Hartford Convention and was twice offered a seat on the state supreme court. Gray's father, William Gray, served as the lieutenant governor of Massachusetts.

3. On the role of marriage and patronage in reinforcing the bonds of this class, see Goodman, "Ethics and Enterprise."

4. Lee, *Memoirs of Buckminster,* 18, 67−68, 70, 83.

5. On the student rebellions of the period, see Novak, *Rights of Youth;* see also Allmendinger, *Paupers and Scholars* and "Dangers of Antebellum Student Life."

6. Joseph Buckminster to Joseph Stevens Buckminster, Sept. 10, Nov. 1797, in Lee, *Memoirs of Buckminster,* 87−90.

7. Joseph Buckminster to Joseph Stevens Buckminster, June 16, 1798, ibid., 90−91.

8. Ibid., 28−33.

9. Joseph Buckminster to Joseph Stevens Buckminster, March 18, 1799, ibid., 93−94.

10. Joseph Buckminster to Joseph Stevens Buckminster, May 1799, ibid., 95−96.

11. On Freeman's atypical brand of Unitarianism and the unusual manner in which this Congregationalist acquired an Episcopal pulpit, see Wright, *Beginnings of Unitarianism,* 210−17.

12. Joseph Buckminster to Joseph Stevens Buckminster, Dec. 3, 31, 1803, July 30, 1804, in Lee, *Memoirs of Buckminster,* 131−33, 135−36, 147−48.

13. Adams, *Life of Sparks* 1:104.

14. Varg, *Everett,* 15−19.

15. Lothrop, "Memoir of Hale"; G. Ticknor, *Life of Prescott;* Chase and Walker, "Journal of James Savage."

16. For Ticknor's early life and these events, see his "Autobiographical Sketch" and letters from George Ticknor to Elisha Ticknor, Dec. 31, 1814, Jan. 21, 1815, in Hillard, *Life of Ticknor* 1:5−16, 27−30.

17. Ibid., 50, 52−68.

18. Ibid., 70−121.

19. Ibid., 121−50.

20. Ibid., 169−83, 185−249.

21. George Ticknor to Elisha Ticknor, Dec. 2, 1818, Nov. 5, 1815, ibid., 251−52, 80.

22. Quoted in Tyack, *George Ticknor,* 83.

23. Long, *Literary Pioneers.*

24. Varg, *Everett,* 21.

25. Quoted in Frothingham, *Edward Everett, Orator,* 51.

26. See A. Ticknor, *Life of Cogswell.*

27. Cogswell to C. S. Daveis, Mar. 5, 1813, to George Ticknor, July 27, 1813, ibid., 19−20, 22−25.

28. Cogswell to C. S. Daveis, Feb. 16, 1817, to John Farrar, Mar. 9, 1817, ibid., 50−54.

29. Cogswell to Dudley Atkins, Dec. 23, 1817, ibid., 77−78; see also Cogswell to George Ticknor, May 23, 1817, to Catherine Prescott, Sept. 2, 1817, ibid., 60−61, 63−64.

30. Cogswell to George Ticknor, Aug. 5, 1820, to Catherine Prescott, July 16, 1818, to C. S. Daveis, Mar. 8, 1821, to Catherine Prescott, Oct. 8, 1819, to George Ticknor, Feb. 18, 1816, Nov. 21, 1819, ibid., 125−26, 84−87, 130−31, 110−11, 44−45, 118−19.

31. Adams, *Life of Sparks.*

32. Ibid., 1:28.

33. Ibid., 32, 40.

34. On the first Unitarian churches in the South, see Howe, "A Massachusetts Yankee."

35. Sparks to Ann Storrow, Dec. 30, 1820, Aug. 3, 1821, in Adams, *Life of Sparks* 1:178–80, 183–85.

36. Ibid., 185.

37. Joseph Stevens Buckminster to Joseph Buckminster, Nov. 12, 1806, in Lee, *Memoirs of Buckminster,* 278–80.

38. Quoted in Frothingham, *Edward Everett, Orator,* 55.

39. W. Tudor, *Letters on the Eastern States,* 53–54.

40. Ibid., 55.

41. Ibid., 50.

42. Lyman, *Diplomacy of the United States* 2:4, 24, 20, 29, 42; Lowell, *New England Patriot.*

43. Ahlstrom, "Theology in America," 253–54; Howe, *Unitarian Conscience,* 6.

44. The following discussion of Unitarian thought relies heavily on Howe's *Unitarian Conscience.* For the history of New England liberalism that fed American Unitarianism, see Wright, *Beginnings of Unitarianism.* For an institutional history of American Unitarianism, see Cooke, *Unitarianism in America.* Robinson's *Unitarians and the Universalists* includes a useful biographical dictionary of Unitarian leaders.

45. William Ellery Channing, "Unitarian Christianity Most Favorable to Piety: Discourse at the Ordination of the Second Congregational Unitarian Church. New York, 1826," and "Unitarian Christianity: Discourse at the Ordination of the Rev. Jared Sparks. Baltimore, 1819," in W. E. Channing, *Works,* 388, 373.

46. On the importance of Scottish intellectuals within the American response to the Enlightenment, see May, *Enlightenment in America,* 337–57.

47. W. E. Channing, "Unitarian Christianity: Discourse at the Ordination of Sparks," 376.

48. William Ellery Channing, "Objections to Unitarian Christianity Considered," in W. E. Channing, *Works,* 406.

49. Lee, *Memoirs of Buckminster,* 338, 336.

50. W. E. Channing, "Unitarian Christianity: Discourse at the Ordination of Sparks," 380.

51. "Inaugural Address of Levi Frisbie," 224–41.

52. For a representative critique of the materialist psychologists, see Norton, "Observations on the Theory of Hartley."

53. Lee, *Memoirs of Buckminster,* 202–3.

54. Buckminster, "The Dangers and Duties of Men of Letters," 148, 150.

55. Lee, *Memoirs of Buckminster,* 391.

56. Quoted in Simpson, *Man of Letters in New England,* 22.

57. Ibid., 18; see also Ferguson, "William Cullen Bryant."

58. For the history of the *Monthly Anthology,* see Simpson, "A Literary Adventure of the Early Republic"; W. Tudor, *Miscellanies,* 1–7; Field, "The Birth of Secular High Culture"; Mott, *History of American Magazines* 1:253–59; McLachlan, *American Boarding School,* 27–31.

59. W. Emerson, "Preface," iii.

60. The North American Club, which assumed ownership of the journal between 1817 and 1820, included John Gallison (b. 1788), Nathan Hale (b. 1784), Richard Henry Dana (b. 1787), Edward Tyrrel Channing (b. 1790), William Powell Mason (b. 1791), Jared Sparks (b. 1789), and Willard Phillips (b. 1784). Although not a member, Francis Calley Gray (b. 1790) regularly attended their meetings. For the details of ownership and editorial staffing, as well as a general history of the *Review,* see Mott, *History of American Magazines* 2:219–61.

61. In 1824 the *North American Review* joined the *Atlantic* in establishing a fixed rate of one dollar per page for most submissions. Many contributors, however, refused to accept payment. See Mott, *History of American Magazines* 1:197–98. One of the very few to complain about the editorial practices was George Bancroft, who separated himself from this circle of intellectuals and this culture in several ways. See Gatell, *John Gorham Palfrey,* 78–90.

CHAPTER 4. *Literature: The Prospects*

1. For a representative collection of articles from the *Monthly Anthology,* see Simpson, *Federalist Literary Mind.*

2. Wells, "Silva, No. 32," 542; Brooks, *Flowering of New England,* 19.

3. J. S. J. Gardiner, *Boston Female Asylum,* 10–20.

4. J. S. J. Gardiner, *A Sermon Preached at the Trinity Church,* 13–14, 16.

5. Walter, "On Pope," 235; J. S. J. Gardiner, "Silva," 15.

6. Buckminster, "Remarker, No. 34," 368–69; J. S. J. Gardiner, "Remarker, No. 35," 417, 419.

7. W. Tudor, *Miscellanies,* 57–58.

8. On the "Paper War," see Mesick, *English Traveller in America.*

9. "History and Present State of America."

10. Ingersoll, *Inchiquin the Jesuit's Letters.*

11. "Inchiquen's Favorable View." The *Quarterly* article was widely but incorrectly attributed to the English poet laureate Robert Southey.

12. Bushman, *Refinement of America.*

13. Dwight, *Remarks on the Review of* Inchiquin's Letters; Walsh, *An Appeal*. Paulding's contributions to this transatlantic argument included *The Diverting History of John Bull and Brother Jonathan* (New York, 1812), *The Lay of the Scottish Fiddle* (New York, 1813), *The United States and England* (New York, 1815), *A Sketch of Old England by a New England Man* (New York, 1822), and *John Bull in America, or the New Munchausen* (New York, 1825).

14. W. Tudor, review of *United States and England*, 62–63, 71, 88. As all articles were published anonymously during this period, to ascertain authorship I have relied on Cameron, *Research Keys*.

15. A. Everett, "Irving's *Life of Columbus*," 109; E. Everett, "England and America," 34.

16. J. S. J. Gardiner, "Silva," 18; Robert H. Gardiner, "Literary Institutions," 115; Buckminster, "Retrospective Notices," 56; A. Everett, "Irving's *Life of Columbus*," 105–6.

17. W. H. Gardiner, review of *The Spy*, 250–82.

18. F. C. Gray, "Phi Beta Kappa Address," 301.

19. E. T. Channing, review of *Charles Brockden Brown*, 58–77.

20. W. H. Gardiner, review of *The Spy*, 251.

21. Bryant, review of *Redwood*, 245–72.

22. W. H. Gardiner, review of *The Spy*, 251.

23. Bryant, review of *Redwood*, 251.

24. A. Everett, review of *Life and Writings of Schiller*, 408.

25. A. Everett, "Lord Byron," 13.

26. A. Everett, review of *Life and Writings of Schiller*, 408.

27. Prescott, "French and English Tragedy," 130, 137–39.

28. Prescott, "Essay Writing," 328–29, 331, 350.

29. W. Tudor, review of *American Academy*, 386–89; Dana, review of *Sketch Book*, 324; Phillips, review of *Letters from the South*, 381; J. C. Gray, "Phi Beta Kappa Oration," 481, 482.

30. W. Channing, "American Language and Literature," 307–14; Sparks, "Professor Everett's Orations," 439.

31. Sparks, "Professor Everett's Orations," 436–39.

32. Bryant, review of *Redwood*, 250, 272.

33. Hillard, *Life of Ticknor* 1:393; E. T. Channing, "On Models in Literature," 207. See also Spencer, *Quest for Nationality*, 81–95.

34. A. Everett, review of *Life and Writings of Schiller*, 403, and "Lord Byron," 43, 40; E. T. Channing, "Moore's *Lalla Rookh*," 3; Phillips, "Godwin's *Mandeville*," 92–94. See also Charvat, *Origins of American Critical Thought*, 7–58; Spencer, *Quest for Nationality*, 32–39.

35. A. Everett, "Irving's *Life of Columbus*," 112.

36. See Nord, "Religious Reading and Readers."

37. D. Scott, *From Office to Profession*.

38. J. C. Gray, "Demosthenes," 36–37.

39. Ibid., 36; E. T. Channing, "Ogilvie's *Philosophical Essays*," 380.

40. J. C. Gray, "Demosthenes," 50; E. T. Channing, "Ogilvie's *Philosophical Essays*," 383.

41. Howe, *Political Culture of the American Whigs*, 31; see also Howe, *Unitarian Conscience*, 160–66.

42. A. Everett, "Mirabeau's *Speeches*," 79, 78.

43. J. C. Gray, "Phi Beta Kappa Oration," 487.

44. Miller, *Life of the Mind*, 3–35; Forgie, *Patricide in the House Divided*, in particular 13–53.

45. Phillips, review of *The Pilot*, 329.

46. Prescott, "Scottish Song," 141; Sparks, "Conventions," 249; J. C. Gray, "Phi Beta Kappa Oration," 488–89.

47. Anderson, *Imagined Communities*, 6–7.

48. John, *Spreading the News*, 1.

49. The disparity in postage rates is evidenced further by an analysis of postal revenues. In 1814 letters constituted 50.9 percent of the mail and generated 91.9 percent of total postal revenues. Newspapers constituted 49.1 percent of the mail while contributing only 8.1 percent of the total revenues. See Kielbowicz, "The Press, Post Office, and the Flow of News."

50. John, *Spreading the News*, 40.

51. Ibid., 59. Michael S. Foley challenges the effectiveness of the postal system in constructing this imagined community in "A Mission Unfulfilled."

CHAPTER 5. *Literature: The Problems*

1. Prescott, "Essay Writing," 350; Sparks, "Recent American Novels," 83.

2. J. C. Gray, "Phi Beta Kappa Oration," 480, 483.

3. See Coultrap-McQuin, *Doing Literary Business*, 2–26; see also Baym, *Woman's Fiction;* Harris, *American Women's Novels*.

4. Baym, *Woman's Fiction*, 17–18, 26–27.

5. As most novels continued to be written anonymously, female authorship was rarely explicit. At times female authorship was acknowledged by the reviewer; at others the author was referred to using male pronouns. But even in these latter circumstances, given the rather close-knit nature of American literary culture, it would be surprising if the specific authors were not fairly widely and accurately identified.

6. Sparks, "Recent American Novels," 80.

7. Ibid., 86–100.

8. Ibid., 104.

9. Lamson, "Works of Mrs. Barbauld," 369; Greenwood, review of *Hope Leslie,* 403–4.

10. See Kelley, "Legacy Profile: Catherine Maria Sedgwick," and "A Woman Alone"; see also Foster, *Catherine Maria Sedgwick;* Baym, *Woman's Fiction,* 53–63.

11. Gardiner, review of *The Spy,* 279; Bryant, review of *Redwood,* 248, 272; Hillard, review of *Clarence,* 94.

12. Gardiner, review of *The Spy,* 279; Bryant, review of *Redwood,* 256, 270; Greenwood, review of *Hope Leslie,* 411–12; Hillard, review of *Clarence,* 75.

13. Hillard, review of *Clarence,* 87; Greenwood, review of *Hope Leslie,* 406–7, 411.

14. Hillard, review of *Clarence,* 74, 76, 89.

15. J. C. Gray, review of *The Rebels,* 401–2.

16. This conclusion is tentative as it is based largely on a survey of Cameron's index of the journal.

17. Lamson, "Works of Mrs. Barbauld," 369–75; Phillips, "Edgeworth's *Harrington and Ormond,*" 154–56; Peabody, review of *Waverly Novels,* 386–421; E. Everett, review of *Works of Maria Edgeworth,* 385.

18. E. Everett, review of *Works of Maria Edgeworth,* 386–89.

19. Ruland and Bradbury, *From Puritanism to Postmodernism,* 76; see also Westbrook, *Literary History of New England,* 102–10.

20. Phillips, "Bryant's *Poems,*" 380; Lamson, "Miscellaneous Poems," 432–34.

21. Contemporary assessments of Brown range from Martin Green who calls it "an exaggeration to talk of Brown as a significant novelist" to Ruland and Bradbury who label Brown "the father of American fiction." See Green, "The God That Neglected to Come," 76; Ruland and Bradbury, *From Puritanism to Postmodernism,* 85–90. Prescott's conclusion was offered in "The Life of Charles Brockden Brown," in Sparks, *American Biography* 7:3–64.

22. C. B. Brown, *Edgar Huntly.*

23. W. H. Gardiner, review of *The Spy,* 281; E. T. Channing, review of *Charles Brockden Brown,* 71–72.

24. This conclusion is supported by the contemporary critical literature, but ironically Cooper argued that America suffered from a "poverty of materials." In his *Notions of the Americans,* he declared that "there is scarcely an ore which contributes to the wealth of the author, that is found, here, in veins as rich as in Europe." See Ruland and Bradbury, *From Puritanism to Postmodernism,* 95–103.

25. Phillips, review of *The Pilot,* 315; W. H. Gardiner, review of *The Spy,* 281.

26. W. H. Gardiner, review of *The Spy,* 276–77; see also "Cooper's Novels," 150–97.

27. Phillips, review of *The Pilot,* 328.

28. W. H. Gardiner, review of *The Spy,* 281–82.

29. Dana, review of *Sketch Book,* 356; A. Everett "Irving's *Life of Columbus,*" 110, 125, 128.

30. Green, "The God That Neglected to Come," 78; Dana, review of *Sketch Book,* 334; A. Everett, "Irving's *Life of Columbus,*" 115, 127–28.

31. See Ruland and Bradbury, *From Puritanism to Postmodernism,* 91–95.

32. Dana, review of *Sketch Book,* 348.

33. On the American publishing industry in relation to American authorship, see Charvat, *Profession of Authorship,* and Cunliffe, "The Conditions of an American Literature."

34. E. Everett, review of *Bracebridge Hall,* 204–24; A. Everett, "Irving's *Life of Columbus,*" 122–24.

35. Blankenship, *American Literature,* 249.

36. Greenwood, "Hillhouse's Hadad," 27; Lamson, "Miscellaneous Poems," 432.

37. Prescott, "Da Ponte's *Observations,*" 214–15; Bryant, review of *Essay on American Poetry,* 199.

38. Palfrey, review of *Tales of My Landlord,* 260; Dexter, review of *Sancho,* 239–40. On the similarly ambivalent feelings of a slightly later group of writers toward the changing literary market, see Gilmore, *American Romanticism.*

39. Phillips, "Edgeworth's *Harrington and Ormond,*" 156; Prescott, "Novel Writing," 193; Dana, "Edgeworth's *Readings on Poetry,*" 71–76.

40. Phillips, "Edgeworth's *Harrington and Ormond,*" 159.

41. E. T. Channing, "On Models in Literature," 202–5.

42. Parsons, "English Writers," 24–32.

43. Greenwood, "Wordsworth's *Poems,*" 356; Dana, "Hazlitt's *English Poets,*" 320, 297.

44. Greenwood, "Wordsworth's *Poems,*" 371; Holley, "Witnessing Scenes of Distress," 66–67; Prescott, "Novel Writing," 184.

45. Dana, "Hazlitt's *English Poets,*" 319.

46. A. Everett, "Works of Madame de Staël," 109, and review of *The Art of Being Happy,* 115–39.

47. A. Everett, "Life of Jean Jacques Rousseau," 9.

48. E. T. Channing, "Moore's *Lalla Rookh,*" 4; Peabody, "The Decline of Poetry," 9.

49. Phillips, "Byron's *Poems,*" 103–4, 109; A. Everett, "Lord Byron," 12, 43; Norton, "Lord Byron's Character and Writings," 359.

50. Phillips, "Byron's *Poems*," 101; Norton, "Lord Byron's Character and Writings," 327−28, 340.

51. Phillips, "Byron's *Poems*," 110; Norton, "Lord Byron's Character and Writings," 359; A. Everett, "Lord Byron," 43.

52. Hunter, *Richard Henry Dana, Sr.*

53. E. T. Channing, "Montgomery's *Poems*," 283.

54. E. T. Channing, review of *Charles Brockden Brown*, 58.

55. E. T. Channing, "Cowper's *Memoir*," 53−54.

56. Greenwood, "Wordsworth's *Poems*," 358, 359.

57. Dana, review of *Sketch Book*, 328.

58. Phillips, "Cowper's *Poems*," 235; A. Everett, review of *Private Life of Voltaire*, 55; Norton, "Lord Byron's Character and Writings," 349.

59. Smith-Rosenberg, *Disorderly Conduct*, 53−76.

60. On the importance of letter writing to antebellum culture, see Zboray, *A Fictive People*, 110−21.

61. Kelley, "Reading Women/Women Reading," 403.

62. Spencer, *Quest for Nationality*, 77.

63. For example, see Pritchard, *Criticism in America*.

64. Gilmore, "Literature of the Revolutionary and Early National Periods," 555.

65. Ibid.

66. The most useful treatment of the numerous journals of this period, especially in terms of their institutional histories, is Mott's *History of American Magazines*. Charvat, *Origins of American Critical Thought*, offers a useful comparison of their philosophical character and critical quality. Spencer's *Quest for Nationality* is also useful, as is J. P. Wood, *Magazines in the United States*.

67. Quoted in Mott, *History of American Magazines* 1:230, 227.

68. Ibid., 235.

69. Dowling, *Literary Federalism*.

70. Ibid., 240.

71. Charvat, *Origins of American Critical Thought*, 168−69; Mott, *History of American Magazines* 1:241.

72. On the Unitarian periodicals, see Cooke, *Unitarianism in America*, 92−123.

73. Mott, *History of American Magazines* 1:292, 284.

74. Charvat, *Origins of American Critical Thought*, 198−200.

75. Mott, *History of American Magazines* 1:275.

76. Charvat, *Origins of American Critical Thought*, 170−72.

77. Mott, *History of American Magazines* 1:282.

78. Ibid., 555.

79. Chase, *American Novel and Its Tradition*, 1–5.

80. Orians, "Rise of Romanticism"; Buell, "Early National Period." See also Timms, "Literary Distances."

81. Spencer, *Quest for Nationality*, 111–21.

CHAPTER 6. *Institutions*

1. J. S. G. Gardiner, *Humane Society*, 13; Kirkland, *Massachusetts Charitable Fire Society*, 7; Porter, *Humane Society*, 14. For a discussion of these efforts among clerical and business elites throughout the country, see Griffin, *Their Brothers' Keepers*.

2. J. S. G. Gardiner, *Humane Society*, 35.

3. *Constitution of the Massachusetts Society for the Suppression of Intemperance*, 4–5, 9.

4. Kirkland, *Massachusetts Society for the Suppression of Intemperance*, 12.

5. Massachusetts Society for the Suppression of Intemperance, *Second Annual Report*, 8.

6. Appleton, *Massachusetts Society for Suppressing Intemperance*, 5; see also Kirkland, *Massachusetts Society for the Suppression of Intemperance*. On this sense of intemperance and the resulting concerns in antebellum America, see Rorabaugh, *Alcoholic Republic*.

7. See Provident Institution for Saving, *Act of Incorporation, 1816; Boston Weekly Messenger*, Nov. 21, Dec. 26, 1816.

8. Kirkland, *Massachusetts Society for the Suppression of Intemperance*, 10–11.

9. Washington Benevolent Society, *Constitution, 1812*, 5, 8; Fischer, *Revolution of American Conservatism*, 121.

10. See Sullivan, *Washington Benevolent Society of Massachusetts;* Quincy, *Washington Benevolent Society of Massachusetts;* Dana, *Washington Benevolent Society at Cambridge;* Bigelow, *Washington Benevolent Society at Cambridge*.

11. T. Harris, *Washington Benevolent Society*, 9, 10.

12. Griffin, *Their Brothers' Keepers*, 13; Gusfield, *Symbolic Crusade*, 36; Tyrrell, *Sobering Up*, 41–42.

13. Tyrrell, *Sobering Up*, 34.

14. Quoted in ibid., 44.

15. Ibid., 54–86.

16. Boyer, *Urban Masses and Moral Order*, 6, 15.

17. Pessen, *Riches, Class, and Power*, 303, 251–80.

18. *Institution of the Boston Dispensary for the Relief of the Poor;* Coffin, *Boston Dispensary*, 6.

19. Circular letter of James Jackson and John C. Warren, Aug. 20, 1810, in Bowditch, *Massachusetts General Hospital*, 3–9; see also Massachusetts General

Hospital, *Report of the Committee of By Laws*; *Address of the Board of Trustees of the Massachusetts General Hospital*. On the development of the hospital system throughout the United States during the nineteenth century, see Rosenberg, *Care of Strangers*.

20. W. Tudor, *Humane Society*, 7, 5; *Boston Weekly Messenger*, Dec. 5, 1816.

21. *Address of the Board of Trustees of the Massachusetts General Hospital*, 14.

22. *Civil, Religious, and Masonic Services*, 7, 6, 3.

23. On the dependence of Boston's upper class upon these new institutions, see R. Story, *Forging of an Aristocracy*. More general treatments of professionalization include Haber, *Quest for Authority;* Bledstein, *Culture of Professionalism*. See also D. Scott, *From Office to Profession*. Thornton's *Cultivating Gentlemen* describes the transitional but still preprofessional model of public service embraced by older Federalists.

24. Schwartz, *Samuel Gridley Howe*.

25. On the series of reforms pursued by Mann and Howe, see ibid., 120–36; Schultz, *Culture Factory*, 132–53. On the link between these reforms and broader social changes, as well as the resistance to these reforms, see Katz, *Irony of Early School Reform*. For an analysis of the public school movement which emphasizes its rural, evangelical character in the early nineteenth century, see Tyack and Hansot, *Managers of Virtue*.

26. McCaughey, "From Town to City"; Hewlett, "Josiah Quincy."

27. Austin, "Penitentiary System" and "Punishment of Crimes"; Cushing, "Livingston's *Penal Code*."

28. For an introduction to Franklin's educational ideas and those of other early American reformers, see Gutek, *Education in the United States;* see also Pulliam, *History of Education*.

29. Rush's most important educational views were laid out in *Thoughts upon the Mode of Education Proper in a Republic* (1786), *To the Citizens of Philadelphia: A Plan for Free Schools* (1787), and *Observations on the Study of Latin and Greek* (1791).

30. Quoted in Gutek, *Education in the United States*, 48.

31. Jefferson's plan would have permitted only the most talented student from each of the elementary schools, unable to afford the tuition, to attend one of the twenty secondary schools established by the state on scholarship. These "public foundationers" would be provided one or two years of subsidized secondary education with the brightest individual in each of these schools allowed to complete the full six-year college preparatory program at the public expense. In this way "twenty of the best geniuses will be raked from the rubbish annually." When their secondary education was completed, ten would be allowed to move on to the College of William and Mary,

while the lower ten would become teachers at the elementary schools (ibid., 40–44).

32. On the progress of education in individual states, see Pulliam, *History of Education;* French, *America's Educational Tradition.*

33. G. Ticknor, review of *Free Schools of New England.*

34. See Schultz, *Culture Factory,* 3–44.

35. For a useful introduction to the educational ideas of Rousseau and the other European reformers, see McLachlan, *American Boarding Schools,* in particular 49–70.

36. Quoted in McLachlan, *American Boarding Schools,* 60.

37. On the centrality of faculty psychology to American thought, and especially American conceptions of human character, see Howe, *Making the American Self.*

38. "Character of Rousseau"; "Neef's Method of Education."

39. Hillard, "Memoir of James Savage," 131.

40. Packard, "College Education," 294–311; Dewey, "Popular Education," 54, 61–62.

41. Sparks, "Mr. Ingersoll's *Discourse,*" 161, 162, 160; Packard, "College Education."

42. Hofstadter and Hardy, *Development and Scope of Higher Education,* 11.

43. See Pickering, "School Education," 188–206; E. Everett, review of *Essays by a Virginian,* 45–58; Frisbie, "Well's Edition of Tacitus," 324–31. On the importance of classical education for the previous generation of Federalists, see Kerber, *Federalists in Dissent,* 95–134; Dowling, *Literary Federalism,* 36–40.

44. On Cogswell's European travels, see A. Ticknor, *Life of Cogswell;* McLachlan, *American Boarding Schools,* 50–63.

45. Cogswell to Elisha Ticknor, Sept. 1, 1818, in A. Ticknor, *Life of Cogswell,* 87–88.

46. On Cogswell's school at Round Hill, see ibid., 138–85; Cogswell and Bancroft, *Some Account of the School;* McLachlan, *American Boarding Schools,* 71–101.

47. McLachlan, *American Boarding Schools,* 62; Cogswell and Bancroft, *Some Account of the School,* 7–8.

48. Cogswell to Charles S. Daveis, March 23, 1828, to Mrs. Ticknor, Sept. 16, 1832, in A. Ticknor, *Life of Cogswell,* 160–61, 175–76.

49. Cogswell and Bancroft, *Some Account of the School,* 5.

50. Cogswell to Catherine Prescott, Oct. 28, 1819, in A. Ticknor, *Life of Cogswell,* 114–15.

51. W. Tudor, *Letters on the Eastern States,* 352–53, 349–50.

52. E. Everett, "University of Virginian," 131.

53. Bode, "Universities," 75.

54. E. Everett, "University of Virginia," 129; Kingsley, "Connecticut School Fund," 392.

55. "Inaugural Address of Levi Frisbie," 225–26.

56. E. Everett, "University of Virginia," 126–30.

57. Haber, *Quest for Authority and Honor,* 45–66; Boston Medical Association, *Rules and Regulations.*

58. *Boston Weekly Messenger,* Nov. 13, 20, 1817.

59. "Inaugural Address of Isaac Parker," 20–21.

60. Kirkland, "Literary Institutions—University," 276; "Inaugural Address of Isaac Parker," 14, 16. On the shifting conceptions of the practice of law, in particular the shift from the lawyer as advocate and maker of law to the lawyer as objective scientist, see Johnson, *Schooled Lawyers.*

61. On the criticism of advanced education, see Butts and Cremin, *History of Education,* 189–235.

62. Sparks, "Internal Improvements of North Carolina," 18; E. Everett, "University of Virginia," 133, 136; Sparks, "Appropriation of Public Lands," 310–42; Kingsley, "Connecticut School Fund," 395.

63. Kingsley, "Connecticut School Fund," 379; Sparks, "Internal Improvements of North Carolina," 17, 34.

64. Veysey, *Emergence of the American University,* 128.

65. Warren, *History of the Harvard Law School* 1:285; Sutherland, *The Law at Harvard,* 45; Gawalt, "Massachusetts Legal Education," 27–50.

66. On the attempts to reform Harvard during these years, see Tyack, *George Ticknor,* 85–128; Hillard, *Life of Ticknor,* 1:353–69. On reform efforts at other institutions during these years, see Cremin, *American Education,* 270–80; Rudolph, *American College and University,* 110–35.

67. George Ticknor to Samuel Eliot, Oct. 29, 1822, Feb. 1, 1823, in A. Ticknor, *Life of Cogswell,* 133–35. For a more thorough description of Bancroft's frustrating early career, see L. Handlin, *George Bancroft,* 82–112.

68. Ticknor was inspired a great deal by the reforms introduced at West Point by Sylvanus Thayer and also was troubled that a military academy should offer a more rigorous education than Harvard. See Hillard, *Life of Ticknor* 1: 372–76.

69. On these events, as well as the reform efforts that followed, see Morison, *Three Centuries of Harvard,* 230–38.

70. In negotiating the terms of his appointment, Ticknor had insisted upon living in Boston. His family home was far more comfortable than the on-campus quarters faculty were expected to maintain, and he had no interest in

supervising student behavior in the dining and living quarters as was usually expected.

71. On the more successful reform efforts of the late nineteenth century, see Hofstadter and Hardy, *Development and Scope of Higher Education*, 29–100; Veysey, *Emergence of the American University*.

72. Sutherland, *The Law at Harvard*, 49.

73. Ibid., 43–91.

74. On the condition of the law and the courts in Massachusetts and the attempts at reform, see Ellis, *Jeffersonian Crisis*, 184–229; Nelson, *Americanization of the Common Law*.

75. For an interpretation of this antilawyer feeling that emphasizes questions more of class than politics, see Gawalt, "Sources of Anti-Lawyer Sentiment."

76. E. Everett, "Code Napoleon," 415–17; Sedgwick, "History of the Law," 201.

77. "Inaugural Address of Isaac Parker," 22; Porter, "Necessity of the Common Law," 168.

78. Haven, "English Common Law Reports," 379–80; see also Cushing, review of *Laws of Massachusetts*, 69–91.

79. Daveis, "Common Law Jurisdiction," 104–41.

80. J. Story, "Hoffman's *Course of Legal Study*," 49; Cushing, "Law Reports," 377; Haven, "English Common Law Reports," 380.

81. Porter, "Necessity of the Common Law," 172.

82. Ibid., 173.

83. "Inaugural Address of Isaac Parker," 21.

84. Cushing, "Law Reports," 378–80; Porter, "Necessity of the Common Law," 180–81.

85. Metcalf, "Wheaton's *Reports*," 119–30; Haven, "Greenleaf's Reports," 29.

86. Metcalf, "Wheaton's *Reports*," 122; Haven, "English Common Law Reports," 387.

87. Cushing, review of *United States Law Journal*, 181–83.

88. See Howe, *Making the American Self*, 158–67. On this vision of emerging educational institutions and the challenge posed to it by more individual-serving educational philosophies, see R. Brown, *Strength of a People*, 118–53.

89. Rantoul, "Education in New England," 318.

90. Katz, *Irony of Early School Reform*; Kaestle and Vinovskis, *Education and Social Change*. See also Melder, "Woman's High Calling."

91. Katz, *Irony of Early School Reform*, 12.

92. G. Ticknor, review of *Free Schools of New England*, and "Griscom's Tour of Europe," 178–92.

93. Precise numbers for the 1820s are difficult to obtain. Kaestle and Vinov-

skis begin tracking the salary differential in 1837. For that year they argue female public school teachers earned 44.7 percent of their male counterparts. Over the next forty-three years this number ranged from 36.5 to 49.7 percent (*Education and Social Change,* 284).

94. Dewey, "Improvement of Common Schools," 164; Bode, "Universities," 71; Sparks, review of *Education in Tennessee,* 222.

95. Sewall, "Suggestions on Education," 323–37.

96. Ibid.

97. Bledstein, *Culture of Professionalism,* 31.

98. Ibid., 80.

99. Ibid., 30, 79.

100. This is Sutherland's argument in *The Law at Harvard,* 92–139.

101. Gawalt, "Massachusetts Legal Education in Transition."

102. Gawalt, "Sources of Anti-Lawyer Sentiment."

103. Nelson, *Americanization of the Common Law,* 29.

104. Ibid., 170.

105. Hurst, *Law and the Conditions of Freedom,* 24.

106. Friedman, *History of American Law,* 100.

CHAPTER 7. *History*

1. Wells, "Silva, No. 32."

2. W. Tudor, *Letters on the Eastern States,* 370.

3. E. Everett, review of *Memoir of Richard Henry Lee,* 387–88.

4. E. Everett, "Flint's *Geography,*" 83.

5. Bloch, *Visionary Republic;* see also Davidson, *Logic of Millennial Thought;* Heimert, *Religion and the American Mind;* Sandeen, *Roots of Fundamentalism;* Tuveson, *Redeemer Nation.*

6. The most useful biography of Cass is Woodford, *Lewis Cass.*

7. Cass, "Schoolcraft's *Travels,*" 375.

8. Cass, "Indians of North America," 55–57.

9. Cass, "Service of Indians," 368.

10. Cass, "Indians of North America," 112.

11. Cass, "Service of Indians," 391.

12. Frothingham, *Edward Everett, Orator,* 109; see also Varg, *Everett,* 42–47.

13. E. Everett, review of *State of the Indians,* 32–35.

14. Ibid., 36–37.

15. Sparks, "Major Long's Second Expedition," 187.

16. Hale, "Heckwelder's Indian History," 167–70, 156.

17. Horsman, *Race and Manifest Destiny.*

18. Ticknor to Walter Channing, May 17, 1816, in Hillard, *Life of Ticknor* 1:94.

19. Pickering, "Fr. Adelung's *Survey*," 128–44; Kingsley, "Webster's *Dictionary*," 433–80; de Wallenstein, "Krusenstern's Voyage," 1–33; Cass, "Indians of North America," 73–92; Pickering, "Dr. Jarvis' *Discourse*," 103–13.

20. E. Everett, review of *State of the Indians*, 41.

21. Bradford, "Lawrence's *Lectures*," 20, 18.

22. Cushing, "Hayti," 112, 115, 119.

23. Cass, "Service of Indians."

24. E. Everett, "England and America," 35.

25. E. Everett, "Mr. Walsh's *Appeal*," 336, 352–53.

26. E. Everett, "Flint's *Geography*," 96.

27. E. Everett, "Schmidt and Gall," 95–97, and "History of Grecian Art," 178–99.

28. E. Everett, "England and America," 37, 39.

29. E. Everett, "Coray's *Aristotle*," 420.

30. E. Everett, "The Greek Frigates," 51–57.

31. E. Everett, "Coray's *Aristotle*," 417–18.

32. Ibid., 423.

33. W. Tudor, review of *A Few Weeks in Paris*, 110.

34. Sparks, "Alliance of the Southern Republics," 163.

35. Sparks, review of *Travels in Columbia*, 154.

36. Sparks, "Alliance of the Southern Republics," 162–63.

37. E. Everett, review of *History of Democracy*, 304–5, 311.

38. Hale, "Mexico," 445–46; F. C. Gray, review of *Europe, by a Citizen*, 190–91.

39. Sparks, "Materials for American History," 275–81, and "Major Long's Second Expedition," 188–89.

40. Sparks, "New Zealand," 339.

41. Sparks, review of *Sandwich Islands*, 353.

42. Sparks, "New Zealand," 352–53.

43. W. Tudor, *Letters on the Eastern States*, 27–29.

44. Ibid., 85–86, 103, 111.

45. Ibid., 136, 137, 133.

46. Kirkland, *Massachusetts Charitable Fire Society*, 8.

47. H. Tudor, "Pedestrian Tour," 180, 185.

48. Mason, *An Oration Delivered July 4*, 25.

49. Ibid., 29.

50. On the contributions of this group, and Jared Sparks in particular, to the evolution of the biography in the nineteenth century, see Casper, *Constructing American Lives*, 135–201.

51. G. Ticknor, "Lafayette," 177.

52. Ibid., 159.

53. Cushing, "Columbus," 420–21.

54. Cushing, "New Documents concerning Columbus," 265–94.

55. Cushing, "Columbus," 417–18.

56. A. Everett, review of *Memoirs of the Queen,* 24.

57. Ibid., 25.

58. W. Tudor, *Life of James Otis,* 60.

59. Ibid., 185, viii, 94.

60. Ibid., 146, 148.

61. Ibid., 364, 486.

62. Hale, "Mexico," 420.

63. Cogswell, "Schoolcraft's *Journal,*" 247.

64. Quincy, review of *A Statistical View,* 345, 346.

65. Webster, review of *Battle of Bunker Hill,* 232.

66. Cushing, "Mr. Webster's *Discourse,*" 22.

67. A. Everett and E. Everett, "European Politics," 152.

68. E. Everett, "Everett's *New Ideas on Population,*" 296.

69. E. Everett, review of *Memoir of Lee,* 374.

70. A. Everett, "Cicero's *Republic,*" 54, 53.

71. E. Everett, "Life of Ali Pacha," 107.

72. F. C. Gray, "Phi Beta Kappa Address," 297.

73. Gray, "Botta's *American Revolution,*" 169. On the influence of Scott, see Orians, "Rise of Romanticism," 210–12.

74. F. C. Gray, "Beginning of the American Revolution," 400.

75. Gray, "Botta's *American Revolution,*" 185–88.

76. Everett to Judge Story, April 13, 1821, in Frothingham, *Edward Everett, Orator,* 71–72.

77. E. Everett, "Phi Beta Kappa Address," 129–31.

78. E. Everett, review of *Speeches of Henry Clay,* 425–51.

79. E. Everett, "Phi Beta Kappa Address," 131.

CHAPTER 8. *Legacy*

1. Tyack, *George Ticknor,* 217.

2. Schlesinger, *The Age of Jackson,* 3.

3. Everett boasted that he had raised circulation from 500 to 2,500 between 1820 and 1823. In 1828 the circulation had risen to 3,063, and by 1830 to 3,200. It would not increase until after the Civil War. See Mott, *History of American Magazines* 2:219–61.

4. "Memoir of William Tudor"; Chase and Walker, "Journal of James Savage"; Frothingham, *Edward Everett, Orator;* "Memoir of Caleb Cushing"; Lathrop, "Memoir of Nathan Hale"; "Memoir of Francis Calley Gray."

5. G. Ticknor, *Life of Prescott,* 339.

6. Prescott to William H. Gardiner, Oct. 4, 1837, to Edward Everett, May 15, 1845, to George Bancroft, April 30, 1831, Dec. 20, 1852, April 3, 1858, in G. Ticknor, *Life of Prescott,* 255, 376–77, 360, 380, 432–33, and 224, 223.

7. Ibid., 141.

8. Otis to George Ticknor, June 4, 1859, ibid., 464–66.

9. Frothingham, *Edward Everett, Orator,* 323, 338.

10. Ibid., 289–90.

11. Ibid., 182.

12. Quoted in Frothingham, *Edward Everett, Orator,* 272.

13. G. Ticknor, *Life of Prescott,* 245. On the intellectual and psychological burden of this inheritance for members of the "post-heroic" generation, see Forgie, *Patricide in the House Divided.*

14. H. Adams, *Education of Henry Adams;* James, *American Scene.*

15. Green, *Problem of Boston,* 19, 87, 101.

16. Ibid., 102–13.

17. Ibid., 141.

18. Ibid., 145–46.

19. Jaher, "Boston Brahmins," 202.

20. Levine, *Highbrow/Lowbrow.*

21. Ibid., 119–32.

22. O. Handlin, *Boston's Immigrants;* Solomon, *Ancestors and Immigrants;* Dalzell, *Enterprising Elite.* See also Farrell, *Elite Families.*

23. Fredrickson, *Inner Civil War,* 1–35.

24. Ibid., 174.

25. Lasch, *New Radicalism in America.*

26. See Fontana, *Rethinking the Politics of Commercial Society.*

27. Ibid., 12.

28. Collini, *Public Moralist,* 53–56.

29. Ibid., 345–54.

30. See Heyck, *Transformation of Intellectual Life.*

31. Collini, *Public Moralist,* 205–24.

32. Ticknor to Charles S. Daveis, Jan. 5, 1835, in Hillard, *Life of Ticknor* 1: 399–401.

33. Ibid., 1:423–24, 2:49, 1:456. In these years Harvard faculty, especially adminstrators, lived in constant fear of arson. One professor wet down his roof every night as protection against these regular attacks. Edward Everett was

moved to the edge of resignation when a bundle of burning straw was thrown inside his front door.

34. Ibid., 1:436, 2:158.

35. Ibid., 1:493, 455.

36. Ibid., 2:13–20.

37. Ibid., 14.

38. Ticknor to Richard Henry Dana, Feb. 22, 1837, ibid., 75.

39. Ibid., 105–9.

40. Ticknor to Earl Fitzwilliam, Oct. 17, 1838, to Maria Edgeworth, March 6, 1839, to Prince John, May 17, 1839, to Maria Edgeworth, July 10, 1840, ibid., 187–90, 193–95.

41. Ticknor to Edward Everett, July 14, 1851, ibid., 303.

42. Ticknor to John Kenyon, June 29, 1843, to Prince John, Oct. 30, 1846, ibid., 212–14, 228–29.

43. Ticknor to Sir Charles Lyell, June 21, 1848, to Prince John, July 22, 1850, ibid., 234, 266–68.

44. Ticknor to Sir Charles Lyell, March 31, 1863, to Edmund Head, April 21, 1861, ibid., 460–61, 433–34.

45. On the emergence of "gender" studies, see Joan Wallach Scott, "Gender"; see also Davis, "'Women's History' in Transition." For a discussion of the usefulness of "gender" as an analytic category, see Hawkesworth's "Confounding Gender," and the "Comments and Reply" by McKenna et al.

46. See Cott, *Bonds of Womanhood;* Kraditor, *Up from the Pedestal;* Welter, "Cult of True Womanhood"; Rotundo, "Body and Soul" and *American Manhood,* 10–30.

47. For a useful introduction to the evolving historiography, see Kerber, "Separate Spheres"; see also DuBois et al., "Politics and Culture."

48. See Johansen, "Before the Waiting Room"; Martin, "Knights-Errant and Gothic Seducers"; Rotundo, *American Manhood,* 75–91.

49. See Griffen, "Reconstructing Masculinity"; Yacovone, "Abolitionists and the 'Language of Fraternal Love'"; see also Gilfolye, *City of Eros,* 92–116.

50. Basch, "Marriage, Morals, and Politics"; K. Wood, "'One Woman So Dangerous'"; Grossberg, "Institutionalizing Masculinity"; Carnes, *Secret Ritual and Manhood;* Clawson, *Constructing Brotherhood;* Cohen, "Unregulated Youth"; Srebnick, *Mysterious Death of Mary Rogers;* Hartog, "Lawyering, Husbands' Rights, and the 'Unwritten Law.'"

51. On the impact of gender on the writers and literature of this next generation, see Leverenz, *Manhood and the American Renaissance;* Baym, "Melodramas of Beset Manhood."

52. See Douglas, *Feminization of American Culture.*

53. Prescott to William H. Gardiner, Oct. 4, 1837, in G. Ticknor, *Life of Prescott*, 255.

54. Cushing, "Legal Condition of Women," 332–33, 318–19.

55. Ibid., 338.

56. Basch, "Equity vs. Equality," 318.

57. Shammas, "Married Women's Property Acts"; Beard, *Women as a Force in History*.

Bibliography

Abbreviations

MA   *Monthly Anthology and Boston Review*
NAR   *North American Review*

Primary Sources

Adams, Henry. *The Education of Henry Adams.* Washington, D.C., 1907.

Adams, John. "A Defence of the Constitutions of Government of the United States of America." In Adrienne Koch, ed., *The American Enlightenment: The Shaping of the American Experiment and a Free Society,* 255–68. New York, 1965.

An Address of the Board of Trustees of the Massachusetts General Hospital to the Public. Boston, 1814.

Ames, Seth, ed. *Works of Fisher Ames.* 2 vols. Boston, 1854.

Appleton, Jesse. *An Address before the Massachusetts Society for Suppressing Intemperance, May 31, 1816.* Boston, 1816.

Austin, James T. "Punishment of Crimes," *NAR* 10 (April 1820): 235–59.

———. "Penitentiary System," *NAR* 13 (Oct. 1821): 417–40.

Bigelow, Andrew. *An Oration Delivered before the Washington Benevolent Society at Cambridge, July 4, 1815.* Cambridge, Mass., 1815.

Bode, George Henry. "Universities," *NAR* 27 (July 1828): 67–89.

Boston Medical Association. *Rules and Regulations.* Boston, 1817.

Bradford, Gamaliel. "Lawrence's *Lectures,*" *NAR* 17 (July 1823): 13–32.

Brown, Charles Brockden. *Edgar Huntly.* Philadelphia, 1799.

Bryant, William Cullen. Review of *Essay on American Poetry, NAR* 7 (July 1818): 198–211.

———. Review of *Redwood, a Tale, NAR* 20 (April 1825): 245–72.

Buckminster, Joseph Stevens. "The Dangers and Duties of Men of Letters," *MA* 7 (Sept. 1809): 145–58.

——. "Remarker, No. 34," *MA* 5 (July 1808): 367–72.

——. "Retrospective Notices of American Literature," *MA* 5 (Jan. 1808): 54–57.

Cass, Lewis. "Indians of North America," *NAR* 22 (Jan. 1826): 53–119.

——. "Schoolcraft's *Travels,*" *NAR* 26 (April 1828): 357–403.

——. "Service of Indians in Civilized Warfare," *NAR* 24 (April 1827): 365–442.

Channing, Edward Tyrrel. "Cowper's *Memoir of His Early Life,*" *NAR* 5 (May 1817): 48–55.

——. Review of *Charles Brockden Brown, NAR* 9 (June 1819): 58–77.

——. "Montgomery's *Poems,*" *NAR* 9 (Sept. 1819): 276–88.

——. "Moore's *Lalla Rookh,*" *NAR* 6 (Nov. 1817): 1–25.

——. "Ogilvie's *Philosophical Essays,*" *NAR* 4 (March 1817): 378–408.

——. "On Models in Literature," *NAR* 3 (July 1816): 202–9.

Channing, Walter. "American Language and Literature," *NAR* 1 (Sept. 1815): 307–14.

Channing, William Ellery. *The Works Of William E. Channing, D.D.* Boston, 1891.

"Character of Rousseau," *MA* 3 (April 1806): 190–91.

Civil, Religious, and Masonic Services, at the Laying of the Corner Stone of the Massachusetts General Hospital, July 4, 1818. Boston, 1818.

Coffin, John Gorham. *An Address Delivered before the Contributors of the Boston Dispensary at Their 17th Anniversary, Oct. 21, 1813.* Boston, 1813.

Cogswell, Joseph Green. "Schoolcraft's *Journal,*" *NAR* 15 (July 1822): 224–50.

Cogswell, Joseph Green, and George Bancroft. *Some Account of the School for the Liberal Education of Boys Established on Round Hill, Northhampton, Massachusetts.* N.p., [1826?].

Constitution of the Massachusetts Society for the Suppression of Intemperance, 1813. Boston, 1813.

Cushing, Caleb. "Columbus," *NAR* 21 (Oct. 1825): 398–429.

——. "Hayti," *NAR* 12 (Jan. 1821): 112–34.

——. "Law Reports," *NAR* 18 (April 1824): 371–82.

——. Review of *Laws of Massachusetts, NAR* 17 (July 1823): 69–91.

——. "Legal Condition of Women," *NAR* 26 (April 1828): 316–35.

——. "Livingston's *Penal Code of Louisiana,*" *NAR* 17 (Oct. 1823): 242–69.

——. "Mr. Webster's *Discourse,*" *NAR* 15 (July 1822): 21–51.

——. "New Documents concerning Columbus," *NAR* 24 (April 1827): 265–94.

——. Review of *United States Law Journal and Civilian's Magazine, NAR* 16 (Jan. 1823): 181–83.

Dana, Richard Henry. "Hazlitt's *English Poets,*" *NAR* 8 (March 1819): 276–322.

——. *Oration Delivered before the Washington Benevolent Society, July 14, 1814.* Cambridge, Mass., 1814.

——. "Edgeworth's *Readings on Poetry,*" *NAR* 7 (May 1818): 69–86.

——. Review of *The Sketch Book, NAR* 9 (Sept. 1819): 322–56.

Daveis, Charles Stuart. "Common Law Jurisdiction," *NAR* 21 (July 1825): 104–41.

de Wallenstein, Jules. "Krusenstern's Voyage and Researches," *NAR* 25 (July 1827): 1–33.

Dewey, Orville. "Improvement of Common Schools," *NAR* 24 (Jan. 1827): 156–69.

——. "Popular Education," *NAR* 23 (July 1826): 49–67.

Dexter, Franklin. Review of *Sancho, or The Proverbialist, NAR* 5 (July 1817): 239–44.

Dwight, Timothy. *Remarks on the Review of* Inchiquin's Letters *Published in the* Quarterly Review; *Addressed to the Right Honorable George Canning, Esq. by an Inhabitant of New England.* Boston, 1815.

Emerson, Edward Waldo, ed. *The Complete Works of Ralph Waldo Emerson.* 12 vols. Concord Edition. Boston, 1904.

Emerson, William. "Preface," *MA* 1 (1804): i-iv.

Everett, Alexander. Review of *The Art of Being Happy, NAR* 27 (July 1828): 115–39.

——. "Cicero's *Republic,*" *NAR* 17 (July 1823): 32–69.

——. "Irving's *Life of Columbus,*" *NAR* 28 (Jan. 1829): 103–34.

——. Review of *Life and Writings of Schiller, NAR* 16 (April 1823): 397–425.

——. "Life of Jean Jacques Rousseau," *NAR* 15 (July 1822): 1–21.

——. "Lord Byron," *NAR* 20 (Jan. 1825): 1–47.

——. Review of *Memoirs of the Queen of France, NAR* 18 (Jan. 1824): 1–33.

——. "Mirabeau's *Speeches,*" *NAR* 15 (July 1822): 73–93.

——. "Posthumous Works of Madame de Staël," *NAR* 14 (Jan. 1822): 101–28.

——. Review of *Private Life of Voltaire, NAR* 12 (Jan. 1821): 38–60.

Everett, Alexander, and Edward Everett. "European Politics," *NAR* 21 (July 1825): 141–53.

Everett, Edward. Review of *Bracebridge Hall, NAR* 15 (July 1822): 204–24.

——. "Code Napoleon," *NAR* 20 (April 1825): 393–417.

——. "Coray's *Aristotle,*" *NAR* 17 (Oct. 1823): 389–424.

——. "England and America," *NAR* 13 (July 1821): 20–47.

——. Review of *Essays by a Virginian, NAR* 16 (Jan. 1823): 45–58.

——. "Everett's *New Ideas on Population,*" *NAR* 17 (Oct. 1823): 288–310.

——. "Flint's *Geography and History of the Western States,*" *NAR* 28 (Jan. 1829): 80–103.

———. "The Greek Frigates," *NAR* 25 (July 1827): 33–62.

———. Review of *History of Democracy in the United States, NAR* 23 (Oct. 1826): 304–14.

———. "The History of Grecian Art," *NAR* 12 (Jan. 1821): 178–99.

———. "Life of Ali Pacha," *NAR* 18 (Jan. 1824): 106–40.

———. Review of *Memoir of Richard Henry Lee, NAR* 22 (April 1826): 373–400.

———. "Mr. Walsh's *Appeal*," *NAR* 10 (April 1820): 334–71.

———. Review of *On the State of the Indians, NAR* 16 (Jan. 1823): 30–45.

———. "Phi Beta Kappa Orations," *NAR* 24 (Jan. 1827): 129–41.

———. "Schmidt and Gall on America," *NAR* 17 (July 1823): 91–118.

———. Review of *Speeches of Henry Clay, NAR* 25 (Oct. 1827): 425–51.

———. "University of Virginia," *NAR* 10 (Jan. 1820): 115–37.

———. Review of *Works of Maria Edgeworth, NAR* 17 (Oct. 1823): 383–89.

Frisbie, Levi. "Wells' Edition of Tacitus," *NAR* 6 (March 1818): 324–31.

Gardiner, John Sylvester John. "Remarker, No. 35," *MA* 5 (Aug. 1808): 416–19.

———. *A Sermon Delivered at the Trinity Church, September 22, 1809, before the Members of the Boston Female Asylum.* Boston, 1809.

———. *A Sermon Delivered before the Humane Society of the Commonwealth of Massachusetts, June 14, 1803.* Boston, 1803.

———. *A Sermon Preached at the Trinity Church in Boston, April 7, 1808.* Boston, 1808.

———. "Silva," *MA* 3 (Jan. 1806): 15–19.

Gardiner, Robert H. "An Essay upon the Multiplicity of Our Literary Institutions," *MA* 4 (March 1807): 113–16.

Gardiner, William H. "Cooper's Novels," *NAR* 23 (July 1826): 150–97.

———. Review of *The Spy, NAR* 15 (July 1822): 250–82.

Gray, Francis Calley. "Beginning of the American Revolution," *NAR* 9 (Sept. 1819): 376–411.

———. "Botta's *American Revolution*," *NAR* 13 (July 1821): 169–200.

———. Review of *Europe, by a Citizen of the United States, NAR* 15 (July 1822): 177–204.

———. "Phi Beta Kappa Address," *NAR* 3 (Sept. 1816): 289–305.

Gray, John Chipman. "Demosthenes," *NAR* 22 (Jan. 1826): 34–52.

———. "Phi Beta Kappa Oration," *NAR* 13 (Oct. 1821): 478–90.

———. Review of *The Rebels, NAR* 22 (April 1826): 400–408.

Greenwood, Francis. "Hillhouse's *Hadad*," *NAR* 22 (Jan. 1826): 13–27.

———. Review of *Hope Leslie, NAR* 26 (April 1828): 403–20.

———. "Wordsworth's *Poems*," *NAR* 18 (April 1824): 356–71.

Hale, Nathan. "Heckwelder's Indian History," *NAR* 9 (June 1819): 155–78.

——. "Mexico," *NAR* 14 (April 1822): 420 – 46.

Hamilton, Alexander, James Madison, John Jay. *The Federalist Papers*. New York, 1787.

Harris, Thaddeus Mason. *An Address Delivered before the Washington Benevolent Society in Dorchester, February 22, 1813*. Boston, 1813.

Haven, Nathaniel. "English Common Law Reports," *NAR* 21 (Oct. 1825): 377 – 88.

——. "Greenleaf's *Reports*," *NAR* 22 (Jan. 1826): 27–34.

Hillard, George S. Review of *Clarence*, *NAR* 32 (Jan. 1831): 73 – 95.

Holley, Horace. "On the Pleasure Derived from Witnessing Scenes of Distress," *NAR* 2 (Nov. 1815): 59 – 67.

Holmes, Oliver Wendell, Jr. *Speeches*. Boston, 1896.

"Inaugural Address of Isaac Parker," *NAR* 3 (May 1816): 11 – 27.

"Inaugural Address of Levi Frisbie," *NAR* 6 (Jan. 1818): 224 – 41.

"Inchiquen's Favorable View of the United States," *Quarterly Review* 10 (Jan. 1814): 494 – 539.

Ingersoll, C. Jared. *Inchiquin the Jesuit's Letters, during a Late Residence in the United States of America*. New York, 1810.

Institution of the Boston Dispensary for the Relief of the Poor. Boston, 1801.

James, Henry. *The American Scene*. New York, 1907.

Kingsley, James Luce. "Connecticut School Fund," *NAR* 16 (April 1823): 379 – 96.

——. "Webster's *Dictionary*," *NAR* 28 (April 1829): 433 – 80.

Kirkland, John T. *An Address Delivered at the Request of the Massachusetts Charitable Fire Society, May 29, 1801*. Boston, 1801.

——. "Literary Institutions—University," *NAR* 7 (July 1818): 270 – 78.

——. *A Sermon Delivered before the Massachusetts Society for the Suppression of Intemperance, May 27, 1814*. Boston, 1814.

Lamson, Alvan. "Miscellaneous Poems," *NAR* 22 (April 1826): 432 – 43.

——. "Works of Mrs. Barbauld," *NAR* 23 (Oct. 1826): 368 – 85.

Lowell, John. *The New England Patriot: Being a Candid Comparison of the Principles and Conduct of the Washington and Jefferson Administrations*. Boston, 1810.

——. *The Road to Peace, Commerce, Wealth, and Happiness by an Old Farmer*. Boston, 1813.

Lyman, Theodore, Jr. *Diplomacy of the United States*. 2 vols. Boston, 1828.

Mason, William Powell. *An Oration Delivered July 4, 1827, in Commemoration of American Independence*. Boston, 1827.

Massachusetts General Hospital. *Report of the Committee of By Laws*. Boston, 1811.

Massachusetts Society for the Suppression of Intemperance. *Second Annual Report*. Boston, 1814.

Metcalf, Theron. "Wheaton's *Reports*," *NAR* 17 (July 1823): 118–30.

"Neef's Method of Education," *MA* 7 (Oct. 1809): 264–71.

Niebuhr, Reinhold. "The Unhappy Intellectuals," *Atlantic Monthly* 143 (June 1929): 790–94.

Norton, Andrews. "Lord Byron's Character and Writings," *NAR* 21 (Oct. 1825): 300–59.

———. "Observations on the Theory of Hartley," *MA* 5 (Oct. 1808): 521–30.

Otis, Harrison Gray. *Otis' Letters in Defence of the Hartford Convention, and the People of Massachusetts*. Boston, 1824.

Packard, Alpheus Spring. "College Education," *NAR* 28 (April 1829): 294–311.

Palfrey, John Gorham. Review of *Tales of My Landlord*, *NAR* 5 (July 1817): 257–86.

Parsons, Theophilus. "Comparative Merits of the Earlier and Later English Writers," *NAR* 10 (Jan. 1820): 19–33.

Paulding, James K. *The Diverting History of John Bull and Brother Jonathan*. New York, 1812.

———. *John Bull in America, or The New Munchausen*. New York, 1825.

———. *The Lay of the Scottish Fiddle*. New York, 1813.

———. *A Sketch of Old England by a New England Man*. New York, 1822.

———. *The United States and England*. New York, 1815.

Peabody, William Bourne Oliver. "The Decline of Poetry," *NAR* 28 (Jan. 1829): 1–18.

———. Review of *Waverly Novels*, *NAR* 32 (April 1831): 386–421.

Phillips, Willard. "Bryant's *Poems*," *NAR* 13 (Oct. 1821): 380–84.

———. "Byron's *Poems*," *NAR* 5 (May 1815): 98–110.

———. "Cowper's *Poems*," *NAR* 2 (Jan. 1816): 233–41.

———. "Godwin's *Mandeville*," *NAR* 7 (May 1818): 92–105.

———. Review of *Letters from the South*, *NAR* 6 (March 1818): 368–82.

———. "Miss Edgeworth's *Harrington and Ormond*," *NAR* 6 (Jan. 1818): 153–78.

———. Review of *The Pilot*, *NAR* 18 (April 1824): 314–29.

Pickering, John. "Dr. Jarvis' *Discourse*," *NAR* 11 (July 1820): 103–13.

———. "Fr. Adelung's *Survey of Languages*," *NAR* 14 (Jan. 1822): 128–44.

———. "School Education," *NAR* 9 (June 1819): 188–206.

Porter, Eliphalet. *A Discourse before the Humane Society of the Commonwealth of Massachusetts, June 8, 1802*. Boston, 1802.

Porter, Jonathan. "Necessity of the Common Law," *NAR* 27 (July 1828): 167–91.

Prescott, William Hickling. "Da Ponte's *Observations*," *NAR* 21 (July 1825): 189–217.

——. Review of *English Literature of the Nineteenth Century, NAR* 35 (July 1832): 165–95.

——. "Essay Writing," *NAR* 14 (April 1822): 319–50.

——. "The French and English Tragedy," *NAR* 16 (Jan. 1823): 124–56.

——. "The Life of Charles Brockden Brown," in Jared Sparks, ed., *American Biography* 7:3–64. 12 vols. New York, 1902.

——. "Novel Writing," *NAR* 25 (July 1827): 183–203.

——. "Scottish Song," *NAR* 23 (July 1826): 124–42.

Provident Institution for Saving. *Act of Incorporation, 1816.* Boston, 1816.

Quincy, Josiah. *An Answer to the Questions, Why Are You a Federalist? and Why Shall You Vote for Governor Strong?* Boston, 1805.

——. *An Oration Delivered before the Washington Benevolent Society of Massachusetts, April 30, 1813.* Boston, 1813.

——. Review of *A Statistical View of the Commerce of the United States, NAR* 3 (Sept. 1816): 345–54.

Rantoul, Robert, Jr. "Education in New England," *NAR* 47 (Oct. 1838): 274–318.

Rush, Benjamin. *Observations on the Study of Latin and Greek.* Philadelphia, 1791.

——. *Thoughts upon the Mode of Education Proper in a Republic.* Philadelphia, 1786.

——. *To the Citizens of Philadelphia: A Plan for Free Schools.* Philadelphia, 1787.

Sedgwick, Henry Dwight. "Correspondence on the History of the Law," *NAR* 23 (July 1826): 197–201.

Sewall, Samuel Edmund. "Suggestions on Education," *NAR* 30 (April 1830): 324–37.

Simpson, Lewis, ed. *The Federalist Literary Mind: Selections from the* Monthly Anthology and Boston Review, *1802–1811, Including Documents Relating to the Boston Athenaeum.* Baton Rouge, 1962.

Sparks, Jared. "Alliance of the Southern Republics," *NAR* 22 (Jan. 1826): 162–76.

——. "Appropriation of Public Lands for Schools," *NAR* 13 (Oct. 1821): 310–42.

——. "Conventions for Adopting the Federal Constitution," *NAR* 25 (Oct. 1827): 249–78.

——. Review of *Education in Tennessee, NAR* 24 (Jan. 1827): 219–24.

——. "Internal Improvements of North Carolina," *NAR* 12 (Jan. 1821): 16–37.

——. "Major Long's Second Expedition," *NAR* 21 (July 1825): 178–89.

——. "Materials for American History," *NAR* 23 (Oct. 1826): 275–94.

——. "Mr. Ingersoll's *Discourse*," *NAR* 18 (Jan. 1824): 157–78.

——. "New Zealand," *NAR* 18 (April 1824): 329–55.

——. "Professor Everett's Orations," *NAR* 20 (April 1825): 417–40.

——. "Recent American Novels," *NAR* 21 (July 1825) 78–104.

——. Review of *Sandwich Islands, NAR* 22 (April 1826): 334–64.

——. Review of *Travels in Columbia, NAR* 21 (July 1825): 153–77.

Story, Joseph. "Hoffman's *Course of Legal Study,*" *NAR* 6 (Nov. 1817): 45–77.

Sullivan, William. *An Oration Delivered before the Washington Benevolent Society of Massachusetts, April 30, 1812.* Boston, 1812.

Ticknor, George. Review of *Free Schools of New England, NAR* 19 (Oct. 1824): 448–57.

——. "Griscom's Tour of Europe," *NAR* 18 (Jan. 1824): 178–92.

——. "Lafayette," *NAR* 20 (Jan. 1825): 147–80.

Tudor, Henry. "Pedestrian Tour," *NAR* 4 (Jan. 1817): 175–86.

Tudor, William. Review of *American Academy of Arts and Sciences, NAR* 1 (Sept. 1815): 370–89.

——. *A Discourse Delivered before the Humane Society, May, 1817.* Boston, 1817.

——. Review of *A Few Weeks in Paris, NAR* 1 (May 1815): 91–110.

——. *Letters on the Eastern States.* 2d ed. Boston, 1821.

——. *Life of James Otis.* Boston, 1823.

——. *Miscellanies.* Boston, 1821.

——. *An Oration Pronounced July 4, 1809, at the Request of the Selectmen of the Town of Boston.* Boston, 1809.

——. Review of *The United States and England, NAR* 1 (May 1815): 61–91.

Walsh, Robert. *An Appeal from the Judgments of Great Britain Representing the United States of America.* Philadelphia, 1819.

Walter, Arthur Maynard. "On Pope," *MA* 2 (May 1805): 235–38.

Washington Benevolent Society. *Constitution, 1812.* Boston, 1812.

Webster, Daniel. Review of *Battle of Bunker Hill, NAR* 7 (July 1818): 225–58.

Wells, Benjamin. "Silva, No. 32," *MA* 4 (Oct. 1807): 542–43.

Newspapers

Boston Spectator
Boston Weekly Messenger
Columbian Centinel (Boston)
Independent Chronicle (Boston)

Published Collections of Letters and Journals

Adams, Herbert B. *The Life and Writings of Jared Sparks.* 2 vols. Boston, 1893.

Gilman, W. H., et al., eds. *The Journals and Miscellaneous Notebooks of Ralph Waldo Emerson.* 16 vols. Cambridge, Mass., 1960–82.

Hillard, George, ed. *Life, Letters, and Journals of George Ticknor.* 2 vols. 6th ed. Boston, 1877.

Lee, Eliza Buckminster. *Memoirs of Rev. Joseph Buckminster, D.D., and of His Son, Rev. Joseph Stevens Buckminster.* Boston, 1849.

Lodge, Henry C., ed. "Letters of Hon. Elijah H. Mills," *Proceedings of the Massachusetts Historical Society* 19 (1881–82): 12–53.

Morison, Samuel Eliot. *The Life and Letters of Harrison Gray Otis, Federalist, 1765–1848.* 2 vols. Boston, 1913.

Ticknor, Anna Eliot. *Life of Joseph Green Cogswell as Sketched in His Letters.* Cambridge, Mass., 1874.

Ticknor, George. *Life of William Hickling Prescott.* Boston, 1864.

Secondary Sources

Ahlstrom, Sydney E. "Theology in America: A Historical Survey." In *The Shaping of American Religion,* ed. James Ward Smith and A. Leland Jamison, 232–321. Princeton, N.J., 1961.

Allmendinger, David F., Jr. "The Dangers of Antebellum Student Life," *Journal of Social History* 7 (Fall 1973): 75–85.

———. *Paupers and Scholars: The Transformation of Student Life in 19th-Century New England.* New York, 1975.

Anderson, Benedict. *Imagined Communities: Reflections on the Origin and Spread of Nationalism.* Rev. ed. London, 1991.

Appleby, Joyce. *Inheriting the Revolution: The First Generation of Americans.* Cambridge, Mass., 2000.

———. *Liberalism and Republicanism in the Historical Imagination.* Cambridge, Mass., 1992.

———. "Republicanism in Old and New Contexts," *William and Mary Quarterly,* 3d ser., 43 (Jan. 1986): 20–34.

———. "What Is Still American in the Political Philosophy of Thomas Jefferson?" *William and Mary Quarterly,* 3d ser., 39 (April 1982): 287–309.

Banner, James M., Jr. *To the Hartford Convention: The Federalists and the Origins of Party Politics in Massachusetts, 1789–1815.* New York, 1970.

Banning, Lance. "Jeffersonian Ideology Revisited: Liberal and Classical Ideas in the New American Republic," *William and Mary Quarterly,* 3d ser., 43 (Jan. 1986): 3–19.

Bailyn, Bernard. *The Ideological Origins of the American Revolution.* Cambridge, Mass., 1967.

Basch, Norma. "Equity vs. Equality: Emerging Concepts of Women's Political Status in the Age of Jackson," *Journal of the Early Republic* 3 (Fall 1983): 297–318.

———. "Marriage, Morals, and Politics in the Election of 1828," *Journal of American History* 80 (Dec. 1993): 890–918.

Baym, Nina. "Melodramas of Beset Manhood: How Theories of American Fiction Exclude Women Authors," *American Quarterly* 33 (Summer 1981): 123–39.

———. *Woman's Fiction: A Guide to Novels by and about Women in America, 1820–70.* 2d ed. Urbana, Ill., 1993.

Beard, Mary Ritter. *Women as a Force in History: A Study in Tradition and Realities.* New York, 1946.

Ben-Atar, Doron, and Barbara B. Oberg, eds. *Federalists Reconsidered.* Charlottesville, Va., 1998.

Blankenship, Russell. *American Literature as an Expression of the National Mind.* London, 1931.

Bledstein, Burton. *The Culture of Professionalism: The Middle Class and the Development of Higher Education in America.* New York, 1978.

Bloch, Ruth. *Visionary Republic: Millennial Themes in American Thought.* Cambridge, 1985.

Bowditch, Nathaniel I. *A History of the Massachusetts General Hospital.* Boston, 1872.

Boyer, Paul. *Urban Masses and Moral Order in America, 1820–1920.* Cambridge, Mass., 1978.

Brooks, Van Wyck. *The Flowering of New England, 1815–1865.* Cleveland, 1936.

Brown, Richard D. *The Strength of a People: The Idea of an Informed Citizenry in America, 1650–1870.* Chapel Hill, N.C., 1996.

Buel, Richard. *Securing the Revolution: Ideology in American Politics, 1789–1815.* Ithaca, N.Y., 1972.

Buell, Lawrence. "The Early National Period and the New England Literary Tradition." In *American Literature: The New England Heritage,* ed. James Nagel and Richard Astro, 29–49. New York, 1981.

Burns, James MacGregor. *Roosevelt: The Lion and the Fox.* New York, 1956.

Bushman, Richard L. *The Refinement of America: Persons, Houses, Cities.* New York, 1992.

Butts, R. Freeman, and Lawrence Cremin. *A History of Education in American Culture.* New York, 1953.

Cameron, Kenneth Walter, ed. *Research Keys to the American Renaissance: Scarce Indexes of the* Christian Examiner, The North American Review, *and* The New Jerusalem Magazine. Hartford, 1967.

Carnes, Mark C. *Secret Ritual and Manhood in Victorian America.* New Haven, 1989.

Casper, Scott E. *Constructing American Lives: Biography and Culture in Nineteenth-Century America.* Chapel Hill, N.C., 1999.

Charles, Joseph. *The Origins of the American Party System: Three Essays.* New York, 1956.

Charvat, William. *The Origins of American Critical Thought, 1810–1835.* Philadelphia, 1936.

——. *The Profession of Authorship in America, 1800–1870: The Papers of William Charvat.* Ed. Matthew Bruccoli. Columbus, Ohio, 1968.

Chase, Richard. *The American Novel and Its Tradition.* Garden City, N.Y., 1957.

Chase, Theodore, and Celeste Walker, eds. "The Journal of James Savage and the Beginning of Frederic Tudor's Career in the Ice Trade," *Proceedings of the Massachusetts Historical Society* 97 (1985): 103–34.

Clawson, Mary Ann. *Constructing Brotherhood: Class, Gender, and Fraternalism.* Princeton, N.J., 1989.

Cohen, Patricia Cline. "Unregulated Youth: Masculinity and Murder in the 1830s City," *Radical History Review* 52 (Winter 1992): 33–52.

Collini, Stefan. *Public Moralists: Political Thought and Intellectual Life in Britain, 1850–1930.* Oxford, 1991.

Cooke, George Willis. *Unitarianism in America: A History of Its Origins and Development.* Boston, 1910.

Cott, Nancy F. *The Bonds of Womanhood: "Women's Sphere" in New England, 1780–1835.* New Haven, 1977.

Coultrap-McQuin, Susan. *Doing Literary Business: American Women Writers in the Nineteenth Century.* Chapel Hill, N.C., 1990.

Cremin, Lawrence. *American Education: The National Experience, 1783–1876.* New York, 1980.

Cunliffe, Marcus. "The Conditions of an American Literature." In *American Literature to 1900,* ed. Marcus Cunliffe, 1–22. 1st American ed. New York, 1973.

Cunningham, Noble E., Jr. *The Process of Government under Jefferson.* Princeton, N.J., 1978.

Dalzell, Robert F., Jr. *Enterprising Elite: The Boston Associates and the World They Made.* New York, 1987.

Dauer, Manning J. *The Adams Federalists.* Baltimore, 1953.

Davidson, James West. *The Logic of Millennial Thought: Eighteenth Century New England.* New Haven, 1977.

Davis, Natalie Zemon. "'Women's History' in Transition: The European Case," *Feminist Studies* 3 (Spring–Summer 1976): 83–103.

Douglas, Ann. *The Feminization of American Culture.* New York, 1977.

Dowling, William C. *Literary Federalism in the Age of Jefferson: Joseph Dennie and* The Port Folio, *1801–1812.* Columbia, S.C., 1999.

DuBois, Ellen, Mari Jo Buhle, Temma Kaplan, Gerda Lerner, and Carroll Smith-Rosenberg. "Politics and Culture in Women's History: A Symposium," *Feminist Studies* 6 (Spring 1980): 26–64.

East, Robert A. "Economic Development and New England Federalism, 1803–1814," *New England Quarterly* 10 (Sept. 1937): 430–46.

Ellis, Richard E. *The Jeffersonian Crisis: Courts and Politics in the Young Republic.* New York, 1971.

Farrell, Betty G. *Elite Families: Class and Power in Nineteenth-Century Boston.* Albany, 1993.

Ferguson, Robert A. "William Cullen Bryant: The Creative Context of the Poet," *New England Quarterly* 53 (Dec. 1980): 431–63.

Field, Peter S. "The Birth of Secular High Culture: *The Monthly Anthology and Boston Review* and Its Critics," *Journal of the Early Republic* 17 (Winter 1997): 575–609.

Fischer, David Hackett. *The Revolution of American Conservatism: The Federalist Party in the Era of Jeffersonian Democracy.* New York, 1965.

Foley, Michael S. "A Mission Unfulfilled: The Post Office and the Distribution of Information in Rural New England, 1821–1835," *Journal of the Early Republic* 17 (Winter 1997): 610–41.

Fontana, Biancamaria. *Rethinking the Politics of Commercial Society: The* Edinburgh Review, *1802–1832.* Cambridge, 1985.

Forgie, George. *Patricide in the House Divided: A Psychological Interpretation of Lincoln and His Age.* New York, 1979.

Formisano, Ronald P. "Boston, 1800–1840: From Deferential-Participant to Party Politics." In *The Transformation of Political Culture: Massachusetts Parties, 1790s-1840s,* 29–57. Oxford, 1983.

Formisano, Ronald P., and Constance K. Burns. *Boston, 1700–1980: The Evolution of Urban Politics.* Westport, Conn., 1984.

Foster, Edward Halsey. *Catherine Maria Sedgwick.* New York, 1974.

Fredrickson, George. *The Inner Civil War: Northern Intellectuals and the Crisis of the Union.* New York, 1965.

French, William M. *America's Educational Tradition: An Interpretive History.* Boston, 1964.

Friedman, Lawrence M. *A History of American Law.* New York, 1973.

Frothingham, Paul Revere. *Edward Everett, Orator and Statesman.* Boston, 1925.

Gatell, Frank Otto. *John Gorham Palfrey and the New England Conscience.* New York, 1963.

Gawalt, Gerard W. "Massachusetts Legal Education in Transition, 1766–1840," *American Journal of Legal History* 17 (1973): 27–50.

——. "Sources of Anti-Lawyer Sentiment in Massachusetts, 1740–1840," *American Journal of Legal History* 14 (1970): 283–307.

Gilfoyle, Timothy J. *City of Eros: New York City, Prostitution, and the Commercialization of Sex, 1790–1920.* New York, 1992.

Gilmore, Michael. *American Romanticism and the Marketplace.* Chicago, 1985.

——. "The Literature of the Revolutionary and Early National Periods." In *The Cambridge History of American Literature,* ed. Sacvan Bercovitch, 1:539–693. 2 vols. Cambridge, 1994.

Goodman, Paul. *The Democratic-Republicans of Massachusetts: Politics in a Young Republic.* Cambridge, Mass., 1964.

——. "Ethics and Enterprise: The Values of a Boston Elite, 1800–1860," *American Quarterly* 18 (Fall 1966): 437–51.

Green, Martin. "The God That Neglected to Come." In *American Literature to 1900,* ed. Marcus Cunliffe, 53–84. 1st American ed. New York, 1973.

——. *The Problem of Boston: Some Readings in Cultural History.* New York, 1966.

Griffen, Clyde. "Reconstructing Masculinity from the Evangelical Revival to the Waning of Progressivism: A Speculative Synthesis." In *Meanings for Manhood: Constructions of Masculinity in Victorian America,* ed. Mark C. Carnes and Clyde Griffen, 183–204. Chicago, 1990.

Griffin, Clifford S. *Their Brothers' Keepers: Moral Stewardship in the United States, 1800–1865.* New Brunswick, N.J., 1960.

Grossberg, Michael. "Institutionalizing Masculinity: The Law as a Masculine Profession." In *Meanings for Manhood: Constructions of Masculinity in Victorian America,* ed. Mark C. Carnes and Clyde Griffen, 133–51. Chicago, 1990.

Gusfield, Joseph R. *Symbolic Crusade: Status Politics and the American Temperance Movement.* Urbana, Ill., 1963.

Gutek, Gerald L. *Education in the United States: An Historical Perspective.* Englewood Cliffs, N.J., 1986.

Haber, Samuel. *The Quest for Authority and Honor in the American Professions, 1750–1900.* Chicago, 1991.

Hall, Peter Dobkin. *The Organization of American Culture, 1700–1900: Private Institutions, Elites, and the Origins of American Nationality.* New York, 1982.

Handlin, Lilian. *George Bancroft: The Intellectual as Democrat.* New York, 1984.

Handlin, Oscar. *Boston's Immigrants, 1790–1880: A Study in Acculturation.* 1949; rev. and enlarged ed., Cambridge, Mass., 1991.

Harris, Susan K. *Nineteenth-Century American Women's Novels: Interpretive Strategies.* Cambridge, 1990.

Hartog, Hendrik. "Lawyering, Husbands' Rights, and the 'Unwritten Law' in

Nineteenth-Century America," *Journal of American History* 84 (June 1997): 67–96.

Hawkesworth, Mary. "Confounding Gender," *Signs* 22 (Spring 1997): 649–85.

Heimert, Alan. *Religion and the American Mind: From the Great Awakening to the Revolution.* Cambridge, Mass., 1966.

Hewlett, Richard G. "Josiah Quincy: Reform Mayor of Boston," *New England Quarterly* 24 (June 1951): 179–96.

Heyck, T. W. *The Transformation of Intellectual Life in Victorian England.* London, 1982.

Hillard, George S. "Memoir of James Savage," *Proceedings of the Massachusetts Historical Society* 16 (March 1878): 117–53.

· Hofstadter, Richard. *Anti-Intellectualism in American Life.* New York, 1963.

——. "The Paranoid Style in American Politics." In *The Paranoid Style in American Politics and Other Essays,* 3–40. New York, 1966.

Hofstadter, Richard, and C. DeWitt Hardy. *The Development and Scope of Higher Education in the United States.* New York, 1952.

Horsman, Reginald. *Race and Manifest Destiny: The Origins of American Racial Anglo-Saxonism.* Cambridge, Mass., 1981.

Howe, Daniel Walker. *Making the American Self: Jonathan Edwards to Abraham Lincoln.* Cambridge, Mass., 1997.

——. "A Massachusetts Yankee in Senator Calhoun's Court: Samuel Gilman in South Carolina," *New England Quarterly* 44 (June 1971): 197–220.

——. *The Political Culture of the American Whigs.* Chicago, 1979.

——. *The Unitarian Conscience: Harvard Moral Philosophy, 1805–1865.* Cambridge, Mass., 1970.

Hunter, Doreen M. *Richard Henry Dana, Sr.* Boston, 1987.

Hurst, James Willard. *Law and the Conditions of Freedom in the Nineteenth-Century United States.* Madison, Wis., 1956.

Jaher, Frederic Cople. "The Boston Brahmins in the Age of Industrial Capitalism." In *The Age of Industrialism in America: Essays in Social Structure and Cultural Values,* ed. Jaher, 188–262. New York, 1968.

Johansen, Shawn. "Before the Waiting Room: Northern Middle-Class Men, Pregnancy, and Birth in Antebellum America," *Gender and History* 7 (Aug. 1995): 183–200.

John, Richard R. *Spreading the News: The American Postal System from Franklin to Morse.* Cambridge, Mass., 1995.

Johnson, William R. *Schooled Lawyers: A Study in the Clash of Professional Cultures.* New York, 1978.

Kaestle, Carl F., and Maris A. Vinovskis. *Education and Social Change in Nineteenth-Century Massachusetts.* Cambridge, 1980.

Katz, Michael. *The Irony of Early School Reform: Educational Innovation in Mid-Nineteenth-Century Massachusetts.* Cambridge, Mass., 1968.

Kelley, Mary. "Catherine Maria Sedgwick, 1789–1867," *Legacy* 6 (Fall 1989): 43–50.

———. "Reading Women/Women Reading: The Making of Learned Women in Antebellum America," *Journal of American History* 83 (Sept. 1996): 403–24.

———. "A Woman Alone: Catherine Maria Sedgwick's Spinsterhood in Nineteenth-Century America," *New England Quarterly* 51 (June 1978): 209–25.

Kerber, Linda. *Federalists in Dissent: Imagery and Ideology in Jeffersonian America.* Ithaca, N.Y., 1970.

———. "Separate Spheres, Female Worlds, Woman's Place: The Rhetoric of Women's History," *Journal of American History* 75 (June 1988): 9–39.

Kielbowicz, Richard B. "The Press, Post Office, and the Flow of News in the Early Republic," *Journal of the Early Republic* 3 (Fall 1983): 255–80.

Kraditor, Aileen S. *Up from the Pedestal: Selected Writings in the History of American Feminism.* Chicago, 1968.

Lasch, Christopher. *The New Radicalism in America, 1889–1963: The Intellectual as a Social Type.* New York, 1965.

Lazarsfeld, Paul F., and Wagner Thielens Jr. *The Academic Mind: Social Scientists in a Time of Crisis.* Glencoe, Ill., 1958.

Lears, Jackson. *No Place of Grace: Antimodernism and the Transformation of American Culture, 1880–1920.* New York, 1981.

Leverenz, David. *Manhood and the American Renaissance.* Ithaca, N.Y., 1989.

Levine, Lawrence. *Highbrow/Lowbrow: The Emergence of Cultural Hierarchy in America.* Cambridge, Mass., 1988.

Lipset, Seymour Martin. *Political Man: The Social Bases of Politics.* New York, 1960.

Livermore, Shaw, Jr. *The Twilight of Federalism: The Disintegration of the Federalist Party, 1815–1830.* Princeton, N.J., 1962.

Long, Orie William. *Literary Pioneers: Early American Explorers of European Culture.* Cambridge, Mass., 1935.

Lothrop, Samuel K. "Memoir of Nathan Hale," *Proceedings of the Massachusetts Historical Society* 18 (Dec. 1880–81): 270–79.

Lubove, Roy. *The Professional Altruist: The Emergence of Social Work as a Career, 1880–1930.* Cambridge, Mass., 1965.

Martin, Robert K. "Knights-Errant and Gothic Seducers: The Representation of Male Friendship in Mid-Nineteenth-Century America." In *Hidden from History: Reclaiming the Gay and Lesbian Past,* ed. Martin Bauml Duberman, Martha Vicinus, and George Chauncey Jr., 169–82. New York, 1989.

May, Henry F. *The Enlightenment in America.* New York, 1976.

McCaughey, Robert A. "From Town to City: Boston in the 1820s," *Political Science Quarterly* 88 (June 1973): 191–213.

McKenna, Wendy, Suzanne Kessler, Steven G. Smith, Joan Wallach Scott, R. W. Connell, and Mary Hawkesworth. "Comments and Reply," *Signs* 22 (Spring 1997): 687–713.

McLachlan, James. *American Boarding Schools: A Historical Study.* New York, 1970.

Melder, Keith E. "Woman's High Calling: The Teaching Profession in America, 1830–1860," *American Studies* 13 (Fall 1972): 19–32.

"Memoir of Caleb Cushing," *Proceedings of the Massachusetts Historical Society* 17 (1879): 7–11.

"Memoir of Francis Calley Gray," *Proceedings of the Massachusetts Historical Society* 47 (1913–47): 529–34.

"Memoir of William Tudor," *Proceedings of the Massachusetts Historical Society* 1 (1791–1835): 429–33.

Mesick, Jane Louise. *The English Traveller in America, 1785–1835.* New York, 1922.

Miller, Perry. *The Life of the Mind in America: From the Revolution to the Civil War.* New York, 1965.

———. *The New England Mind: The Seventeenth Century.* Boston, 1939.

Morison, Samuel Eliot. *Three Centuries of Harvard, 1636–1936.* Cambridge, Mass.,1936.

Mott, Frank Luther. *A History of American Magazines.* 5 vols. Cambridge, Mass., 1938–68.

National Endowment for the Humanities Website. <http://www.neh.fed.us/>.

Nelson, William E. *The Americanization of the Common Law: The Impact of Legal Change on Massachusetts Society, 1760–1830.* Cambridge, Mass., 1975.

Nord, David Paul. "Religious Reading and Readers in Antebellum America," *Journal of the Early Republic* 15 (Summer 1995): 241–72.

Novak, Stephen. *The Rights of Youth: American Colleges and Student Revolt, 1798–1815.* Cambridge, Mass., 1977.

Orians, G. Harrison. "The Rise of Romanticism, 1805–1855." In *Transitions in American Literary History,* ed. Harry Hayden Clark, 161–244. New York, 1967.

Parrington, Vernon L. *Main Currents in American Thought.* 3 vols. New York, 1927.

Pessen, Edward. *Riches, Class, and Power: America before the Civil War.* Lexington, Mass., 1973; rept. with new Introduction, New Brunswick, N.J., 1990.

Prince, Carl E. "The Passing of the Aristocracy: Jefferson's Removal of the

Federalists, 1801–1805," *Journal of American History* 57 (Dec. 1970): 563–75.

Pritchard, John Paul. *Criticism in America: An Account of the Development of Critical Techniques from the Early Period of the Republic to the Middle Years of the Twentieth Century.* Norman, Okla., 1956.

Pulliam, John D. *History of Education in America.* 5th ed. New York, 1991.

Robinson, David. *The Unitarians and the Universalists.* Westport, Conn., 1985.

Rodgers, Daniel T. "Republicanism: The Career of a Concept," *Journal of American History* 79 (June 1992): 11–38.

Rorabaugh, W. J. *The Alcoholic Republic, an American Tradition.* New York, 1979.

Rosenberg, Charles E. *The Care of Strangers: The Rise of America's Hospital System.* New York, 1987.

Rotundo, E. Anthony. *American Manhood: Transformations in Masculinity from the Revolution to the Modern Era.* New York, 1993.

——. "Body and Soul: Changing Ideals of American Middle-Class Manhood, 1770–1920," *Journal of Social History* 16 (Summer 1983): 23–38.

Rudolph, Frederick. *The American College and University: A History.* New York, 1962.

Ruland, Richard, and Malcolm Bradbury. *From Puritanism to Postmodernism: A History of American Literature.* New York, 1991.

Sandeen, Ernest. *The Roots of Fundamentalism: British and American Millenarianism, 1800–1930.* Chicago, 1970.

Sandel, Michael J. *Democracy's Discontent: America in Search of a Public Philosophy.* Cambridge, Mass., 1996.

Schlesinger, Arthur M., Jr. *The Age of Jackson.* Boston, 1953.

Schultz, Stanley. *The Culture Factory: Boston's Public Schools, 1789–1860.* Oxford, 1973.

Schwartz, Harold. *Samuel Gridley Howe: Social Reformer, 1801–1876.* Cambridge, Mass., 1956.

Scott, Donald. *From Office to Profession: The New England Ministry, 1750–1850.* Philadelphia, 1978.

Scott, Joan Wallach. "Gender: A Useful Category of Historical Analysis," *American Historical Review* 91 (Dec. 1986): 1053–75.

Shalhope, Robert E. "Republicanism and Early American Historiography," *William and Mary Quarterly,* 3d ser., 39 (April 1982): 334–56.

Shammas, Carole. "Re-Assessing the Married Women's Property Acts," *Journal Of Women's History* 6 (Spring 1994): 9–30.

Simpson, Lewis. "The Era of Joseph Stevens Buckminster: Life and Letters in the Boston-Cambridge Community, 1800–1815." Ph.D. diss., University of Texas, 1948.

——. "A Literary Adventure of the Early Republic: The Anthology Society and the Monthly Anthology," *New England Quarterly* 27 (June 1954): 168–90.

——. *The Man of Letters in New England and the South: Essays on the History of the Literary Vocation in America.* Baton Rouge, La., 1973.

Smith-Rosenberg, Carroll. *Disorderly Conduct: Visions of Gender in Victorian America.* New York, 1985.

Solomon, Barbara M. *Ancestors and Immigrants: A Changing New England Tradition.* Cambridge, Mass., 1956.

Spencer, Benjamin. *The Quest for Nationality.* Syracuse, N.Y., 1957.

Spiller, Robert, Willard Thorp, Thomas H. Johnson, Henry Seidel Canby, Richard M. Ludwig, and William M. Gibson, eds. *Literary History of the United States.* New York, 1946.

Srebnick, Amy Gilman. *The Mysterious Death of Mary Rogers: Sex and Culture in Nineteenth-Century New York.* New York, 1995.

Story, Ronald. *The Forging of an Aristocracy: Harvard and the Boston Upper Class, 1800–1970.* Middletown, Conn., 1980.

Sutherland, Arthur E. *The Law at Harvard: A History of Ideas and Men, 1817–1967.* Cambridge, Mass., 1967.

Thornton, Tamara Plakins. *Cultivating Gentlemen: The Meaning of Country Life among the Boston Elite, 1785–1860.* New Haven, 1989.

Timms, David. "Literary Distances." In *The End of Anglo-America: Historical Essays in the Study of Cultural Divergence,* ed. R. A. Burchell, 160–83. Manchester, Eng., 1991.

Tuveson, Ernest Lee. *Redeemer Nation: The Idea of America's Millennial Role.* Chicago, 1968.

Tyack, David B. *George Ticknor and the Boston Brahmins.* Cambridge, Mass., 1967.

Tyack, David B., and Elisabeth Hansot. *Managers of Virtue: Public School Leadership in America, 1820–1980.* New York, 1982.

Tyrrell, Ian. *Sobering Up: From Temperance to Prohibition in Antebellum America, 1800–1860.* Westport, Conn., 1979.

Varg, Paul A. *Edward Everett: The Intellectual in the Turmoil of Politics.* Selinsgrove, Pa., 1992.

Veysey, Laurence. *The Emergence of the American University.* Chicago, 1965.

Warren, Charles. *History of the Harvard Law School and of Early Legal Conditions in America.* 3 vols. Boston, 1908.

——. *Jacobin and Junto; or, Early American Politics as Viewed in the Diary of Dr. Nathaniel Ames, 1758–1822.* Cambridge, Mass., 1931.

Westbrook, Perry D. *A Literary History of New England.* Bethlehem, Pa., 1988.

Welter, Barbara. "The Cult of True Womanhood, 1820–1860," *American Quarterly* 18 (Summer 1966): 151–74.

Wills, Garry. *Inventing America: Jefferson's Declaration of Independence.* Garden City, N.Y., 1978.

Wood, James Playsted. *Magazines in the United States.* 2d ed. New York, 1956.

Wood, Kirsten E. "'One Woman So Dangerous to Public Morals': Gender and Power in the Eaton Affair," *Journal of the Early Republic* 17 (Summer 1997): 237–75.

Woodford, Frank B. *Lewis Cass: The Last Jeffersonian.* New Brunswick, N.J., 1950.

Wright, Conrad. *The Beginnings of Unitarianism in America.* Boston, 1955.

Yacovone, Donald. "Abolitionists and the 'Language of Fraternal Love.'" In *Meanings for Manhood: Constructions of Masculinity in Victorian America,* ed. Mark C. Carnes and Clyde Griffen, 85–95. Chicago, 1990.

Zboray, Ronald J. *A Fictive People: Antebellum Economic Development and the American Reading Public.* New York, 1993.

Index

Italicized page numbers refer to illustrations.

Everett, Edward (*cont.*)
    Lee, 205; on Napoleon, 206; on
    Ali Pacha, 206; on the scholar's
    life, 207–8; political career, 213,
    216–19; as Harvard president, 216,
    218; as secretary of state, 216–17; as
    orator, 219–20, and father's gen-
    eration, 238
Everett, Oliver, 74

Faculty psychology: within Unitarian-
    ism, 69–70; and oratory, 94; and
    Fellenberg, 151; and Cogswell, 153–
    54; and Mann, 173
Farm School for Boys, 142
Farrar, John, 54
Federalism, 3–9; as political culture, 3–
    4; ideology of, 4–7, 8–9, 70, 183–
    84; provincialism of, 6–7; and
    democratic ideology, 12; genera-
    tional differences, 77–79; and phil-
    anthropic institutions, 136–41, 142.
    See also Federalist intellectuals;
    Federalist Party; Federalists
Federalist intellectuals: criticism of, 9–
    11; literary and social circles, 45–
    46; marriage, 47; and Unitarian-
    ism, 50, 61–70; in Europe, 51–57;
    on partisanship, 59–60; on War of
    1812, 60; and Federalist culture, 61;
    and the *Monthly Anthology,* 72; and
    the *North American Review,* 73–75;
    and European critics of America,
    79–81, 189–193; and national lit-
    erature, 82–100, 101–2, 109, 122–
    23, 124–27, 133–34, 209–10, 212; on
    British literature and language,
    85–88; and Romantic theories of
    language, 88–89, 124–26; and
    neoclassicim, 89, 124–26; on ora-
    tory, 90–95; on literature and na-
    tional feeling, 96–97; on literary
    criticism, 101–2, 113–16; and
    women writers, 102–9; on Bryant,

109–10; on Brown, 110–11; on
Cooper, 111; on Irving, 111–13; on
the role of literature, 114–18; on
genius, 115, 119–22, 212; on aesthetics and morality, 118–22; literary
contribution, 122–26, 131–32, 133–
34, 209–10, 212, 222; and philanthropic institutions, 141, 211; and
professionalization, 145, 175–79; on
the university, 145, 156–62, 163, 211;
on education, 151–67; on professional education, 158–60, 163, 178–
79, 212–13; reform efforts at Harvard, 163–67, 211; and legal reform,
168, 169–72, 179–81, 211; and female teachers, 174–76; on Jefferson, 182; on western expansion,
182; on history and historical
progress, 183–208, 210; on Native
Americans, 184–87, 188, 189, 190–
91; on race, 187–89; and the revolution in Greece, 191–92, 193; on
South American revolutions, 192–
94; on self-interest, 197–98; on
the role of the individual in history, 198–208, 212; achievements
and legacy, 208–13, 227–28, 245–
46; and cultural isolation, 226–
27; and British intellectual life,
228–33; and manhood, 239–45;
and women, 241–45. *See also*
Federalism
Federalist Party, 3, 22; decline of, 2;
political adaptation, 7–8, 29;
in Massachusetts, 24, 40–42;
relationship to Whigs, 43; and
Washington Benevolent Society,
138–39. *See also* Federalism;
Federalists
Federalists: Federalist clergy, 5, 8, 22;
influence in early America, 11; on
Jefferson, 16, 23, 25–26, 31–32; on
the Louisiana Purchase, 24; on the
three-fifths clause, 24; and con-

Massachusetts Peace Society, 141
Massachusetts Society for the Suppression of Intemperance, 137–38, 139, 140
May, Henry, 26
Mayhew, Jonathan, 202
McCarthyism, 17
McLachlan, James, 154
Melville, Herman, 241–42
Metcalf, Theron, 171–72
Metternich, Prince Klemens von, 235
Milan Decree, 60
Miller, Perry, 95
Mills, Elijah, 39–40, 75
Missionary Magazine, 129
Monroe, James, 38, 39
Monroe-Pinckney Treaty, 25
Monthly Anthology, 11, 72–73, 75, 125; compared to *North American Review,* 76–78, 100; literary dispute in, 78–79; and *Port Folio,* 128; on education, 151
Moore, Thomas, 89
Morison, Samuel, 39
Morse, Jedidiah, 129, 130
Mott, Frank Luther: on the *Port Folio,* 129; on the *Christian Disciple,* 130; on the *American Quarterly Review,* 130; on the *Analectic,* 131; on *Graham's,* 131

Napoleon, 51
National Endowment for the Humanities, 19
National literature, 127; calls for, 76, 81; impediments to in America, 82; and the *North American Review,* 82–100, 101–2, 109, 122–23, 124–27, 133–34; relationship to British literature and language, 86–88; benefits of, 88–90; and national feeling, 95–97; and women writers, 109; and literary standards, 113–14; romanticism and neoclas-

sicism, 124–27, 131–33; and other journals, 128–31
National Science Foundation, 19
Native Americans, 184–87
Neef, Joseph, 151
Nelson, William, 179–80
Neoclassicism, 78, 89–90, 100, 122, 127, 130; and romanticism, 124–27, 131–33
New Deal, 13, 18
New England, 2, 6, 9–11. *See also* Boston
New England Farmer, 129
New England Marine Insurance Company, 72
New England Tale (Sedgwick), 106
New Haven, 129
New Princeton Review, 129
New York, 80, 131, 225
New York Mirror, 131
New York Review, 131
Niebuhr, Reinhold, 16
Niles' National Register, 130
Niles' Weekly Register, 130
North American Club, 73, 254 n. 60
North American Review, 1, 2, 7, 8, 20, 254 n. 61; criticism of, 9–10, 11, 214; and a conservative tradition, 14; generational character, 73–75; editorial philosophy, 74–75; compared to *Monthly Anthology,* 76–79, 100; defense of American culture, 81; romanticism and neoclassicism, 125–126; American journals compared, 127–131; circulation, 211, 267 n. 3; compared to British journals, 228–231. *See also* Federalist intellectuals
Northwood (Hale), 108
Norton, Andrews, 119–20, 122, 166
Norton, Charles Eliot, 75, 222, 226

Oratory, 90–95
Orians, G. Harrison, 133